Social Policy and Planning for the 21st Century

The greatest problems facing humanity today are climate change, poverty, and the increasing separation between the rich and poor. The aim of this book is to examine the social constructions that have led to these breakdowns and provide potential solutions that are based on a fundamental change in the structure of society and the values on which a new and better social system can be built.

Unless we as a society set a drastically different course soon, human life as we know it will suffer greatly, perhaps even cease altogether. Excess consumption is becoming anti-social as the effects of global warming and increasing poverty become apparent. What, then, will form the new social values on which society replaces the present emphasis on work and material consumption that now prevail? This book's answer to that question is accomplishment and aesthetic consumption. The proposed refocused existence will necessitate a new economic order that provides access to a livelihood beyond the market system.

This groundbreaking book will appeal to students and scholars of sociology, leisure studies, political science, and social work.

Donald G. Reid is University Professor Emeritus in the School of Environmental Design and Rural Development at the University of Guelph, Canada.

Routledge Advances in Sociology

177 **The Decent Society**
Planning for Social Quality
Pamela Abbott, Claire Wallace and Roger Sapsford

178 **The Politics and Practice of Religious Diversity**
National Contexts, Global Issues
Edited by Andrew Dawson

179 **São Paulo in the Twenty-First Century**
Spaces, Heterogeneities, Inequalities
Edited by Eduardo Cesar Leão Marques

180 **State Looteries**
Historical Continuity, Rearticulations of Racism, and American Taxation
Kasey Henricks and David G. Embrick

181 **Lesbian, Gay, Bisexual and Trans* Individuals Living with Dementia**
Concepts, Practice and Rights
Edited by Sue Westwood and Elizabeth Price

182 **Family, Culture, and Self in the Development of Eating Disorders**
Susan Haworth-Hoeppner

183 **Origins of Inequality in Human Societies**
Bernd Baldus

184 **Confronting the Challenges of Urbanization in China**
Insights from Social Science Perspectives
Edited by Zai Liang, Steven F. Messner, Youqin Huang and Cheng Chen

185 **Social Policy and Planning for the 21st Century**
In Search of the Next Great Social Transformation
Donald G. Reid

Social Policy and Planning for the 21st Century
In Search of the Next Great
Social Transformation

Donald G. Reid

NEW YORK AND LONDON

First published 2017
by Routledge
711 Third Avenue, New York, NY 10017

and by Routledge
2 Park Square, Milton Park, Abingdon, Oxon OX14 4RN

Routledge is an imprint of the Taylor & Francis Group, an informa business

© 2017 Taylor & Francis

The right of Donald G. Reid to be identified as author of this work has been asserted by him in accordance with sections 77 and 78 of the Copyright, Designs and Patents Act 1988.

All rights reserved. No part of this book may be reprinted or reproduced or utilised in any form or by any electronic, mechanical, or other means, now known or hereafter invented, including photocopying and recording, or in any information storage or retrieval system, without permission in writing from the publishers.

Trademark notice: Product or corporate names may be trademarks or registered trademarks, and are used only for identification and explanation without intent to infringe.

Library of Congress Cataloging-in-Publication Data
Names: Reid, Donald G., author.
Title: Social policy and planning for the 21st century : in search of the next great social transformation / Donald G. Reid.
Description: Abingdon, Oxon ; New York, NY : Routledge, 2017. | Series: Routledge advances in sociology ; 185
Identifiers: LCCN 2016007994 | ISBN 9781138674059 (hardback) | ISBN 9781315561530 (e-book)
Subjects: LCSH: Social policy. | Social planning. | Social problems—History—21st century.
Classification: LCC HN18.3 .R449 2017 | DDC 303.3—dc23
LC record available at http://lccn.loc.gov/2016007994

ISBN: 978-1-138-67405-9 (hbk)
ISBN: 978-1-315-56153-0 (ebk)

Typeset in Times New Roman
by Apex CoVantage, LLC

Contents

List of Illustrations vii
Acknowledgements viii

PART I

1 Introduction 3
2 The Human Crisis 11
3 Culture and False Consciousness in Human Evolution 32
4 The Context for Policy Making 51
5 Planning Theory in Social Policy Development 61

PART II

6 Poverty and Marginalization in the Keynesian State 75
7 Beyond Poverty: Major Areas for Active Social Policy 100
8 Social Policy in the Developing World 118
9 Community Building 126
10 The Role of Research in Social Policy Formation 141

PART III

11 Decentring Work: The Role of Meaningful Activity and Leisure in Social Policy Development 161

12 The Way Forward: The Great Transformation 176

Index 201

Illustrations

Figures

5.1	Domains of Social Policy Theory	64
6.1	Roots and Outcomes of Poverty	90
7.1	The Homelessness Crisis	111
9.1	Three Major Components to Community Building	127
10.1	Stages in the Research and Planning Process	151
12.1	Transition from the Status Quo to a New Social Contract	181

Table

6.1	The Basic Welfare State in Canada	81

Acknowledgements

A number of people have been very helpful in developing the ideas contained in this book. First, I want to thank Tim Brookes for helping me clarify many of my thoughts on the subjects elaborated herein. Tim and I spent many interesting hours overlooking the ocean, drinking coffee as we talked and debated these ideas. Thanks to Patricia MacPherson for her continued support. Patricia's ongoing encouragement is greatly appreciated. I wish to thank Nicole Gosselin for the many hours she spent editing this book. Editors are underappreciated but add much to the final product. Also, a number of people, including Hilary Black, Jennifer Burns, Shawn Filson, Sarah Mahato, Maanpreet Sian, Rana Telfah, and Nicole Vanquaethem, read the draft manuscript and made valuable comments, many of which contributed to the final version of this book.

Part I

1 Introduction

The social and environmental basis on which modern life is constructed is deteriorating. News, including print, broadcast, and social media, is increasingly concerned about the consequences of climate change, growing poverty, and increasing separation between the rich and poor. The aim of this book is to examine the social constructions that have led to these failures in modern society and provide some ideas with regard to how civilization might set a different course; one that requires a fundamental change in the structure of society and the values on which a new and better social system could be built. Let there be no mistake—unless we as a society set a drastically different course soon, human life on this planet may suffer greatly, perhaps even cease to exist altogether.

The first part of this book sets out the present condition of society and highlights some of the major entanglements that have caused the problems facing humanity today. It focuses on identifying the issues that accompany climate change, the drastic separation of the rich and poor, and the underlying basis for poverty in the face of increasing affluence for some. These conditions have become embedded in our modern culture.

Culture is the organizing force that provides structure to human individual and social existence, and this book examines the role it plays in constructing social life. Culture is the lens through which *Homo sapiens* interpret and create their everyday social world. As cultures mature, many false consciousness are created to help society reaffirm itself in the face of changing social environments. False consciousness is an inevitable by-product of culture as humans attempt to hang on to the aspects of their lives that give them comfort even though they may now be inhibiting the proper functioning of society. These practices may spell the doom for a society that is unable to see the negativities for what they are and search out more appropriate explanations for the changing conditions they confront. One such false consciousness is our notion of wealth creation and the process we have created for its distribution. The overwhelming focus of society on wealth creation at the expense of other life-sustaining values is an issue that needs to be addressed if social and environmental integration is to be sustained. Culture and the values it creates are major evolutionary devices in the lives of humans that play a deterministic role in social change, much like genes play in biological evolution. In fact, culture may now be more important than biology in determining the future of humankind. What gets established as humanity's culture in the future will determine the fate of society over the near and long term.

Social and environmental policy plays an intricate part in implementing the values of society. The context for policy making is extremely important and provides the framework for social discourse. There are a number of competing views about not only what form social policy should take in modern society, but also how much of it should be produced and for whom. The issues of eligibility are critical to social justice. Most people possess an underlying perspective about where the root causes of human frailty lie. This worldview determines the need for social policy and what should or should not be done about it by the collective. Most of these views are built on a vision of fundamental human nature and human society. At the most fundamental level of this debate are the competing ideas of biological influence on human makeup and those of environmental determinism. These concepts shape the core of the social debate in society today and will be discussed at great length later in this book.

A person's theory of society dictates what social interventions should be considered in order to address the inadequacies that plague his or her individual life and the broader social condition. For some, intervention in the human system is seen as social engineering and to be minimized at best, if not avoided altogether. For others intervention in the social system is seen as the way to create a modern civilization. It is important to this discussion to lay out the theories that direct the policy and planning process and what outcomes these differing views of the world have on social construction. Culture influences, and perhaps dominates, the social development discourse. The domination of culture, which has been appropriately strong in the social policy discussion, may now need to recognize the increasing importance of the nature side of the argument, given the recent advances in genetic mapping and neurological science. No longer can nature be ignored, given the recent advances in genetics and other biological discoveries, including a greater understanding of the function and role of the brain in human consciousness. These ideas and their potential contribution to human development are provided in more detail in later chapters in this book.

Any text on social policy must address the substance of the domain with which it is concerned. Issues of poverty and the marginalization of an increasing number of individuals in society will be examined in later chapters of this book. It is often claimed that a critical measure of a civilized society is how it treats its minorities, including its marginalized and disadvantaged citizens. Although some progress has been made in a few quarters, such as gender equality and race discrimination, it has fallen behind on other measures, such as poverty. It is evident that at least one marginalized group, the poverty stricken, have not made much, if any, progress in overcoming their predicament since the end of World War II, and, their condition continues to deteriorate today. Poverty in both the developed and in many parts of the developing world is not being eliminated in spite of constant economic growth across the globe and governments' continuing rhetoric about eradicating its presence.

In its present form poverty is gaining ground because the growth in the economy is being consumed by fewer and fewer people, particularly in the developed world, leaving an ever-growing poorer population and a widening of the income gap. Some predictions have suggested that in a decade or so the poor in the United States will be as visible as it is today in many of the developing countries. The issue of poverty is as much about the equal distribution of resources and social justice as it is about the ability of populations to consume sufficient calories to maintain life, although that dire level of poverty continues to exist as well.

A large part of social policy is about poverty, either in attempting to reduce its consequence for those who find themselves experiencing its ferocity or in attempting to protect the general population from falling into it. Poverty is viewed as either a system problem, in that the economy is unable to supply a means for making a living to those unemployed and marginalized, or an individual problem whereby those in poverty may simply lack the skills to find a job, and those who are designated as lazy by society and thought to lack all motivation for working and taking responsibility for themselves. In the latter case, the poor and those on social assistance are frequently characterized by society as social deviants, the undeserving poor, and a drag on the economy. One of the objectives of this book is to challenge those myths and stereotypes, which are designed to denigrate and blame those experiencing poverty for the failures of society. I intend to provide a more realistic picture of its true structure.

In addition to poverty, social policy addresses a number of social issues in society. These concerns can be classified in many ways, but they will be categorized in this book as healthcare, housing and homelessness, education, and justice and democracy. Although this book views poverty as a key problem for social policy to address, these other related issues need to be dealt with as well. Many of them are the result of poverty or, in some cases, the cause of it. Some of these problems may be related to poverty directly; however, they can also stand on their own and constitute concerns that society might want to address as separate public questions. Many of these domains may affect the entire population or a specific group within society and if treated or enhanced will provide a desired benefit to the general public. Many of these efforts can be remedial or developmental in nature—remedial in that if eradicated, society will be better off; developmental in that their adoption by society will enhance individual functioning directly or social solidarity generally.

This book's focus is mainly on Western nations; however, the developing world requires some attention as well. Given the upheaval throughout the world and the resulting mass migration of populations produced by conflict and hunger, social problems produced in one country are no longer the exclusive domain of that single country, but are shared throughout the globe. Consider those fleeing conflicts in their home countries and the resulting migration throughout the globe. Europe has been particularly inundated with migration and is having difficulties integrating those new arrivals into their societies. Because globalization has become a dominant force in the world, it is necessary to compare and contrast poverty in the developing world with the developed countries across the globe. There may not be much difference between the poor in the so-called developing world and the marginalized in developed countries, given the recent condition of marginalized populations, such as the First Nations people in Canada, recent ethnic migrants to Britain, and some inner-city neighbourhoods and rural parts of the United States. In some ways their struggle is not much different than communities in Africa and elsewhere.

That said, the origin of social policy development in the developing world is dramatically different than in the more affluent countries of the West. Perhaps the most telling feature of this difference is that many developing world countries were not constructed on, or have subsequently adopted, Keynesian principles. Additionally, a number of these countries entered the modern era as colonies of European nations, and therefore, did not develop a tradition of social welfare based on any notion of equity, nor were the colonial masters particularly concerned about the domestic economy and the welfare of the people in the countries they occupied. These occupied countries were seen as peripheral to the homeland, and their major purpose was to supply the colonizer with natural riches, as far as the colonials were concerned. The role of the colony was to serve the occupying country by providing cheap raw materials and even cheaper labour to the colonial power. Little thought by the occupiers was given to the welfare of the host people; in fact, many of the local inhabitants were not seen as human, and if they were given that status, they were believed to be a substandard or primitive people. Servitude and slavery were thought to be legitimate and condoned throughout many parts of the so-called modern world. Only when it suited the colonizer were social programs, mainly rudimentary healthcare, provided to the locals. This healthcare was not necessarily provided in a spirit of benevolence, but so those in servitude could be more productive in their work for their colonial masters.

That said, the picture of poverty in the developing world is changing. On some measures, it is said that poverty is abating in a number of the countries in the developing world. China, India, South Africa, and Brazil are good examples where gross domestic product (GDP) is increasing. Whether or not all citizens in these countries are benefiting from this GDP growth and their general quality of life is improving is questionable, however. The changing nature of social progress and policy in the developing world is important to recognize. All countries are unique with a set of exceptional problems and potential solutions, but some concerns are shared throughout the world.

Engaging citizens in the development of policies that affect them is critical to sound policy formation. Community building and citizen participation are critical to social policy development and are major contributors in the pursuit of democracy and social justice. Most discussions on the subject identify democracy as a vital link in the social policy universe. Other than simply stating that it is important, identifying how democracy is enhanced or achieved through social policy construction is often neglected, but I focus on it in some depth later in this book. Engaging the populace in the development and provision of social policy is an essential characteristic of the policy construction process. Theoretically, citizen engagement occurs at all levels of policy making, including at the international, national, and local levels. However, it is most likely that, beyond voting for national representatives or in belonging to a political party, most of us engage with democracy at the community and local levels, and it is here where most citizen action occurs. It is in communities where our lives are lived and the provision of social policy gets played out. Although senior-level governments are the most likely developers of social policies such as healthcare, social assistance, and housing, it is usually the local government that implements these policies at the community level. The local community is the space where social policy gets delivered. Additionally, discussions about the adequacy of social policy and the required changes to it should be generated at the community level if these programs are to be bottom up and not top down. It is in the community where needs are identified and the best ideas about how to satisfy those needs get created. Community building is not just a byproduct of social policy but a development goal in its own right.

The idea of community building has become the mechanism for playing out the notions of democracy and social justice at the local level. In addition to the responsibility of government to create social policy, civic institutions have become features on the social policy landscape and active in its development and delivery. Whether or not this has always been in the best interests of society is a matter of debate, but it is a reality nonetheless. It is generally thought that the creation and delivery of social policy is a partnership between governments and civil society. The balance in that relationship is always a concern and needs to be constantly debated and adjusted. A major contributing factor to community building is research and social impact assessment. This part of the process is not always recognized and often circumvented in community-building activity.

Social impact assessment and research are critical to sound policy development. This book may be slightly different from other social policy texts in that it addresses social impact assessment and research as methods for determining what ought to exist in the long-term future, as well as for dealing with present conditions. Most texts addressing research and impact assessment form a here-and-now perspective. Social policy needs to address the large-scale social and human problems looming on the horizon in addition to attending to present and immediate difficulties. It needs to be active in advancing the human condition, and not simply focus exclusively on the historic situation or current inadequacies. Social policy in this book is not only meant to be remedial, but also developmental, which can generate a profound influence on how research and social impact assessments are completed and interpreted. This volume also presents the overarching ontological positions that support the appropriate level of research and social impact assessment for present and potentially future social policy construction.

Critical to this discussion on social policy is the idea that society will need to decentre work in the new economy and increase the importance of other forms of meaningful activity in everyday life, particularly the use of meaningful nonwork activity or leisure. In this book the case is made that in the postindustrial, information age we are entering, work cannot play the exclusive role in providing life's purpose as it did in the industrial age, even though the marketplace continues to operate on this flawed principle. I argue that human society is in the midst of a significant series of crises—social, psychological, environmental, and economic—and that in order to overcome these challenges human society will need to transition to a new way of existing, much as it did when it leaped from an agrarian way of life to the industrial society. It is my position that nonremunerated meaningful activity or leisure will play a heightened, perhaps central, role in a new economy and social contract if life on this planet is to flourish. It is the purpose of this book to outline what that role might look like and how it will enhance the human condition and the physical environment in which we live.

Increased consumption and work will also become more and more antisocial as the effects of global warming and increasing poverty become apparent. What then will form the new social values on which society replaces the present emphasis on work and material consumption that now prevail? My answer to that question is accomplishment and aesthetic consumption—much of it gained through nonremunerated meaningful activity or leisure. The focus for those without work in the market system is to find purpose and construct a meaningful life outside the market economy. Those not engaged in the market economy will rely more on serious leisure as outlined by Stebbins (Stebbins, 1982) to find one's purpose in life and self-actualization. The locus for developing a sense of life's purpose and self-worth will need to change for some, if not many of us. This refocused existence will necessitate a new economic system that requires providing access to a livelihood beyond the market system. Such schemes as a guaranteed annual income (GAI) need to be seriously considered as an option for not only increasing social justice, but also as a legitimate mechanism for distributing the wealth society creates. As this book is being written, Finland is initiating a GAI and other European countries such as Switzerland are considering it.

Finally, this book attempts to be prescriptive. Much of the early sections of the book identify the critical issues facing society and what needs to be done about them. The last part focuses on setting out scenarios to remedy those problems. It rejects the notion that life in general and the social system in particular is completely controlled by economics and embraces the idea that only through leadership and public policy can society move toward creating a radically new poverty eradication strategy, social organizing system, and a reconstruction of the natural environment.

I posit that the cultural values that were acquired at the beginning of human existence and throughout the evolution of humanity, although once necessary for the survival of the species, are now a threat to our continued existence and must be unlearned and a new set of appropriate values incorporated into a more sustainable culture. This is no mean task. Because humans are emotionally attached to cultural patterns that proved valuable in the past, it will now take great effort to assist society in transitioning to new ideologies and behaviours that may be more beneficial for continuing life on this planet.

What is the basis for this argument? As the Nobel laureate Krugman (2007) points out, extensive inequality has run rampant since the early 1970s. This change in the social condition, according to him, is a result of 'movement conservatives' (the neoconservative movement) who have gained political control, particularly in the United States, but also in other Western nations, including Britain and Canada, and more broadly in Europe. The recent economic and environmental crisis has made this fact apparent. Recent fledgling social movements in multiple countries have identified the inequality that exists in the United States and, to a lesser extent, in Canada and in Europe. The failure of the largest firms on Wall Street such as Lehman Brothers and others has laid bare the overlarge compensation packages, including unwarranted bonuses paid to top executives that exist in the system. The enormous differences between the compensation of the top executives and those working on the factory floor have been exposed. It is estimated that the CEOs of the largest corporations will make as much money by noon on the first day of the year as the average worker will make in the whole year. Additionally, these same executives have been so reckless in their risk taking they have endangered the economic system, and no one seems to be reining them in in any meaningful way. All of these conditions have created the opportunity and potential for dramatic change to the social safety net. Greed is now running unchecked. The public may be ready to alter the social contract in favour of the majority of its citizens, and they must bring their politicians into the struggle.

The basic argument here is that, contrary to conventional wisdom, politics and public policies are the vehicle for social and organizational change and not classical economic theory. Mature industrial societies have moved from a manufacturing focus to a technological information-based society. This transition demands a change in the social system that may not be favourable to the traditional capitalist system and those who have profited handsomely from it. A potentially catastrophic series of events can stimulate and give impetus to change. The great economic and social separation of society that has been occurring since the 1970s, and the challenge of climate change, may be the beginnings of such a crisis. Witness the recent Occupy movement in North America and Arab Spring in North Africa as the potential beginnings of that unrest and eventual change.

What is being argued here is that affluent times do not provide an environment for dealing with inequality, but rather stimulate greed that causes large and increasing differentiation within society and leaves many people behind and in poverty. The 2008/2009 economic crisis and other recessions shone light on the exorbitant amounts of money many on Wall Street and in multinational corporations across the globe continue to pay themselves in spite of their complicity in causing great calamity in the economic and social system. Technological innovation has exacerbated the unemployment problem that accompanied the financial catastrophe. There seems to be little recognition on the part of the financial and business community that many of their excessive pay packages are unjustified, and perhaps even immoral, and are symbolic of the rot in the system. Certainly, they do not appear to recognize their detrimental role in the deteriorating condition of the economy or in society generally. This behaviour points to a systemic problem of great urgency for society to address. At the same time many of these wealthy people are promoting the disbandment of unions and providing resistance to such crucial policies as raising the minimum wage, which is so vital to the existence of working people at the lower end of the economic continuum. Public policies such as limited inequality, strategies for creating a guaranteed annual income, life skills coaching, support mechanisms for those in difficulty, and natural resource consumption reduction are some of the main themes addressed throughout this book.

References

Krugman, P. (2007). *The Conscience of a Liberal.* New York: W.W. Norton & Company.

Stebbins, R. A. (1982). Serious Leisure: A Conceptual Statement. *Pacific Sociological Review,* 25 (2), 251–272.

2   The Human Crisis

Global society is currently confronted with colossal social and environmental crises that appear to be irresolvable by our present social and political system. The warming of the earth's atmosphere by the rapid, uncontrolled, and escalating injection of human-created CO_2 emissions into the atmosphere and the increase in poverty and inequality in the social and economic system are destabilizing the natural and social world.

The industrial era is giving way to a new, yet undefined, social organizing system resulting from the scientific and technological advances gained by society over the last few decades. The rapid rise in population growth over the last century and the advanced technology with which we are now exploiting the planet's resources is putting great stress on the globe's environment and social system. This new era has changed how we live in the world and our relations with each other with at least the same magnitude as occurred during humanity's transition from the agrarian to the industrial society. In fact, Redner (2013) tells us that we are leaving the condition of civilization and entering into a new way of life yet undelineated, but extremely different. Although the science and technological revolution has and will continue to provide great benefits to society and the human condition, it has the potential to greatly damage the important advances gained through human civilization from both an environmental and social perspective. Whether or not the end result of this technological revolution will be a new golden era for humanity or a catastrophic Armageddon is yet to be determined. I'm betting on it being a new golden age, but there is potential for it to destroy us. However, there is no doubt that the two areas of life that will be most affected by these developments are the environment on which life depends and the social system that sets out the framework for democracy and social justice. This book attempts to address these important issues and views them as critical to humanity's continuing and future existence. It views social and environmental issues such as poverty and climate change as inclusive and integrated areas of life—conditions that need to be addressed interdependently and simultaneously.

This book is about social policy in the large sense. At the macro level, social policy provides the pattern for how we organize our lives in cooperation with one another and denotes our aspirations for future social and individual life conditions. Social policy says something about the state of our civilization and how we relate to one another and the physical environment in which we live.

This book treats the subject of social policy in two ways. First, it reviews the dimensions that constitute social policy in present society. This part of the discussion is based on the premise that until we understand our present reality, we cannot create a more desirable future. And, if we don't mindfully create our future, we are bound to suffer from democratic drift; that is, we will follow familiar patterns and institutions unquestioningly, such as unfettered markets and other inappropriate behaviours, no matter where they may lead and who benefits and disbenefits from them. To suggest we suffer from democratic drift at present would be redundant. Democratic drift recycles the same old solutions to the same old problems and takes us where most of us don't want to go. Engaging the same solutions to resolve recurring problems when they didn't work in the first instance is a definition of insanity and is particularly relevant today. We as a collective society need to reflect on our present condition and decide how we want life to be structured in the short and long term and then put mindful policies and plans into place to achieve those goals rather than relying on old remedies to solve society's present problems when they clearly haven't worked previously. The second objective of this book is to sketch out society's present and anticipated social problems and suggest policy solutions to meet those challenges. It is critical to keep our eye on the macro end goal, but it is also imperative to address immediate issues given their impact on the day-to-day lives of many of our fellow citizens. To that end, this book challenges the appropriateness of present social policy and sets out ways to address its shortcomings.

Social policy is often talked about but little understood. Most think it is short-term social insurance fashioned exclusively to support those out of work and in poverty. The focus on poverty is certainly a major issue of disquiet in society and will consume many pages of this book, but social policy is also concerned with various aspects of modern existence that are basic to achieving a quality of life worth living for everybody in society, including the idea of social justice. A modern civilization possesses needs greater than simply the alleviation of poverty. Although it is not difficult to create a potential catalogue of those requirements, it is more useful to come to a collective consensus on what should be included in the social policy inventory and then determine to what extent each item should be supplied through public expenditure and what can be left to the private marketplace. Social policy is essentially about things that are wrong in society and what needs to be done to fix them and the social aspirations of a population.

***

Many authors have provided definitions of what constitutes social policy. Some of these definitions address domains of life that are in deficit, and a number of them include notions of individual and community developmental. The main groupings of social policy will be identified further along in this book, but it is important to stress here that there are many different components to social policy formulation that do not deal specifically with concrete individual issues, but with processes and activities that are intricately connected to realizing the aspirations of society and in achieving continued social development. Further, social policy is fundamentally about the aspirations of society and the emotional, social, and physical well-being of all individuals in it. The social policy debate is a discussion about how society should express its values generally and organize itself specifically. Processes and activities that facilitate social policy development often get lost in the debate when people focus prematurely on generating potential solutions to unclearly defined problems without proper reflection on the context and substance of the issue to be addressed, or at the expense of constructing an inadequate structure for policy making and program delivery. The unforeseen side effects of individual social policies must also be considered before launching into a program that may do more damage than it remedies.

In its most basic form, social policy is about making choices and the processes involved in making them. These choices and the processes by which they are made rely on identified social purposes and the various ideological ideas that lay behind alternative options. Social policy is also about resolving conflict inherent in decision making by, in the first instance, including all segments of society in the decision-making process through some form of citizen participation. Social policy construction is fundamentally about engagement and inclusiveness in addition to the resolution of substantive social and individual problems in society.

Social policy formulation rests on acting or not in society. If a particular identified need is not addressed, then that, too, constitutes a form of social policy. Social policy formulation involves all segments of the public, either formally or informally, in decision making. Decisions are not limited to what services will be provided to the public, but also with who will provide them. As a consequence, it is not only governments at all levels that are involved, but also civil society, the voluntary nongovernment organization (NGO) sector, and private enterprise.

Other authors add elements to this definition. Finkel (2006), for example, adds dynamics when he defines social policy as a "set of non-market decisions, public and private, that determine the distribution of wealth to individuals and families and the degree of availability of human services to all members of society" (p. 3). Gilbert (2002) weighs in on the subject of social policy and planning when he suggests "social planning is often finding the appropriate mix of public investments, economic sanctions and social incentives to create the social environment desired" (p. 62).

What is wrong in society is often a matter of individual perception and choice, as the previous definitions suggest, and not a widely agreed-upon specific catalogue of deficiencies or desires. Social aspirations are as wide and as varied as the number of people who constitute society. It is often relatively easy to reach agreement on social policies that are clearly dedicated to sustaining a minimum standard of life for those in need, but once social policy leaves the minimum standards realm and approaches the social development spectrum, agreement is much harder to achieve. Additionally, social policy is viewed by those who see human relations in strictly economic terms as an impediment to the efficient functioning of the market. For those in this camp, social policy is best left minimal, if not avoided entirely, and, in their view, life—social life included—should be directly tied to market forces. On the other hand, many of us take a much more pragmatic approach to social policy provision and see a spectrum of needs and services as the responsibility of the public enterprise rather than simply leaving social decision making completely to the market.

For most, if not all, countries in the developed world, it can be said that they do not regularly let their citizens die of starvation, but resistance to social payments stiffens when social policy enters into less clear areas. However, the devil, as they say, is in the details. All of us have different standards and ideas about what constitutes a sufficient quality of life and how that should be achieved. Negotiating an agreement that gives substance to that objective is a major task for policy makers. The debate that eventually produces the fundamental standard for social policy forms the platforms and defines the differences among the political parties at election time and the various personal views on the subject within society more generally. Suffice it to say that what gets enunciated as social policy in the end is frequently a result of a most contentious debate. Compromise is needed to reach a conclusion and, as a consequence, often results in a less-than-adequate solution to the original problem. An important but often lost step in the process is to return to the original vision initiating the policy debate to determine if the final solution is the best one possible or even partially adequate to address the task. A good example of this problem is President Obama's healthcare reform in the United States known as 'The Affordable Care Act'. The final policy solution gained through hard compromise turned out to be a long way from what was originally envisioned, and one needs to wonder whether or not the act will take the country any closer to solving the healthcare problem that gave impetus to the original effort. Although Obama Care, as it is euphemistically referred to, is demonstrating its potential to advance medical care in the United States, the final judgment of its true success can only be made some time in the future and after it has had sufficient time to become part of the social fabric. In some instances no policy may be a better alternative than to accept something that does not address the problem sufficiently just for the sake of political cache or to avoid the appearance of failure.

In addition to the processes and activities inherent in social policy making enunciated earlier, social policy development must be committed to generating wide-ranging citizen input into the decision-making process, including those who will be most affected by the eventual policies that result from the discussion. This is such a critical area of concern that an entire chapter of this book is devoted to that subject. Citizen participation is another one of those phrases that are often spoken but little understood by those who are responsible for policy formulation and decision making.

Tensions between politicians and the public frequently increase when social policy strays into areas that are not seen to be directed exclusively to the disadvantaged. Health is often one of those domains that generate the greatest amount of rancour. There are those who argue that healthcare can be supplied more efficiently through the market mechanism than by the public system. The other side contends that health is not a commodity to be consumed but a right to be enjoyed by all citizens and, therefore, should be left in the public domain and not in the hands of those whose primary interest is profit. Health is but one example of the debate about what should be in or out of the public social policy arena when it comes to formulating the public's social agenda. The healthcare debate, among others, is addressed in greater detail in later parts of this book.

What is noticeable about the discussions and definitions provided earlier is that they do not speak specifically about alternative solutions to social problems or outcomes resulting from social policy, although these realizations are critical in the final analysis. The discussion to this point has been entirely concerned with making choices and determining the actors (sectors) in the system and not subject areas that need attention. A sound policy-making process will determine what is included or not in the eventual repertoire of social policies and services to be delivered to a targeted population. And it should not be assumed that all jurisdictions will focus on the same entities or with equal intensity if they do happen to coincide. Social policy is an individual response to a set of unique conditions experienced by a specific location and context. Without a sound and clearly enunciated unique vision to be achieved and an identified process for achieving it, the social policy debate will break down and result in less than a satisfactory conclusion.

***

Social policies are based, in part, on social problems. I say 'in part' because social policies may also be developmental rather than purely remedial. For example, social policy resulting in an art gallery is often not thought of as remedial but as an opportunity to advance appreciation for humanly created aesthetics. It is therefore a developmental activity rather than a remedial one, but could very well be considered part of the social policy agenda. That aside, a very critical first step in the policy process is to formulate the problem statement and vision for action on which all activity will be eventually concentrated. Although the policy formulation process is addressed in detail later in this book, it is important to state here that how a problem is perceived and articulated is critical to the eventual resolution of the undesired condition. If the problem is not conceptualized and enunciated accurately and many people will perceive the issue slightly differently, then the risk of not achieving the desired end state is high. Additionally, the way a problem is visualized determines the range of possible solutions to it, and the way it is conceived determines the kind of strategy that is appropriate for its resolution. For example, the eradication of poverty, if seen as a problem of economic growth, will produce strategies to grow the economy. If, on the other hand, poverty eradication is viewed as a matter of wealth distribution and not growth, then that will lead to altogether different strategies for resolving the problem. Clear problem descriptions that are agreed to by all players in the system are absolutely critical to the successful resolution of any problem. If there is no clear agreement on what needs resolving, then technical arguments among the stakeholders in the process will arise constantly and throughout the course of the decision-making and planning activity. Neglecting this part of the process often results in a frustrating experience for those involved and a less-than-adequate resolution to the problem. In effect, those working on the issue will continually attempt to clarify what they are trying to achieve because it constantly appears to them that the deliberations do not speak to their conception of the problem. Agreement on the definition of the problem by those who will be the recipients of the eventual policy is also critical. Leaving the constituency out of the process is often experienced in the developing world where the donors or Western-based NGOs determine the problem to be addressed and when the real needs of those living in country are left unidentified and consequently unaddressed. Leaving those experiencing the problem out of the decision-making process is a constant recurring problem in the West as well as in the developing world.

***

Social policy formulation and implementation have many complicated aspects, and they can be boiled down to three main areas of concern. First, are the technical processes and resulting information that needs to be understood and made a part of the social policy formulation process. Original research is often undertaken to provide measures on the condition to be resolved. In addition to primary data collection methods such as surveys and interviews there are other methods for gaining important technical information as well. Data can be obtained through reviews of pertinent existing documentation that may have been collected for a previous social policy decision, or information contained in documents that were constructed for entirely different purposes. All of this data, properly analyzed, will provide decision makers with valuable technical information on which to make the right decision when the issue is presented to them for their consideration. Many people, including politicians, often think they have the common-sense solution to all social problems and don't require research to expand their view. However, their intuition on many of these issues has been clearly demonstrated to be inadequate and half-baked in the past. Research must be undertaken and its results made part of the social policy construction process if all aspects of the problem, who it might affect, and in what ways is to be made clear. Although research will not provide decisions in and of itself, it will certainly help decision makers greatly in reaching well-informed decisions.

Social policies also need to be motivational and inspirational. Unless the decision makers and general public are inspired and understand fully and agree with the rationale for the specific policy under consideration, there will be little or no support for its eventual acceptance and implementation. Important to the process is a public discussion that results in understanding and enthusiasm for the policy. Policies should appeal to the imagination of the target community and cause individuals in that setting, and the public at large, to be enthused about the potential of the social policy to make life better. In addition to being inspiring, policies need to create confidence in their ability to resolve the issue under review.

Finally, policies must be constructed so that they can fit into the established bureaucratic system. It is often the bureaucracy that is charged with policy implementation on a daily basis, so policies must be constructed so that they can be delivered with great ease and not formulated so that they cause roadblocks and reduce accessibility to those in need. The simpler the implementation strategy, the more likely it is to be accepted and implemented successfully.

In a time of severe government financial restraint and cutback, policy makers should also look to civil society, particularly voluntary organizations, to assist with policy implementation. Caution in this regard is needed, however. It may be expedient for governments to turn over too much social policy implementation to the voluntary and private sector, and we must not allow governments to abdicate their responsibility for addressing social problems through overreliance on the nongovernment sector. Food banks established by well-meaning voluntary organizations became a permanent fixture on the social landscape shortly after they were originally designed as a stop-gap measure in the fight against hunger and until the public sector could deal permanently with the poverty problem. These institutions are still with us today and may now be an impediment to dealing with poverty in a comprehensive manner by the public sector. Twentieth-century civilization proceeded through the charitable approach to social policy formulation and responsibility and opted for state involvement in order to provide a service that was comprehensive and nonpartisan. It is important not to retreat to the charity model stage of development, which would be a backward step. Increasing reliance on food banks may be just such a retrograde step in that direction. Certainly, voluntary agencies and volunteers can be a part of the social policy mix in many ways, but not with the intent of letting governments off the hook for producing a just and acceptable standard of life for all citizens.

***

Social policy encompasses a number of areas that affect the health and well-being of the human population. Collectively, issues such as health, including mental health, pensions (more specifically adequate sustenance and personal care in old age), adequate housing, equality and justice, and the construction of and access to democratic institutions, determine the quality of life for individuals and are frequently part of any comprehensive social policy set that gets established by governments on behalf of its citizens. It is often said that one catastrophic event can throw a life into turmoil, and without social policy to provide assistance and support in such circumstances, an individual's existence may be severely and negatively affected and may even be placed in jeopardy.

Although all of the aforementioned themes are critical to quality of life, poverty is a central issue in the social policy debate. There are many countries throughout the world where lives are negatively affected due to the lack, or complete absence, of formal social policy. At a minimum, and in its barest form, social policy is dedicated to supporting citizens who encounter an extraordinary event that causes upheaval and damage to their existence or lifestyle, be it related to health, housing, lack of income, or a myriad of other fundamental quality-of-life issues. At the other end of the spectrum social policy can increase social development and functioning by concentrating on universal provision of services that improves the quality of individual lives and social functioning. Social policy is fundamental to providing a system that supports its citizens in satisfying the fundamental needs society has deemed necessary for its citizens to live an adequate life. What constitutes an adequate life, however, is a matter for citizens of all countries to determine through debate and deliberation. The responsibility of government is to provide leadership to and operationalize the results of that deliberation. Finally, social policy is devoted to producing or increasing social solidarity among its citizenry. Social solidarity is the glue that binds society together by creating a sense of belonging to the larger body of society, and social policies are a primary method for achieving that cohesion.

Although many of the subjects addressed by social policy appear to be unrelated, a closer look exposes their interdependence and relationships. Certainly a catastrophic health incident could very well thrust an individual or family into absolute poverty if they do not have adequate private health insurance or, more likely, live in a country that provides such insurance publically. On the other hand, poverty can lead to poor health. The interrelation of many social conditions is complex but undeniable.

All of the domains that constitute social policy can be either a cause or an effect, depending on the situation encountered, but poverty more often than not acts as an independent variable and is frequently a great influence on whether or not the other problems outlined earlier are present or absent in a person's life. For example, a person in poverty often suffers from inadequate housing and poor health because of that poverty. Access to higher education is problematic for someone stricken with poverty. On the other hand, a person suffering from mental illness may become dysfunctional and succumb to poverty as a result. All of this demonstrates how the major domains of social policy relate to one another and are intricately entwined. The position of this book is that poverty has an overwhelming causal effect on many of the other domains in social life at both the individual and societal level and, as a result, will form the major entry point in this volume for examining present and future social policy. Poverty is a pervasive and dominant issue in our modern world, be it in the affluent countries of the globe or in the developing and less prosperous parts of the world. Not considering war or the death and destruction perpetuated by tyrannical governments, poverty stands as the single most social evil in the world today.

***

This book includes many of the issues often thought to be the exclusive domain of environmental policy. Certainly subjects such as climate change and global warming are indeed rightfully discussed as environmental policy independent of social policy, but this book suggests that social and environmental problems are related and connected and need to be addressed interdependently. As Homer-Dixon (2006, p. 295) reminds us, "Our global problems are not technological ones: they are political problems fraught with conflicts over values, interests, and power; surrounded by scientific uncertainty, and burdened with deep moral implications." What society establishes as a *raison d'être* or guiding principle affects both social and environmental policy equally. The human animal historically focused its effort either collectively or individually on eking out a living. Many of today's institutions devoted to this task are now wreaking great havoc on the planet because of overconsumption and the dominance of economics in human relations. It would not be a surprise if future anthropologists term our generation of *Homo sapiens* '*Homo economicus*' given our single-minded focus on economic relations through exploitation of the environment and overconsumption. This is all to suggest that until we harmonize social and environmental policy, human society will remain in great peril, not only from a social but also from an environmental perspective.

***

The modern economy is skewed so that humans have not only become sheepishly greedy, but admire greed, and some accumulate great amounts of wealth, leaving others, maybe half the population or more, destitute or severely behind those at the top end of the economic ladder. It is difficult to countenance the huge multimillion-dollar bonuses paid annually to CEOs. At the same time these huge bonuses are being handed out, many social programs that are vital to the well-being of a large number of individuals are being cut and reduced drastically. It seems ludicrous for the U.S. Congress, and other governments throughout the world, to continually insist on cutting the so-called entitlements when numerous individuals are being remunerated so exorbitantly. The gap between the rich and the poor is greater now than before the First World War (Piketty, 2014), when the world's wealth was held in the hands of the aristocracy. Why are we so protective of those at the top of the economic ladder and at the same time willing to let those at the bottom drift further into poverty?

Although inequality among some nations seems to be decreasing (perhaps with the obvious exception of the African countries), inequality within countries is on the rise. As a result, we see the spontaneous rise of the Occupy movements and other similar social action forces throughout the world that are dedicated to shining light on this increasing inequality. Equity in sharing the world's resources in a sustainable manner, both among individuals and between nations, is urgently needed and is an issue for social policy to address. This does not mean there should be no variation in wealth, but the notion of 'limited inequality' needs to be considered and held as a social principle in both advanced and less developed countries. This idea could form the basis on which social policy is formulated in the future. Only by pursuing a concept such as limited inequality will we deal effectively with the growing and demoralizing separation of the rich and poor that exists in society at present. How this idea gets defined is yet to be determined, and its construction would warrant widespread discussion in the public domain. Nonetheless the idea of limited inequality needs focused attention in any attempt at resolving this social justice issue that continually plagues society. The idea of limited inequality is a vital concept and will be discussed in detail in later chapters of this book.

***

Until now capitalism has been good at growing the economy, but has failed miserably at dealing adequately with the distribution of that wealth and with reducing the high levels of poverty faced by all countries in the world today. In spite of great rhetoric to eliminate deficiency in all parts of the world, including in the affluent countries, high levels of poverty have not deteriorated sufficiently, in spite of enormous wealth creation since the end of the World War Two. The market economy has had trouble dealing equitably with the constant increase in healthcare needs and costs and housing requirements for many citizens worldwide. The popular idea that a rising tide lifts all boats in a capitalist economy is now thoroughly discredited. Creating a society that relies on overconsumption has also led to massive climate change and other environmental disasters producing great environmental stress in addition to heightened anxiety about the general state of the economy. The capitalist economy neglects to address the environmental externalities that its activity produces causing poisoned air, water, and land. As a consequence we are now faced with a severe environmental crisis, including global warming and climate change. These environmental conditions directly affect the health of the population.

Western nations have created an exaggerated, if not dysfunctional, economy, and the resulting expectations of reproducing this extravagance in all other countries throughout the world will be not only hard to duplicate, but will inflict great havoc on the environment. What is generally considered to be the American dream—that all individuals in society can prosper through hard work and ingenuity—could become the world's nightmare, particularly if it means developing the same type of affluence in India and China as was produced in the Western world during the nineteenth and twentieth centuries.

As we approach the third decade of the twenty-first century and rebound from the great recession produced in the latter part of the first decade, the major economies of the Western world are in the midst of a severe economic restructuring. The middle class in the United States and in other Western nations is quickly disappearing and, as the disparity in incomes becomes more pronounced, these countries are in jeopardy of taking on many of the social characteristics of the developing world. This eventuality is particularly apparent in many U.S. cities. Not being able to create or perpetuate a middle class is one of the main reasons why many developing world countries have not been able to climb out of their economic malaise. This situation in the United States is partly due to the inability to construct adequate social policy to address the decline of the middle class and the abandonment of the poor. In his book *The Conscience of a Liberal*, Nobel Laureate Paul Krugman (2007) chronicles the history of the rise and decline of the middle class; the people on whom the advance of the economy has come to depend. As Krugman chronicles, the poor dominated the American landscape in the latter part of the nineteenth and early part of the twentieth century, giving rise to social policy and social welfare generally. Progressive political policies throughout the Great Depression and World War Two created a middle class by the 1950s. Since then, however, Krugman demonstrates that North American society and the West generally have once again reduced their middle class and created an enormous separation between the rich and poor. What was once a compressed society with reasonable separation between the rich and poor (limited inequality) has become severely unbalanced again. There now appears to be an economically unacceptable distance between the have and have-nots in society and among countries. As Krugman (2007) dramatically concludes,

> Now we live in a second Gilded Age, as the middle-class society of the postwar era rapidly vanishes. The conventional wisdom of our time is that this is a bad thing, and it is the result of forces beyond our control. But the story of the Great Compression is a powerful antidote to fatalism, a demonstration that political reform can create a more equitable distribution of income—and, in the process, create a healthier climate for democracy.
> (p. 39)

Creating a more egalitarian and balanced lifestyle for all humans and respecting the needs of the ecological system are major themes of this book. This volume examines the social safety net in general and rests on the premise that structural economic inequality and high levels of poverty provide the origin for the present crisis in society and not the entitlements or social policies that are in place today, as some would have us believe.

The purpose of this book is to examine present-day social policy with the aim of determining if society is on the right path to achieve a sustainable environment within a balanced social system inside a sustainable and equitable economic order. The following chapters in this book will not only examine the present social issues within society, but also determine the basis on which a healthier society could be built and how that goal might be achieved. As briefly explained earlier, this volume views social policy to include macro issues such as the health of the environment as well as micro concerns such as poverty reduction and supplying sufficient housing and adequate healthcare to all. It also examines the role of leisure and democratic participation as inputs to, and outcomes of, social policy. The book basically takes the position that the present version of the capitalist system is worn out; it has produced huge income inequality and widespread corruption over the recent past. It is in bad need of revision if issues such as environmental protection and satisfactory social provision are to be adequately addressed. This book postulates that the time-honoured tradition of unfettered exploitation of the globe's natural resources through hard work and for economic gain may now be leading humanity to catastrophe, and a great social transition to a 'new economy' and a remake of the social contract is needed in order to produce a system that changes the old paradigm drastically, resulting in a more sustainable environmental and social system. Some ideas of what that system might look like are attempted in later chapters of this book.

***

This book also aims to examine social policy in light of analyzing the present and future needs of society that are anticipated to result from the 'new economy'. The new economy is taking form in the developed world as the transition of manufacturing to the emerging economies such as China, Brazil, and India takes place. The movement of manufacturing to parts of the developing world from Europe and North America is necessitating the expansion of the service, technological, and financial sector to replace manufacturing. A short description of what the new economy looks like and how it is being created will provide an adequate foundation for the discussion of social policy formulation that shapes the focus for the remainder of this book.

This writing could get swallowed up very easily in describing and addressing the economic landscape, but the intent here is to set the stage for a more in-depth discussion of the need for a new social contract, so a short description of the characteristics of the present economy will suffice. The 'new economy' is creating uncertainty and turmoil as it transitions from manufacturing to a technological, finance, and service-based economy, and it is assumed that social policy will address the inadvertent anxieties and tensions that this change produces. The intent is to construct a postmodern social system that provides more equity and less variance in incomes and quality of life than it was ever possible to do in the industrial age. Eventually social policy in this new environment will not only be remedial, in the sense that it addresses social problems that are produced by the present economic system, but will, in fact, focus much of its attention on creating an egalitarian society where aesthetic consumption and accomplishment replace material consumption and accumulation as the major social values in society. That said, it is understood that the conditions of poverty, need for universal healthcare, adequate housing to house the homeless, justice and equality for all citizens, and, particularly, the protection of the environment on which we all depend for our existence will be addressed as the transition spoken about earlier takes shape. The intent of this book is to address those immediate problems in addition to advocating for a new social contract and social order that makes the short-term issues redundant over the long term as these problems will no longer be an externality of the new economy. Social policy, in this author's view, must be proactive in creating the future organization of society based on principles of justice and equality (limited inequality) in society and the production of a sustainable environment, not simply reactive policy that deals remedially with social problems as they arise through the externalities and negative forces inherent in the present economic system.

It is understood that the environmental and social order that accompanies the new economy will not take on the orientation described earlier unless it is intentionally guided in that direction. To leave such important matters to what has become known as 'the invisible hand of the market' will simply lead to more of the same corruption, greed, and malaise that have led society to where it is today. Society must plan its way out of this dilemma and create a social order that respects the environment and provides equality to all its citizens in order for humanity to continue to flourish on this planet. As a consequence, the intent of this book is to provoke a discussion that places humans above the economy and is based on the notion that the function of any economy is to serve humans and not the other way around, as it has tended to do over the later stages of industrial age.

With the dangers of such environmental catastrophe as climate change staring us in the face, there is great motivation to create a new social order that lives in harmony with the planet and transitions away from life-threatening practices that are a result of an unfettered and inequitable economic system that depends on continual and exaggerated growth for its existence. In addition to climate change, intractable poverty threatens us and the planet. As long as there is exaggerated poverty in society due to the unequal distribution of wealth within and among societies, there continues to be the production of excessive goods and services in an attempt to satisfy the basic needs of those at the bottom of the economic ladder and create greater wealth for those at the top. The basic idea here is that the economy should be devoted to satisfying the basic needs of all people on the planet and not dedicated to producing extravagant wealth for the few. Overcoming these fundamental problems are the key factors on which the new economy is based, and they will form the underpinnings of the suggested social policies, programs, and strategies provided in this book. Fundamentally, the new economy will emphasize 'effectiveness' over 'efficiency' as defined by classical economics.

The transition to the new economy and hence 'new society' will depend on the creation of theoretical frameworks and blueprints to guide that change. This book provides a discussion on current and new theoretical frameworks for achieving the daunting task described herein. And, although the task may seem truly daunting, maybe unachievable to some readers, it must be stressed that the present course of society and its economy is no longer a viable option and will spell the demise of the human species unless it is transitioned to something more in keeping with the physical limits of the planet. In addition, the new economy must be dedicated to reversing the trend of increasing disparity among countries and within populations. Many respected commentators and scientists such as Steven Hawking have taken a more pessimistic view of the situation when suggesting that it may be already too late to save the environment and the future of humanity lies in colonizing another planet and abandoning this one. This book does not take such a dire tone, but it does understand the enormity of the problem and realizes that a huge economic transition is needed, which is not too dissimilar from the great leap humans made centuries ago when they evolved from a hunting and gathering existence to agriculture or from an agrarian to a manufacturing economy. This book assumes that a transition is inevitable and focuses its effort on what principles the economy and society could embrace rather than leaving it entirely up to those who want to reproduce the status quo or something close to that tradition. The stance of this book is that tinkering with the present system is not sufficient to take humanity into the next great leap forward, but a new society founded upon principles that reflect the true interests of all humanity and a better balance of the life-world[1] with the system-world is necessary if that goal is to be accomplished.

***

As Western society moves toward the third decade of the twenty-first century, social policy and planning for social development have become a heightened focus of attention by governments and citizens alike, but usually as a subset of economic policy. Social policy has become a target for deficit fighting just at a time when it is most needed in support of those at the bottom of society and without the means to support themselves to any reasonable standard. Recessions traditionally produce high levels of unemployment, making many of our citizens vulnerable and reliant on the public wage. It is important to bolster social policy at these times and not diminish its role. However, modern social policy in this complicated era must transcend the reactive approach that politicians took to it in the past and move to a forward-looking comprehensive policy that tackles a number of social goals and overlapping objectives in allied domains. As more and more people become alienated from the capitalist labour market, social policy will need to focus less on stop-gap measures—social insurance—designed to tide the unemployed over until they reengage in traditional work, and focus more on creating an alternative to paid work—social development—that provides for a meaningful lifestyle that is both stimulating to the individual and of benefit to the community in which they live. If a transition from the classical capitalist arrangement does not occur in a timely and orderly fashion, then social collapse and revolution can be expected. People in formerly affluent countries will not sit by and be subjected to 25 to 50 percent unemployment rates or employment that keeps them in perpetual poverty and, at the same time, watch others enjoy unprecedented wealth.

Social analysis and policy must focus on revamping the economy and not simply centre on short term measures to protect against starvation. Society should not be asked to rely on economic growth over the long term to address this issue. This latter approach has not worked in the past and needs to be completely rethought. The idea that the economy must serve humanity rather than the other way around is needed as a beacon to modern social policy formation. The perpetual growth scenario that has formed the framework for social development during modern times has produced catastrophic environmental implications that need to be addressed in tandem with concerns of economic inequality. The globe can no longer tolerate the ideology that allows economic growth to trump all other social and environmental concerns as it has to this point in history. The environmental health of the planet must be viewed as a priority, and a social concern and be incorporated into an overarching social policy.

***

We live in a time of unprecedented planetary peril due to climate change, which can be directly related to the relentless push for economic growth. Most of the returns produced by this increase in economic growth are being appropriated by the upper 10 percent of the population. This is occurring at a time when the middle class in America, and in other affluent countries, is in decline and about to partially replicate developing world living standards. To many observers, the increasing inequality in wealth is no longer related to one's contribution to the social good, but to unfettered greed and the imposition of a class system that protects its wealthy and exploits the mass population. There is too cozy a relationship between the wealthy in society and the politicians that govern it. Politicians rely on the wealthy to fund their campaigns, and the wealthy are given too much access to the corridors of power as their reward for that financing.

There is no relationship between the huge bonuses paid to bankers and the manipulators of the market system and achieving a healthy economy. This unhealthy relationship was clearly exposed when bankers and related industries paid themselves huge bonuses at a time when they were responsible for the near collapse of the economy and a looming depression in 2008. It may be one thing to pay bonuses in a year when the firm does well, but it is simply untenable to do so in a time that produces huge losses to investors and taxpayers alike. It doesn't seem morally right or socially healthy to provide a small group in society with astronomical remuneration for questionable practices when governments at all levels are cutting back on social expenditures, causing hardship among the larger population. It is clear that a rethinking of how society organizes its financial affairs is needed rather than relying on historic platitudes and ideology, much of which is skewed in favour of the wealthy. More of the same kind of thinking that narrowly escaped a depression will only lead to the same conclusion, and maybe we won't be so lucky in narrowly escaping the catastrophe next time. It seems that we have attempted to drag social and economic practices that may have been appropriate for an industrial society into a new economy that requires original thinking and fresh ways of practicing economics and social life.

At the time this book is being written, North America and Western European countries have been struggling to recover from a deep recession and general economic malaise. In fact, it is not completely clear yet that the world is safe from falling into another recession or worse in the near future. The last recession was accelerated unduly by the added burden placed on the financial system by the unwarranted and exorbitant risk taken by many of its largest financial institutions or what is euphemistically dubbed 'Wall Street' in the United States. The continual erosion of regulations governing the operations of the banking system, problematic practices such as the subprime housing mortgage market, and the bundling of these mortgages into mortgaged-backed securities that were then sold to unsuspecting secondary security holders caused the financial system to lapse into turmoil once housing prices declined. The mortgages that secured those properties were all of a sudden worth more than the property itself, essentially causing the recession to deepen. Although these schemes reduced the risks for those who sold the bundled mortgages initially, it transferred the burden to unsuspecting investors, usually banks and subsequent secondary holders of this toxic paper. Those selling these toxic instruments may have known full well that the mortgagee had no possibility of fulfilling their obligation over the long term; however, this was of little or no concern to them because they knew they would not hold these mortgages to maturity. When housing prices were increasing in value, this practice did not present a mortal danger to society, but once the housing market and prices began to correct and pull back, many of the mortgage holders possessed an asset that was worth less than the price of the original mortgage. Making this toxic brew even more deadly was the fine print in the mortgage documents, which called for an escalation of interest rates to the mortgagee after a short honeymoon period. As a result of these practices the housing market collapsed, causing many banks and trusts to foreclose on their mortgage holders, throwing the whole housing system into chaos. This turmoil resulted in severely declining housing prices that effectively closed down the housing market for an extended period.

As the supporters of the capitalist system are quick to remind us, the banks that essentially went bankrupt should have been allowed to fail and go out of business. But that is not what happened. Many of these banks were deemed 'too big to fail' and, as a result, their debt was nationalized through government bailouts. Effectively, we now have a situation where profits are privatized for banks but the consequences to society if this risky behaviour turns sour is nationalization of the debt through government intervention and bailouts by the taxpayer. Essentially, the risk has been permanently transferred to taxpayers. This practice is tantamount to handing these institutions a blank cheque, which is commonly referred to as 'moral hazard'. This practice by U.S. banks was not allowed to happen in Canada. A far-sighted former finance minister was not persuaded by the Canadian banks to open up this lethal practice, as was the case in the United States and in other parts of Western Europe, so during the 2008 recession Canadian banks remained fairly unscathed, as did the Canadian taxpayer.

As alluded to earlier, the banking system, equity markets, and small and large businesses have been recently rocked by the near collapse of the capital system, which provides the foundation for the local and global economies. As a result, attention to the social safety net is again receiving heightened attention in both a positive and negative way. Large numbers of people have been thrown out of work and, as a result of the collapse of the subprime mortgage market in the United States and elsewhere in the world, many people have lost their homes through foreclosure. All of these events have put great pressure on social welfare budgets at a time when economic indicators are also showing a slow and lagging economy apparently for the foreseeable future. Federal and central banks around the world have reduced their interest rates to near zero, which does not leave them many alternatives when it comes time to fight the next economic slowdown. All of this is to say that we live in a time when the economy is fragile, and there is great concern about the possibility of a long-lasting recovery.

***

Recent global events have radically challenged the way we view and act in the world today. The current economic meltdown has brought a new reality to the consumptive, destructive behaviour that led to society's idea of a decent 'quality of life'. The overreliance of the economy on increasing consumer consumption is now being seen as a flimsy house of cards on which the future environmental and economic system rests, making many economists, pundits, and social commentators uneasy about the future. Exacerbating this situation is the consumer who has retreated from the market because of high unemployment rates and what has been termed a 'jobless recovery'. It is now recognized that the high standard of living in the United States and other Western countries has been based on individual borrowing and debt over the last decade rather than wage increases and wealth creation by the middle class. In fact, the captains of industry continue to call for more efficient labour markets, which is code for reducing wages to workers. This mind-set is a prescription for a continued spiral of descent for the middle class, possibly resulting in its death. Society is experiencing the hollowing out of the middle class, and some of our wealthy citizens are becoming wealthier on the backs of those who are becoming poorer. McMurtry (1999) has identified this state in the title of his book as the Cancer Stage of Capitalism. Although the economy seems to be recovering slowly for large businesses that export most of their goods abroad, it is not having the same effect for the average citizen who labours for a living. It seems that hefty bonuses and other forms of exorbitant remuneration are still being paid to the upper-tier executives in the financial sector, regardless of whether or not their companies turn a profit. However, Britain and Europe are now limiting the bonuses paid to bankers, so bonuses can no longer exceed what employees make in wages. This is a step in the right direction, and hopefully this practice will spread to North America and beyond.

It is reported that the jobless recovery is a result of decreased domestic spending, but there is another variable at work here as well, and that is the continuation and expansion of the technological revolution. Technology devoted to speeding up business and increasing exploitation of natural resources is outstripping society's ability to control and manage the environment in a sustainable way. It is fair to say that the technological revolution is now advancing faster than social institutions can keep up, leading to many practices that will have severe detrimental effects on the environment and social conditions in the future.

Since the last recession corporations have mainly focused their effort on improving productivity in the workplace by increasing the use of technology in the production process. Human input in production is being relied on less and less, and labour is being replaced in the manufacturing process with new technologies. It is arguably this new technology that is increasing productivity in manufacturing and other sectors of the economy and not the continued discipline of labour, as has been the case traditionally.

Additionally, we see a major shift in manufacturing from the developed world to China and other parts of Asia, leaving manufacturing at about 20 percent of the economy in Europe and North America. It seems that manufacturing in the developed world is going into decline, as did agriculture in the earlier part of the twentieth century. The decline in manufacturing is causing North American and Western Europe to develop a new economy based on the financial sector, services, and knowledge industries. What is not known at the present time is whether or not the new industries will be capable of generating enough employment to replace the jobs lost in manufacturing and whether or not these new sectors can provide wages at the same level of those traditionally seen in the former industries. Regardless of these new issues, the industrial age and the capitalist economy has always had difficulty fulfilling some aspects of its early promise.

***

Some general issues provide an undercurrent to this discussion and are affecting the social policy debate at the present time. At least in Great Britain and Canada, if not the United States, the intent of social policy was originally intended to provide social insurance in times of need and to protect the general public from the vagaries of everyday life. Social policy may not be seen in that light any longer.

Rivaling security as the underlying principle of, and motivation for, social policy is the concept of 'adjustment'. Some policies such as unemployment insurance are not only providing a short-term wage to those who find themselves out of work, as it has done since its inception, but has introduced into the system skill upgrading programs to assist unemployed workers to gain new skills appropriate for a fast-changing economy and work environment. The Employment Insurance Program in Canada, for example, has increased eligibility requirements to get onto the system and lessened the number of weeks that a worker is insurable in order to find funds to develop these new adjustment initiatives. The transference of emphasis from insurance to adjustment has come at the expense of the security traditionally provided to unemployed workers by this program. The restructured approach is grounded in the belief that there are available jobs waiting for workers, but the barrier to taking those jobs is the lack of skill in the workforce. This may be an erroneous assumption if the job statistics provided by other government departments charged with monitoring such issues are to be trusted. So it would appear that the transition from security to adjustment in the unemployment system is an example of a trend that may prevail throughout the whole system.

In addition to the adjustment vs. security clash, an even greater struggle is taking place inside the social policy arena. Over recent years the private market vs. public provision of service debate has heated up, with great strength being exerted by those in favour of privatization and the market approach to social provision. In Canada, for example, universal healthcare has always been under attack by those who favour the private approach to human relations. They contend that private enterprise would be more efficient in service provision than the public sector. We can see what form this efficiency takes when we look at the American system. Defining efficiency is a critical activity in the debate. If we think that eliminating subscribers to private health insurance due to preexisting illness provides the definition for efficiency, then the advocates for privatization may be right. Other efficiency measures are found in driving down wages of workers in the industry and reducing the size of the workforce where possible. Some of these practices have produced questionable outcomes where health is concerned. If we believe that healthcare is a privilege and not a right, then the privateers may be right. If, on the other hand, we believe that health is a basic human right and that all people should have equal access to healthcare, then those who favour the public system will prevail in the end.

America and other countries have introduced privately run prison facilities either partially or in total. From time to time Canada has considered contracting out many of the day-to-day operations of their prisons rather than operate them themselves, and this debate continues. This arrangement has been seen as a healthy public/private partnership and a way for governments to reduce their expenditures on the prison system. There is great controversy about this practice, however. Should people be incarcerated by a private company instead of a publicly run and accountable public body? Incarceration restricts the freedom of individuals, and many citizens believe that such a drastic measure should be the sole responsibility of the public's government. Will the privatization of prisons create a new lobby group that will push governments to create new and more laws and to take other measures such as expanding minimum sentences as a way to increase their profits? This occurs in other sectors of the economy, so why not in the prison system?

In addition to the public vs. private debate is the creeping role of religion into the system. The presidential era of George W. Bush saw the transfer of responsibility for administering much social policy to the religious sector in the United States. Funds were transferred to the religious sector for training of the unemployed, for example. Money for providing assistance to the poor was also transferred to religious institutions. President Bush was quite convinced there was a legitimate role for the religious sector to play in social welfare policy. The days of separation between church and state came to an end. This approach was also a throwback to the charity model of social policy development and service provision, and we shouldn't want to retreat to that era again.

Finally, the last undercurrent issue that needs to be address is the decentralization vs. centralization question. Certainly in Canada and the United States, this debate is hotly contested because of their political histories. Generally speaking, decentralization and putting the decision-making power at the local level and closer to people who rely on social policy makes sense when viewed that way. The problem, of course, is that those who want to privatize the entire system would have greater power to do so at the local level. It is easier for special interests to get their way in a smaller arena than at the senior government level. It is not inconceivable that power from the quarter that usually prefers the market approach rather than government intervention would have undue sway in the debate. Captains of industry and free market advocates are quite familiar with exerting their inflated influence in persuading governments to view the issue as they see it. Private capital has undue sway in the affairs that affect all of humanity. Weight of voice in the decision-making process is another exceedingly important issue to address in the social policy debate.

How the division of power in social policy provision between the various levels of government is determined will change the entire nature of the social policy that exists today. That is not to say that present social policy is adequate for the near- and long-term future. It clearly is not. How those changes come about and who is involved in making them and with what weight is critical to this question of change, however. These and other questions of importance will form the remaining content of this volume. That said, it is not sufficient simply to ask questions or present a critique. It is imperative that potential answers and action steps be offered to remedy what is identified as in need of change. The remainder of this volume will attempt to do just that.

Note

1 Life-world and system-world are ideas first discussed by the Frankfurt School. The system-world represents the forces and interests of the social institutions that pervade society. The life-world represents the basic parts of life that are endemic to enhancing the individual life force. Many members of the Frankfurt School would suggest that in modern society the life-world is dominated by the system-world, and a balance between these two forces needs to be struck in order for the enhancement of everyday life for humans to improve or flourish.

References

Finkel, A. (2006). *Social Policy and Practice in Canada: A History.* Waterloo, Ontario, Canada: Wilfrid Laurier Press.
Gilbert, N. (2002). *Dimensions of Social Welfare Policy.* Boston: Allyn and Bacon.
Homer-Dixon, T. (2006). *The Upside of Down.* Toronto: Knopf Canada.
Krugman, P. (2007). *The Conscience of a Liberal.* New York: W.W. Norton & Company.
McMurtry, J. (1999). *The Cancer Stage of Capitalism.* London: Pluto.
Piketty, T. (2014). *Capital in the Twenty-First Century.* Cambridge, MA: The Belknap Press of Harvard University Press.
Redner, H. (2013). *Beyond Civilization: Society, Culture, and the Individual in the Age of Globalization.* New Brunswick, NJ: Transaction Publishers.

3 Culture and False Consciousness in Human Evolution

The idea of culture and the role it plays in the design of social policy is critical to the central focus of this book. Have you ever considered how we humans make sense of the world around us every minute of the day? Certainly, we do not analyze each event or activity that we constantly encounter as we navigate through everyday activities. Much of our actions are governed by rote. That is, we are preprogrammed to conduct our everyday affairs without thinking about them in minute detail, but act through habit. Much of this preprogramming is a result of generations of our forbearers building up knowledge as they encountered their environment and passed on their interactions with it to us through cultural practices. This has worked well for us in the past, but we are entering a new, drastically changed world, and many of those practices do not fit our present or future conditions, but they remain comfortable to us nonetheless. This makes culture slow and hard to change. Over the last century or more, many, if not all, of our behaviours and beliefs have been manufactured or preserved by those who have a stake in the present system, and particularly by those who want to shape human relations to their advantage. They are a small but wealthy group of people who profit from the way things are and appear to be willing to sacrifice the future to maintain their present position. As a consequence they maintain and attempt to perpetuate an elaborate set of beliefs and myths about how the world should operate and employ sophisticated mechanisms for the transmission and maintenance of those ideas.

Culture is the framework through which humans transact everyday life. It is a lens through which humans view the world. Some of society's traditional cultural practices are no longer applicable to our present world, but we hold on to them nonetheless. Also, some of these practices may never have been in the best interest of the mass of society but only benefited the few. McNamara (2004) has termed these bits of manufactured cultural practices that don't serve our collective interest any longer 'false consciousnesses'. The idea of false consciousness is raised as an inevitability of culture and how it distorts truth. Culture is seen as a major evolutionary devise in the life of humans that plays a deterministic role in social change, much like genes play in biological evolution. Culture may now be more important in determining the future of humankind than is biology. In fact, culture may now be changing biology rather than biology determining human behaviour, but more on that later.

Present-day and future societies will need to harness their technological development, which is now predominant in directing human culture, and turn their attention away from the production of consumer goods to helping society address an extremely fragile and deteriorating physical and social environment. Culture to this point in time has helped humans to be successful in exploiting the environment in an attempt to eke out a living and to accumulate wealth. It has done so without much regard for the physical health of the planet or for promoting equality throughout society. The day of reckoning for this reckless disregard for the environment and social system is here in the form of an exaggerated separation between the rich and poor and the warming of the earth's atmosphere. Notions of sustaining the environment will need to influence cultural patterns in the future if humans are to sustain life on this planet over the long term. The idea of equality between countries and among populations will also need to be part of this reorganizing.

Darwin (1859) in *On The Origin of Species*, as well as other notable modern evolutionary scholars such as Dawkins (2004), made the case for evolution's role in human development and the advance of life on this planet. Although there may be those who Dawkins describes as 'history deniers' who refuse to acknowledge the role evolution and natural selection play in human development and prefer to attribute all of existence, including the construction of the planet itself, to a supernatural being or intelligent designer, it is now clear that Darwin essentially had it right. Following on Darwin's incredible insight, it has become unambiguous that genes and DNA contain the context and rules of duplication that reproduce life in an evolutionary course and in a steady but changing pattern. It has been demonstrated that the isolation of individuals eventually causes new species to arise through segregation and natural selection and the consequent mutation of genes. It is also known that the recombination of genes over centuries and millennia will alter the organism significantly.

The role of biology, genes, and DNA in the evolution of all species is apparent, but what is less understood is the influence culture has on human evolutionary processes. The question of whether or not culture is now shaping biology is an important focus for research in academia today. In spite of some resistance, it is also becoming understood that culture is now a vital force for either continued human existence or its peril. The present consensus would suggest that the future success of humanity and the globe is in the hands of society and its cultural development.

***

Culture often gets defined in terms of a society's artifacts, such as its technology, food, and unique expressions found through such practices as dance and art; but it is much more than that. It is as deep and complex as how a society interprets the world. This interpretation is often constructed through generations of learned behaviour and supposedly directs a person's daily actions and provides structure to society. It explains how a particular society elucidates and interprets the world. Classical definitions of culture provided a focus for anthropological studies in the 1950s, '60s, and '70s when culture became recognized as a primary force in human social relations. Cultural anthropologists Keesing and Keesing (1971) define human culture "as the totality of learned, accumulated experience. Culture refers to those socially transmitted patterns of behaviour characteristic of a particular social group" (pp. 20–21). Kroeber and Kluckholn (1952) define culture as "patterns, explicit and implicit, of and for behaviour acquired and transmitted by symbols, constituting the distinctive achievement of human groups, including their embodiments in artifacts" (p. 1). Peacock and Kirsch (1970) add their ideas to the discussion. They suggest that "culture is a system of logically related ideas and values shared by participants in a social system, which in turn is a system of interacting roles and groups" (p. 26). Spradley and McCurdy (1975) in their definition of culture focus on the cognitive dimension of experience. They contend that "culture is the acquired knowledge that people use to interpret experience and to generate social behavior. This definition restricts the concept to what people know, the codes and rules that are socially acquired. Our definition involves a theory of meaning" (p. 5). They continue to say that "culture is that human experience and behavior that are largely products of symbolic meaning systems" (p. 5). A more contemporary definition of culture is given by Burns (1999) who defines culture as a "linked set of rules and standards shared by a society which produces behaviour judged acceptable by that group" (p. 57). Classical or contemporary, what all of these definitions share in common are the ingredients of shared values, cognitive experience and ideas, defined roles, and a mechanism for individuals to employ in their effort to interpret the world and their place in it.

***

Genes and culture have provided a complimentary mechanism to DNA in the evolutionary success of the human species. Culture is the mechanism that created the behaviour that assured human survival in the past. It has allowed humans to be so successful that we now dominate the planet, or at least we think we do. We hold dominion over all the animals as the Christian Bible would have it. In fact, we hold dominion over the entire planet. However, like other forces in evolution, culture will not guarantee continued success if the environment changes and culture does not adapt to those changes.

Culture through humanly constructed social institutions such as the economic system has an undeniably and profound effect on daily life. Some want to think about such institutions as part of the naturally occurring, organic world, such as in the concept of the invisible hand of the market. But on more sober thought, it can be seen that the economy and other such institutions are clearly constructed by humans and not naturally occurring at all. It is conceivable that humans can produce alternative ideas to the capitalist system if the situation warrants. After all, former societies existed on completely different subsistence and social arrangements. Feudalism and the mercantilism system successfully played solid, if short, roles in human affairs until they were no longer useful in supporting or advancing society. Other modern systems such as socialism also had its minute on the world stage. Although socialism has been largely discredited because of the bastardization of its principle tenets by the Soviet system, it is still useful today as an analytical and critical perspective that is becoming quite helpful in shining light on the foibles of capitalism as it matures and becomes exaggerated and hence, less relevant to the needs of all modern humans. Marx's comments about the eventual collapse of capitalism may yet prove prophetic.

Culture is also demonstrating its influence on biology as technological advances begin to control biological systems. Here I am referring to such ideas as genetic engineering and its influence on food production and the control of individual characteristics through cloning and the manipulation of genes. Certainly our consumer and throwaway culture which was made possible by the technological revolution is clearly having a huge detrimental effect on the climate of the planet. These quick examples very pointedly demonstrate the increasing influence of culture on shaping biological systems for both good or ill. Culture may now have greater influence on the future success or failure of the human species and the planet than biological processes will. With that in mind, it is worth exploring how culture works and its relationship to biological evolution.

***

Biological evolution is said to provide the mechanism for reproducing adaptive behaviour and characteristics for all species of animals, including humans. Simply put, when a characteristic allows an individual to survive successfully and reproduce, there is a good chance that characteristic will show up in its offspring and predominate over future generations. After a few generations the successful characteristic will surely be a feature of the species until new adaptations occur, making the original advantage less useful. This adaptive characteristic is said to be backward looking in that it helps the originator of it survive and reproduce offspring based on past circumstances. As Dawkins (2004) reminds us, it is the gene that is in competition for survival, not the individual.

It can be said that culture works in a similar, if not exact, fashion. Many of our cultural practices have been constructed to solve present and historic problems and, therefore, are entrenched in our patterns of living and relationships with the world. The capitalist system was an adaptation to a set of production and consumption problems that were prevalent at a particular time in human history. The human species adapted to a newly emerging set of technologies that the existing system could not exploit.

The mercantile system was a class-based arrangement with prescribed individual roles in a structure handed down from one generation to another. One's social position in the mercantile system was based on heritage, not necessarily on skill or aptitude. These practices did not fit the requirements of the Industrial Revolution. As new technologies proliferated, the rigid structure of the mercantile system was unable to accommodate the new reality. Capitalism placed no limitations on the advancement of the individual as did mercantilism, and it also generated the idea of comparative advantage, which championed the notion that one person or region could produce a single product more efficiently than others could and then trade that product for the things they needed from other individuals or regions who were competitive in that speciality. This became known as comparative advantage. Voila, capitalism was born. Of course it was much more convoluted and complex than this simple portrayal suggests, but suffice it to say that capitalism was born at a particular period in history because it was better suited for a technological environment that the old system could not accommodate. A new system was needed, and capitalism was considered at the time to be the best adaptation available.

What is new in the world that makes this process less likely to repeat the successful adaptive mechanism of the past? It is the speed with which change is now occurring that makes the present backward-gazing process of cultural evolution less likely to work in the fast-changing environment produced by the technological and scientific-driven society. Present society may be engaged in a life race against time. It is also now extremely difficult for society's institutions to keep up with the social, technological, and environmental change that is occurring today. Time is extremely critical in the new environment. We now require an adaptive mechanism that anticipates problems and is future looking and in some ways adaptive to where we are going, not where we are at this moment in time. One of the characteristics that made Wayne Gretsky such an outstanding ice hockey player is that he went to the point on the ice where he anticipated the puck was going to be in the next moment, not where it was at that particular time. This is described as anticipatory play, and that is the type of cultural mechanism society needs more of today. Metaphorically speaking, our culture needs to be skating to where the puck is going to be, not where it is at present. This quick-moving adaptation will allow us to retrieve ourselves from the social and environmental chasm we have created through the abuse and bastardization of the capitalist economic system and our futile attempts to adapt it to entirely new social and environmental requirements.

Many, including myself, would suggest we are at another critical turning point in human history, much like we were when mercantilism was in full swing but showing its weaknesses as the social and economic environment changed. The mechanisms and instruments of culture that are likely to prove adaptive in this fight for survival, for not only the human species but for the entire planet itself, will need to be determined based on anticipation of the problems that are emerging and likely to be dominant in the future. But suffice it to say that the present economic system is not likely to provide the needed organizational structure to address these new and anticipated problems. It certainly doesn't seem to be able to deal successfully with climate change or the increasing separation of the rich and poor.

Although culture may provide the arena and adaptive mechanism for our species, it is not without its difficulties in this regard. McNamara (2004) suggests that

> Every culture is the product of generations of survival and reproductive success because culture is the expression of the collective learning (memes as Dawkins and Blackmore would define it) of a reproductive community's ongoing adaptation to a particular natural and social environment.
>
> (p. 5)

Culture, as McNamara portrays it, has all the markings and characteristics of an evolutionary process. If McNamara is right in that any particular culture is a product of history, and there is no reason to doubt him, present cultural practices may now be detrimental to the sustainability and ultimately to the existence of the human species and perhaps the planet itself unless it can leave its reflective predisposition and become more anticipatory. The deficiencies of a backward-looking culture that is relied upon as the adaptive evolutionary mechanism in the ongoing battle to save humanity from the present climate problems and social deterioration poses a serious problem. McNamara's ideas strongly suggest that culture is formed by adapting to a previous generation's situation and their solutions to a particular set of life's problems and then carrying those forward into the present reality. Technological culture as we experience it today may be changing so rapidly that the present process of cultural evolution and its resulting institutions may not be able to keep up with such rapid change. The challenge for culture to remain as an adaptive mechanism in the life course of humans is to determine if it can be anticipative rather than simply reflective and backward looking.

Not all scholars see culture as so hard to move as does McNamara. Harari (2014), for example suggests,

> Since large scale human cooperation is based on myths, the way people cooperate can be altered by changing the myths—by telling different stories. Under the right circumstances myths can change rapidly. In 1789 the French population switched almost overnight from believing in the myth of the divine right of kings to believing the myth of the sovereignty of the people.
>
> (p. 32)

Only time will tell who is right, and hopefully Harari wins the argument.

Present-day problems require huge-scale changes and not simply tinkering at the margins, which has been the modus operandi of past cultural evolutionary practice. This puts a new set of requirements and parameters on culture that it has not had to deal with previously. Rather than allowing decision makers to make decisions based on past experience, we now need them to make decisions in anticipation of future problems, including those of a social and environmental nature. Culture must become adaptive to problems and stresses that society may not have yet experienced fully but can anticipate based on evidentiary trends. The same can be said about employing solutions that worked in the past to new problems. Although they worked in the past, they may not possess the same positive effect under present or future changed circumstances. For example, based on past experience there is some notion that new technologies will eventually materialize to deal with the climate-warming problem that is dominant today. That is how we have previously solved our environmental problems. There is no evidence of an approaching technological solution to the climate-warming problem but we want to have faith in its eventuality because it has provided solutions to most of our environmental problems in the past. Technology's past performance gives us feelings of confidence and comfort, if not arrogance.

***

Gardenfors (2003) suggests, "Man (sic) seems to be the only animal that can plan for future needs" (p. 74). This notion seems to counter evolutionary thinking. But is it really true? If it is true, then why is it that the economy trumps the environment when the environment's precarious state is so well documented? Gardenfors interprets the literature on experiments with monkeys to conclude that when given choices animals will make decisions based on the present situation, but humans can make decisions based on perceived future needs. Why then do humans consistently attend to immediate economic needs and not consider the looming environmental catastrophe and dire social problems that have made themselves evident and whose consequences are certain if society stays on the present course, rather than switching priorities at least until the more pressing social and environmental problems are resolved? Could it possibly have something to do with how cultural patterns are learned and how they are transmitted from one generation to the next? We know that anticipatory planning is located in the neocortex of the brain where all executive functions are to be found in humans. Proportionately, humans have the largest frontal lobe of all the animals, which, it is argued, is the distinguishing feature between us and them. Is there a battle going on between learned culture and the human ability to examine and plan for the future in the abstract? Perhaps Gardenfors (2003) got it right when he said, "The dilemma is that actions required to satisfy future needs often conflict with those that satisfy our current desires" (p. 80).

The argument as to whether or not evolution, including cultural evolution, occurs in a slow-moving fashion as Darwin suggested, or whether it develops in leaps and bounds (punctuated equilibrium) and then remains dormant for periods of time, as Gould (2002) proposed, is still an unanswered question. If it is the latter, it may play a determining role in culture's success as an adaptive mechanism. If it is the former, then culture may have some difficulty in maintaining human existence given the technological revolution sweeping the social world and the fast-paced changes to the environment that are afoot. If it is the latter, then there is something positive to be said about culture's ability to eventually lead human society out of its present-day and future dilemma.

Blackmore (1999) and Dawkins (2004), among others, have coined the term 'memes' (pronounced like genes) to describe how culture evolves. It is worth outlining in some detail what Blackmore (1999) tells us about memes and how they operate as a mechanism for reproducing human culture: "Memes are instructions for carrying out behaviour, stored in brains (or other objects) and passed on by imitation. Their competition drives the evolution of the mind" (p.15). Memes, then, are replicators, as are genes. Genes replicate biological characteristics, and memes reproduce cultural practice. Blackmore goes on to explain, "For something to count as a replicator it must sustain the evolutionary algorithm based on variation, selection and retention (or heredity)" (p. 14). Blackmore and Dawkins see genes as the first replicator and memes as the second. Given that the future of humankind rests on being able to anticipate the future rather than dealing solely with the present or past, perhaps human evolution will depend on a third force, not a replicator but a 'transformer', of culture. As Blackmore (1999) says about genes and memes, "[T]hey are just mindless replicators. They have no foresight and they could not plan according to the consequences of their actions even if they did care" (p. 42). Given the present dilemma, memes are of no use in creating the future in the short time that is required, if I understand the severity of the situation correctly. It may be evolutionary in our case to connect 'reason' to the mechanism of meme replication, rather than relying totally on present and historic stimulus and response to create the social organization strategy of society as, apparently, we do today. Maybe our future society and the future of this planet will need to be designed by an intelligent designer after all, but in this case the designer will be us, not some supernatural force. Rather than purely adapting to the present environment as we apparently do today through the replication mechanism of memes, it would be prudent, even compulsory, if human life is to be sustained on this planet, to reason out future possible trends built from present reality but also taking into account the consequences of our current behaviour. These projections would need to be based on the assessment of potential future technological discoveries, those that are actually in the pipeline but not those that are mere speculation or pure hope, and on the environmental and social needs of the population including social justice issues. Of course, these projects would be directed at solving humanity's collective problems that are determined by consensus among the populations and supported by scientific analysis, including social and environmental examination. It is suggested here that relying on memes solely as the mechanism for replicating cultural traits that direct future decision making is no longer serving humanity well and, in fact, may be antithetical to continuing life on this planet. In a sense memes are emotional intelligence and what is needed at present is rational and analytical astuteness more than anything else.

***

Culture is truly a powerful force in society. Many enlightened societies have adopted relativism as a way for defining truth. It is recognized that truth, like beauty, lies in the eye of the beholder. Truth is said to be individually constructed. But is there a truth that lies external to the human mind? If the answer is no and every person possesses his or her own truth, then social policy may simply be a matter for those who subscribe to the majority myth. In fact, we may have done that with the myth of capitalism and the suballegories that define it. These are profound and perplexing questions. In the not too distant past, I was one of those persons who subscribed to the notion that truth lay individually inside each and every one of us. I am in the process of changing my thoughts on this idea somewhat. For example, cultural relativism allows for truth and interpretation to be culturally held, but I believe that girls should have equal access to education in accordance with privileges of the male child. Given this basic personal belief is it equally OK for me to allow cultural practices in societies that do not behave that way and exclude girls from being educated to go unchallenged? Is this way of thinking acceptable in this day and age? I don't think so. However, Chris Hedges (2001) in *American Fascists: The Christian Right* suggests absolute tolerance breeds intolerance. He argues, and I think rightly so, that, to allow the Christian Right in America to work toward a Christian Nation that would exclude all other religions and all forms of humanists ideas is to accept self-destruction through intolerance on the part of those who deny the idea of cultural relativism and multiple truths. So, it seems clear that the globe is at present in such dire condition environmentally, coupled with the abject failure of past and present social policies to address absolute poverty, that a new approach needs to be constructed through open dialogue. This open dialogue must first dispel the myths and false consciousness that have kept society from achieving the eradication of poverty in the past and environmental destruction. This type of cultural dialogue may initiate the next leap forward in the human condition through cultural change. We must come to an agreement on what constitutes truth in society. In doing so we may deny some forces that perpetuate false consciousness to work toward implementing their view of the world, and some may term this culture intolerance. I would argue that it may truncate Hedge's ideas about tolerance breeding intolerance and disallow culture to perpetuate discrimination.

***

So what are the weaknesses in our present cultural processes that inhibit us from implementing reasoned transformations of our present deeply held cultural practices? Several ideas explain the weakness of culture in the transition of society. Consciousness, the single most important element in creating culture and the modern human species, lies at the root of the problem.

Thomas McNamara (2004) instructs,

> [W]e will never be able to understand, or develop, human consciousness until we also understand the functions of what I call the preconscious mind . . . our present form of consciousness was produced by evolutionary forces in response to a prehistoric environment that no longer exists: so our present form of consciousness is no longer a successful form of adaptation.
>
> (p. 17)

Many of the stories (or our self-conception as a species) on which society is constructed are built on past events and environments that do not anticipate a future with new problems to address. It was probably useful for prehistoric humans to interpret the success of the hunt as dependent on some unseen but imagined hunter god, but that way of thinking is no longer useful and has been rejected. Understanding the backward-looking nature of our gaze brings into question many of our present-day social foundations leading to false consciousness. One of the most pressing false consciousness issues facing us today is how we view the role of the present economy and natural environment in maintaining or advancing the human species. Again, as McNamara (2004) explains,

> [I]f all social institutions are ultimately the products of a past stage of evolution, then we can see the fundamental dilemma built into the foundation of the modern world. The individualism of our modern consumer oriented culture constantly advocates individual fulfillment; yet, most contemporary institutions; including modern consciousness itself, did not evolve for, nor serve, that purpose.
>
> (p. 22)

False consciousness is created when an entire culture or species is told a story that is held to be an unqualified truth but which may no longer be so, and the holders of that truth carry it forward as a cultural certainty without questioning its premise over successive generations. The practicality of the American Dream is such a false consciousness. The story may have had relevance in the past but lost all effectiveness as conditions changed over time. Do we truly believe that everyone in American society can achieve the same level of success in life simply through hard work? There is a very poignant story attributed to Bhagwan Shree Rajneesh (1994) that provides an example of false consciousness. The guru was born into a religion where eating after sunset and before sunrise was made taboo. He lived in that culture exclusively until he was eighteen years old and never questioned any of the traditions of his society. He tells the story: "when I was eighteen my friends were going to see a beautiful castle very close by, a few miles away. I went with them" (p. 33). He continues to tell us that they traveled all day without preparing or eating any food. By the time they quit hiking that day, it was dark and none of them had eaten. Then after sunset the group began to prepare a meal and, of course, offered a share to Rajneesh. As he tells it,

> [T]here is great difficulty. I have never eaten in the night, and the religion in which unfortunately I have been born, thinks that if you eat in the night, you will go to hell. I don't want to go to hell just for one night's food, but I cannot sleep either. Moreover, the smell of your food is too much! They persuaded me saying, we will not tell your parents or anybody. Nobody will ever know that you have eaten in the night. I said, that is not the point—I will know. The question is not my parents or anybody. You can tell the whole world, that's not the problem. The problem is that I cannot conceive of myself eating at night, after eighteen years of continuous conditioning. But they persuaded me—and I had to be persuaded.
> (Rajneesh, 1994, pp. 31–33)

He continues by telling us that after eating in the night he was unable to sleep and in fact threw up all of the food he had eaten. He explains that the others who ate it did not react in the same manner but slept comfortably. It was only he who was sick and felt it was directly tied to the taboo he had broken.

The taboo was generated early on in Rajneesh's culture. The culture was also a meatless society. Because of the lack of artificial light the culture was concerned that bugs and other forms of unhealthy meat might wind up in what they were eating, so it was best to eat in daylight. This rational concern wound up as a taboo in that society and has been carried forward, although the original light issue no longer exists to warrant such behaviour. As Rajneesh explains, "[O]nce you accept something, this creates a false conscience that goes on telling you, don't do this, do this. This is not consciousness" (p. 26). This story has great relevance for the discussion here. Our society also has many false consciousnesses particularly with regard to economic theory. As Sam Harris (2010) tells us in *The Moral Landscape*, "the mere endurance of a belief system or custom does not suggest that it is adaptive, much less wise" (p. 20).

We accept without question that our cultural truths and taboos explain absolutely how the economy works. We believe in the invisible hand of the market without seeing it operate, and we are told that it guides the economy and our everyday lives. As a society we believe unconditionally in the truth and power of classical economic theory, although its practice has not had positive effect for many people in the world since the invention of capitalism. Modern humans spend inordinate amounts of time and energy focused on an economy that provides meagre benefit to many people. Without questioning the basic premises of orthodox economic theory, or the profound changes in our technologies, we have simply dragged the economic myths of the nineteenth and twentieth centuries into the twenty-first. It is conceivable that present-day humans will become known in posterity as *Homo economicus* because of the singular focus on classical economics as the method for solving all of humanity's problems and for constructing so many of our social relationships.

We continue to believe that every person needs to work in the market economy in order to be a productive citizen. The notion of the supreme value of work to individual identity, purpose, and worthiness does not take into consideration the overexploitation of the natural resources on which this imperative depends and its consequential effect on the planet. Much of the focus of the economy is on creating jobs, whether the products produced by those jobs are absolutely needed by society or not and whether they are neutral or have negative effects on the environment. The goal today is to create jobs without regard for the consequences of those jobs on the lives of all citizens, the community, and the planet. For example, the many private companies that now control and administer our prison system lobby fiercely for increased penalties to crime so their businesses will expand and their companies will show increased profits. One needs to ask if that activity is truly in the best interest of the public. It was once clear that production of needed goods and services was the goal of society, and job creation was the means to achieving that production, but we may now have the goals of society and the vehicles for achieving them confused. The goal is now on creating jobs, not on what needs to be produced by those jobs in order to subsist well. We have created a huge marketing industry to tell us what we need and want rather than figuring out what our basic needs are ourselves. And, like Rajneesh's taboo against eating after sunset, we leave our welfare up to the enigma of the market, which interferes with our ability to act rationally in spite of those who would argue that the market is irrational and purely a matter of perception, not reality, and one more false consciousness. One does not need to focus only on unique and complex cultures like the one from which Rajneesh comes. We can see the same kind of false consciousness in the United States today in the gun debate. Ideas such as 'everybody needs to be armed in order to reduce mass killings by guns' fits the criteria of false consciousness unequivocally.

One of the major false consciousnesses that permeate the human psyche is the notion that the gross domestic product (GDP) is an adequate measure for how a society and individuals in it fare in terms of their standard of living and overall wellness. The GDP is a gross measure of central tendency and uses the mean as the measuring statistic. This method of measuring the economy has a number of shortcomings. Those who are extremely wealthy, often referred to as the top 1 percent, have incomes sufficiently large to skew the mean, giving a false impression of how the middle and lower segments of society live. Poverty may be rampant within a society, although the GDP portrays that society as doing well. In fact, this is what is happening in the United States today.

The GDP is purely an economic measure that defines wellness by using money and expenditure as the medium for measurement. There are many variables that denote standard of living beyond anything that can be measured using currency as the unit of measure. Such areas as democratic participation and individual and social health are examples. Finally, the GDP includes what most would consider negative events and treats them as positive in its calculation. For example, expenditures that are made in recovering from a natural disaster are seen as a positive contribution to the social order in the GDP calculation, when most people would think that these monies would be better spent if put to more positive use if the natural disaster had not occurred. The growth and manufacture of tobacco products, which is not only detrimental to society's health but also an economic drain through unneeded healthcare, is also considered a plus in the GDP computation.

Perhaps the greatest false consciousness that pervades society today is the notion that all problems are created by government and the way to solve them is to hand them over to the private sector and the market economy. This false consciousness is created by the wealthy and powerful in society in order for them to perpetuate the myth of the superiority of private enterprise and individual ownership over collective action. This myth continues to keep wealth in the hands of those who have it now and away from a more equal distribution throughout society. On the other hand, Mazzucato (2014) in her book argues that the state is an entrepreneurial agent that takes risks during the beginning of a technological development that may be too risky for the private market to engage in. She cites the early years of Silicon Valley that would not have occurred without initial support by government. But government today is characterized as a bloated bureaucracy that only gets in the way of moving society forward and not the positive force it is in actuality.

Our environment and society are much too fragile and complex for that kind of unthinking acceptance of commonly held beliefs and their perpetuation through false consciousness. Ideas that guide our life through the invisible hand of the market are much too important to be unquestioned and trusted without reflection. The idea that a person is dependent if he or she is receiving some form of government support but not so if receiving life sustenance from General Motors or some other multinational company is a ludicrous premise when you stop to think about it, but it is accepted dogma in our everyday life. In fact, General Motors is less transparent than the government and, therefore, it may be that workers at GM are more dependent on forces they cannot control than those receiving government social assistance.

Our civilization can no longer accept these 'systems of belief' created in the past without rethinking their effect on the present and future social system and the environment. The notion of the invisible hand of the market, for example, does not consider the negative externalities that our economic activity pours into the environment every day, or the poor that our wealth-creating system leaves permanently behind and marginalized in society. The idea that a rising tide lifts all boats is another of those antiquated beliefs that reward the few at the expense of the many. These are all false consciousnesses that our society must expel as we move toward the new social contract. We need a new set of stories based on present and future realities to guide modern-day society, and they need to be very different from the myths that direct and control our society today. Once again, as Harris (2010) instructs, "human wellbeing entirely depends on events in the world and on states of the human brain" (p. 7). He continues,

> [O]ur brains were not designed with a view to our ultimate fulfillment. Evolution could never have foreseen the wisdom or necessity of creating stable democracies, mitigating climate change, saving other species from extinction, containing the spread of nuclear weapons, or of doing much else that is now crucial to our happiness in this century.
>
> (p. 50)

Rationality created through public discourse and science must provide the answers we are looking for, and the conditions faced by our society demand that we abandon faith and myth to establish the morals and values on which the future will be built. Again as Harris (2010), states, "Faith, if it is ever right about anything, is right by accident" (p. 23). Human continuance on this planet will not happen by accident; it needs to be planned in a very thoughtful and methodical way based on science and knowledge, not on myth and religion. A culture that is based on antiquated myths and without possibility of solving our most pressing existing and future problems is a millstone around our necks, not a mechanism for protection or for moving society forward to the next level of human existence.

Why is it so hard to dismiss false consciousness in favour of truth? Again we can turn to Rajneesh (1994) for an explanation when he suggests that "truth makes you utterly naked—naked of all lies, naked of all hypocrisies. That's why nobody wants the truth; everybody believes that he has got it" (p. 9). As Jack Nicholson in the motion picture *A Few Good Men* said so forcefully when referring to the distasteful and hidden practices that many armies engage in when protecting their country, "You can't handle the truth" because it may not conform to commonly held thoughts or present standards and the reality of the situation. Societal-wide myths provide a structure around which we conduct our everyday affairs, and it is disconcerting to discard those structures until others are built and become proven and familiar. The truth is that some people in society have gained enormously from the myths that led to false consciousness, and they are not going to be willing to give them up easily.

How can the irrationality of the present condition be explained? There is a well-developed mechanism for creating false consciousness in capitalism known euphemistically as Madison Avenue. Society is swimming in a sea of propaganda created by the elites of society and the false consciousness they have created in order to preserve their power and position at the top of the socioeconomic order. To solidify their position they have created the big lie that basically accentuates the notion that all in society can achieve through hard work and sacrifice what the privileged have attained. This has been referred to as 'The American Dream'. To maintain their power and dominant position in society, the barons of capitalism have created Madison Avenue and its large marketing firms as the mechanism for selling the myth of the American Dream and their ideas about the natural order of society. And, for the most part, they have been successful in having that myth, or its equivalent in other countries, accepted, which keeps the general public psychologically engaged in the status quo.

That is why the banking system has been able to prevail in the battle over regulating their industry, the market, and their dubious practices. The powerful have too much to lose and they can rationalize their self-interest and legitimize their override of the general good of society. They would be the first to tell you that they are not a social welfare institution but are responsible to their shareholders only and need not worry about the common good. There are a few rich souls amongst us who would not be so rich if our false consciousnesses were exposed. Their wealth, however, comes at the expense of the rest of us in society and all others on the planet. So, the way forward must be through public dialogue and debate, and it must centre on exposing the fundamental underlying myths that our society holds onto but may be antisocial in this new age. The dialogue must expose those who are determined to be antisocial because of their exploitation of the environment and society in general. This would include those who are making unreasonable salaries and bonuses that do not fit the definition of limited inequality as discussed elsewhere in this book. A planned society that embraces a rational approach to problem solving must replace an antiquated culture that is based in present reality and not anticipatory of future problems and the consequences of our present behaviour. It must replace a culture that simply allows greed to prevail through the so-called invisible hand of the marketplace, and planning must take into account the welfare of all citizens and not simply those with power.

***

Our present thoughts about our society's economic system encourage false consciousness. The idea that all of us need to be in the market economy requires examination. The idea of 'productivity' itself needs to be redefined. At present, productivity is essentially centred on the market economy and one's participation in it. If you don't have a job then you are not seen as a productive member of society. This, of course, leaves a great many of the positive human activities that are carried out every day that are outside of the market economy out of the equation. Avocations such as being a house wife or house husband are not considered in the notion of productivity. Volunteerism, where much of the important social and environmental work gets accomplished, is not seen as positive or productive; in fact, Canada's former Minister of Natural Resources at the time labeled those in the environmental movement as radicals and ecoterrorists in an attempt to create, yet again, a false consciousness. So our basic idea of how we reward and compensate people to a reasonable standard requires alteration. It is now time to abandon a monetary distribution system that leaves allocation decisions up to some 'invisible hand,' as advocated by the capitalist economic system. This system rewards those who do not necessarily produce positive results for society but leaves some in society with more of the resources than they could ever productively use in a lifetime and excludes many whose basic existence is in constant jeopardy. Such schemes as a guaranteed annual income need to be considered as a replacement for at least the present social assistance system, if not as a basic principle of a revamped economic system. This idea will be discussed at length in the last part of this book.

***

Some of these ideas about human social construction require a review of our present ideas about democracy. We in the Western world do not live in the same democracy that was initially conceived at the beginning of its construction. We live in a world that significantly favours the upper economic class as it did at the beginning of the last century. If we continue on this present path, the rich will continue to get richer and the poor poorer (Piketty, 2014) until the whole system implodes upon itself. A democracy that views individual freedom above all other values, including some form of environmental and social justice, is now destructive to the human condition. Although this may have been prudent when there was a smaller number of people on the globe who were unaware of how others lived, it is no longer appropriate today when there are now 7 billion people on this planet and a transportation and communication system that lays bare how all live throughout the world.

A democracy that allows those at the upper end of the income scale to continue to oppress those at the other end must implode. More balance between individual freedom and collective interest is required as humanity moves into the next social contract in order to create a society that includes all citizens and preserves the environment. After all it is the collectivity that underpins and allows for individual freedom. In order to accomplish the task of creating a new social contract, we may need to revisit the objections to the notion of collective action as described by Hayek (2007) and others. We will need to dispel the myths that surround collective ideas, including the mythical march toward fascism that is thought to occur when restraining individual freedom in favour of collective action.

***

McNamara (2004) suggests that

> If the ultimate purpose of the mind is to aid in the survival and reproduction of its organism, which is a fundamental promise of evolutionary psychology, then this result is best achieved by learning the collective wisdom of the tribe, that is, the local culture in a way that increases the probability of repeating the successful behaviours of the group.
>
> (p. 11)

Although I agree with the notion of the purpose of the mind in aiding the survival and reproduction of the organism, it is no longer advantageous to limiting ourselves to learning the culture of the local group when present-day problems are global in nature as Redner (2013) instructs us in his book *Beyond Civilization*. Culture, at least some fundamental parts of it, will need to become homogenized across the globe. Some will see this as interference in sovereign cultural development. It may be, in fact, cultural interference, but the social and environmental problems that plague humanity's existence no longer respect boundaries of any sort, let alone local traditions. We are in this together.

Additionally, modern culture has not been successful when it has categorized and approached problems in a reductionist manner. Most, if not all, of society's institutions are established in, and as, silos, and in a hierarchical form. We have set up knowledge areas in university departments or in government ministries, for example, which act in isolation to other like interests and with mandates that are exclusionary. Modern economic and environmental problems may not lend themselves well to this type of institutional arrangement. Decisions made about the economy will affect the environment and vice versa, so not only are the problems our present culture have to address different, they also need an alternative operating system and institutional arrangements to be addressed effectively. Systems thinking throughout horizontal institutions that support this kind of wisdom will need to form society's foundation. At the very least we require horizontal, not vertical, institutions to address the interconnectedness of the issues we are confronted with today and will be more so in the future.

Established ideologies are perhaps society's strongest institutions but least useful thinking systems. Each ideology is firmly entrenched in a set of ideas about how the world works or should work. They provide a road map and foundation of how problems are to be resolved, most notably by government interventions or left to the so-called 'free market' mechanism. It is not likely that the present set of ideologies and views of how the world does or should work will be of much use in solving present and future problems. Why should they? They really haven't worked all that well for us in the past either. Recently, the political arena has become paralyzed and not very good at getting present problems resolved. It suffers greatly from gridlock. Politics, which is underpinned by ideology, is the cultural space where ideas and problems get discussed and, hopefully, resolved, but given the present reality, there may be need to alter the political system to make it more effective, as well.

The cultural institution that superimposes itself on all other institutions, including the economic system, is the political system. In the case of present society the two appear to be fused. Politics is now dominated by the economy, particularly by the wealthy, and it is out of control and serving a narrow set of interests. In the United States corporations have now been given the status of a living individual when it comes to contributing money to political parties and influencing the ideas being enunciated during elections and campaigns. What this has ushered in is the highest spending on an election in the United States ever. This has allowed the wealthy to dominate the airwaves with myths that promote their agenda and the status quo of an unequal society. Money dominates the culture and protects its myths and false consciousnesses.

This chapter has attempted to lay out the fundamental impediments to society's success in overcoming the basic problems it is facing in perpetuating the human species into the future. It has argued that present cultural practices and its derivative false consciousness may now be limiting humanity's ability to wrestle and overcome the huge environmental and social tasks confronting it. The rest of the book will attempt to not only explain some of the weaknesses in our social policy system, but also begin a discussion of what a successful and sustainable future society might look like. In saying this, I will be the first to admit that what the future will turn out to be will likely not look much like what is being offered here. But there is need to think about the future in a radical way and not leave its creation to those forces that dominate the system-world today. Let there be no mistake—those forces are quite willing and able to create a future that suits them if we let them, but it will not likely turn out to be what is in our best interest. What is important is that all citizens engage in a dialogue that will eventually create a scenario that is more egalitarian and environmentally sustainable than what we seem to be steering toward at present. But first the question to address must be: What is the basis on which social policy often gets established? The next chapter will begin to examine that issue.

References

Blackmore, S. (1999). *The Meme Machine.* New York: Oxford University Press.
Burns, P. (1999). *An Introduction to Tourism.* New York: Routledge.
Darwin, C. (1859). *Origin of the Species by Natural Selection.* London, UK: John Murray.
Dawkins, R. (2004). *The Ancestors Tale: A Pilgrimage to the Dawn of Life.* London, UK: Phoenix.
Gardenfors, P. (2003). *How Homo Became Sapiens: On the Evolution of Thinking.* Oxford, UK: Oxford University Press.
Gould, S. J. (2002). *The Structure of Evolutionary Theory.* Cambridge: Harvard University Press.
Harari, Y. (2014). *Sapiens: A Brief History of Humankind.* Toronto, Ontario: McClelland & Stewart.
Harris, S. (2010). *How Science Can Determine Human Values.* New York: Simon and Schuster.
Hayek, F. (2007). *The Road to Serfdom* (Vol. 2). Chicago: University of Chicago Press.
Hedges, C. (2001). *American Fascists: The Christian Right and the War on America.* New York: Free Press.
Keesing, R. M., & Keesing, F. M. (1971). *New Perspectives in Cultural Anthropology.* New York: Holt, Rinehart and Winston Inc.
Kroeber, A. L., & Kluckhohn, C. (1952). *Culture: A Critical Review of Concepts and Definitions. Peabody Museum Papers.* Cambridge: Harvard University Press.

Mazzucato, M. (2014). *The Entrepreneurial State: Debunking Public vs. Private Sector Myths*. London, UK: Anthem Press.

McNamara, T. (2004). *Evolution, Culture and Consciousness: The Discovery of the Preconscious Mind*. Dallas: University Press of America.

Peacock, J. L., & Kirsch, A. T. (1970). *The Human Direction: An Evolutionary Approach to Social and Cultural Anthropology*. New York: Appleton-Century-Crofts.

Piketty, T. (2014). *Capital in the Twenty-First Century*. Cambridge, MA: The Belknap Press of Harvard University Press.

Rajneesh, B. S. (1994). *Freedom in All Dimensions*. New Delhi: Diamond Pocket Books.

Redner, H. (2013). *Beyond Civilization: Society, Culture, and the Individual in the Age of Globalization*. New Brunswick, NJ: Transaction Publishers.

Spradley, P., & McCurdy, D. W. (1975). *Anthropology: The Cultural Perspective*. New York: Wiley.

4 The Context for Policy Making

There are a number of competing views about how much social policy should be offered by a modern society, to whom it should be provided, and in what form. Most people possess an underlying perspective about where the root causes of human frailty lie that forms the basis for individual need and what should or should not be done about it through public expenditure. It is understood that all members of society benefit from social policy by way of increased social solidarity, and although this book focuses on the direct benefits provided to individuals through social policy, it also explores the direct and indirect benefits to the larger social context. And most of these views are built on a vision of the fundamental nature of human beings and their responsibility to society.

At the most fundamental level of this debate are the competing ideas of biological influence and the role of the social environment in forming human behaviour. Biological determinism has had a long and sordid history in explaining human behaviour and motivation—sordid in the sense that some societies have engaged this notion to justify the most grotesque of human practices. One only needs to cite the history of eugenics and the extermination of the Jews by the Nazis in the 1930s and '40s, or the early notion in the United States that blacks were not fully human and therefore could be held as slaves and traded as commodities. Similar attitudes prevailed at the time many European nations were colonizing Africa and various other countries around the globe. Although these notions are horrid and have been thoroughly discredited, one must be cautious in associating these ugly and dark practices with the contributions of biology to understanding human behaviour and development.

Fundamentally, biological determinism contends that human motivations are mostly shaped by biological inheritance that dates from the beginning of our history as a species, when we were at an early stage of development and our lifestyle was not too far removed from the practices of our primate relatives. This concept attributes human relationships and motivations predominantly to the nature side of the nature/nurture argument. This school of thought contends that culture has recently become a contributing factor in determining human behaviour. Humans are basically governed, or limited, by their biology. Certainly the recent advance in the science of genetics is giving more credibility to biological forces as a contributor to human makeup and behaviour today than it has over the recent past. It is fair to say that biological determinists have a point when they argue that human potential is limited by biology. For example, humans are unable to hear certain frequencies that are available to other species of animals because of their biological makeup and, therefore, this limitation causes humans to act or not in accordance with these parameters. Notwithstanding the darker side of this concept, biological determinism continues to play a role in the social and public policy debate. Many of those on the biological side of the argument embrace the idea that biology influences behaviour and therefore should influence the decisions made by society about such matters as social policy. Most of the proponents of this school of thought have come from the disciplines of sociobiology and environmental psychology. Both of these disciplines bring the theory of culture into play but give prominence to the fundamental idea of biological evolution in human social makeup. These scholars would contend that humans not only react to present environmental circumstances through currently constructed concepts, but also by responses that were ingrained in the genes during prehistory days. At the policy level, human nature is often invoked as a major determinant in the need for social assistance by the segment of the population that are constant or repeat recipients of social services, euphemistically referred to as welfare repeats in most societies. This determination is much too simplistic a rationale and needs to be challenged; however, its potential contribution to the analysis of the problem should not be summarily dismissed.

On the other hand, some view the idea of biological impulse as a key contributor to human behaviour as an idea long jettisoned in favour of relying completely on the cultural environment as the controlling factor in human social development. Environmental determinism rejects any notion that biology plays an important or primary role in modern human behaviour. This side of the argument contributes all human action to culturally determined practices. Those of this persuasion suggest that humans have completely broken the tie to our biological past, arguing that human evolution is now mostly controlled by culture and that the fundamental ways of thinking and acting are passed down from one generation to the next through cultural practices. People such as Richard Dawkins (2004) have championed the term 'meme' to describe how culture is duplicated and transmitted in a similar manner as the 'gene' operates, which is standard practice for describing the mechanism for the evolution of physical attributes. This is not to suggest that cultural observances are static and never changing, but are in fact dynamic and altered by each generation, perhaps grudgingly, as they attempt to adapt to changes in the environment. As Susan Blackmore (1999) instructs us, "memes are instructions for carrying out human behaviour, stored in brains (or other objects) and passed on by imitation. Their competition drives the evolution of the mind" (p. 17). That said, culture can be quite rigidly held and become antifunctional in spite of a changed environment, as can be observed through such abhorrent practices as the honour killings of female children by some immigrants to a new homeland that abides by different cultural observances than those left behind in the old culture. Often those in transition from a traditional to a modern culture find the adopted behaviour of their children intolerable and an affront to their previous worldview, although the new practices may be quite acceptable in the new culture. These events certainly attest to the power of culture as a human motivation and social control mechanism. The nurture school of thought contends that human behaviour is learned through the nurturing of each individual by society and is culturally determined through the socialization process. Accumulated culture determines what is right and wrong for a society and the sanctions that are put in place to curb what is deemed to be inappropriate or taboo.

So, what view should influence or dominate our decision-making process when one looks at the competing ideas of biological and cultural determinism? The answer to that question given by most people is—both. As Blackmore (1999) suggests

> [N]othing is purely genetically determined and nothing purely environmentally determined. We human beings, like all other creatures, are a complex product of both—and this is true of the way we behave as well as the shape of our legs.
>
> (p. 33)

Chapter 2 in this book attempts to explain the role that culture plays in social system development and how it may be limiting society's reactions to the real threats of climate change and poverty today. From that discussion we can say that culture is very complex and slow to catch up to the advances in technology and other influences that are shaping our world today.

***

Since the nature/nurture debate first took shape, ideas about their relationship have changed considerably. This change in connection may be due to the cumulative and increasing power of culture in everyday life. It is now conceivable that today, culture is changing biology. The selection of traits during the creation of test tube babies is a good example. With the mapping of the human genome, it is conceivable that gene therapy will become eventually paramount in treating and curing the most deadly biological and neurological diseases of our age. It is fair to say that technologically driven healthcare has extended the life of affluent individuals considerably over the last decade or two.

On a more practical level, culture is exclusive to the human species and exerts an overwhelming force on human behaviour. As mentioned earlier, memes are thought to act like genes, but from a cultural point of view. What is critical to this discussion is to confirm culture's role in human existence in transmitting a repertoire of behaviours that have proven useful in the past to a new generation. This can explain, for example, why our society continues to hold onto the imperative of economic growth when all social and environmental indicators suggest that this concept needs to be replaced with something that is more environmentally sustainable and might also provide a better mechanism for the distribution of resources on a more equitable basis. Because the present economic system is part of our cultural past, it gets replicated with modification (perhaps not enough modification) within each new generation of human society. In spite of an intellectual understanding of the truths of unsustainability, humans are experiencing great difficulty in reordering the social system to eliminate destructive economic behaviour in favour of more sustainable practices. As McNamara (2004) tells us:

> For most of its history, the human species was engaged in hunting and gathering in a natural and social environment that did not significantly change within a life span of any one generation. Therefore, in order to achieve the best balance between social stability on the one hand and adaptability to change on the other, natural selection favored a developmental process that made the personality highly adaptable during its formation, but very resistant to change thereafter. From an evolutionary perspective, resistance to change after childhood was essential because the collective set of values and behaviors we call culture was far too vulnerable to be allowed to be contaminated by individual preferences. That collective wisdom had to be from each generation to the next without distortion because it was the key to successful adaptation to that particular environment. . . . Since the industrial revolution however, the pace of social and environmental change has been accelerating at an ever increasing rate.
>
> (pp. 25–26)

The stability function of culture, as McNamara goes on to explain, may now be inhibiting our ability to adapt to today's fast-changing environment due to the rapid innovation and implementation of new technology. Culture makes us unique as a species, but its slow adaptation mechanism may contribute to our extinction unless we can alter how practices are established and the timeframe for their formation and alteration.

Dawkins, Blackmore, and others see genes as the first replicator and memes as the second. Given that the future of humankind rests more and more on being able to anticipate not only the future needs of humans but also the requirements of the environment on which our species depends, perhaps a third replicator will be needed, possibly one that rationally anticipates fast-changing technological and environmental conditions as they occur, instead of replicating outdated, ineffective behaviours. This would provide a transforming mechanism that could speed up the evolutionary process and be anticipatory rather than based on hindsight. Given the speed at which technology changes today and the slow adaptation by our culture to those advances, our species is now at great risk. Humans must now anticipate the consequences of rapidly changing

The Context for Policy Making 55

environmental conditions and make quick adjustments to those circumstances in order to address the inevitable future problems our present behaviour is generating.

***

Whether or not the ideas contained in biological determinism and culture are at work consciously in the minds of policy makers as they create policy alternatives and choose among them is debatable. What is likely the case is that these fundamental ideas on how humans and society operate work at the subconscious level. This may be particularly evident when the basis for social policy development is deeply ingrained in the psyche and driven by emotion. The nurture or cultural deterministic position is more often than not held by those who hold society responsible and accountable for marginalization and the root cause for such issues as the growing poverty in society. On the other hand, those who see poverty as a failing of the individual often bring a biological deterministic approach to their thinking that focuses on the inadequacy of the individual and not on the shortcomings of society. Differing points of view as to the root causes of poverty play out in the policy-making process, frequently resulting in much angst in a heated debate at the policy decision table and throughout society generally. I think it would be important to say that decision makers probably do not think in absolute terms when making decisions. It is likely the case that individuals take into consideration both the nature and the nurture perspectives when making determinations, but not in equal quantities. It is likely that one perspective dominates, although it may be ever so slightly.

***

The problems that challenge the human condition today require citizens and policy makers alike to rethink the bases on which decisions are made. This process needs to begin with self-reflection and an analysis of how one views such matters. Each of us needs to understand our present worldview and how that colours how we think about world affairs and human relations. In some cases our dominant worldview may not be helpful in solving the issue at hand. We may need to consider and weigh all philosophical paradigms before reaching a conclusion on the issue of concern and before reaching a final conclusion. Likewise we should not take it for granted that others see the world exactly as we do. Whether one acts on ideas of biological or environmental determinism needs to be apparent to the individual actor and others in the decision-making process. That said, it may be that neither of these approaches focuses on the future as much as they do on the past and therefore are not pertinent to solving humanity's imposing problems. Being attached to a worldview without understanding how we came to that choice and whether or not it remains appropriate for the social policy question under review may be the reason why society continues to plan its future inappropriately by employing old paradigms to new problems. We tend to recycle the same ideologies and solutions in an attempt to solve complex problems, regardless of whether or not these actions have worked historically or are even appropriate for today's circumstances. We think and act in this manner because it is psychologically comfortable and maintains a consistency to our thought process. As a consequence we establish for ourselves a whole set of myths about how the problem/resolution process should work in our conception of the world. Whether it does or not has little consequence on how we think. Humans tend to want to adhere to an integrated and consistent notion of how the world works, or should work. This way of acting in the world brings stability and regularity to one's life, although it may not be effective in solving our social and environmental problems.

Additionally, we seem to be unable to connect individual problems and their resolution to narrowly mandated administrative units. For example, we continue to see job growth as the solution to poverty and conservation as the solution to the environmental problem. When both of these problem and solution sets are connected, they quickly appear complex and incompatible, and although they need to be integrated into problem resolution, they are often addressed in isolation to each other. Rarely, if ever, do decision makers step outside the single dimensional box and attempt to determine an integrated set of solutions to a multifaceted repertoire of problems. Governments work in silos, making integrated multiple problem resolution difficult, if not impossible. In the present social context the public would likely rank job creation ahead of the environment for attention rather than seek an interdependent and complex set of conditions and pursue an integrated approach to the resolution of these multiple problems. Often, we rank-order problems, and resolving one in isolation makes the others worse. The human community seeks simplicity in problem identification and resolution and is therefore subject to simplistic political analysis and rhetoric, which often relies on or perpetuates false consciousness. This situation is certainly evident in the continued deterioration of the environment when governments continually talk about job creation as the single, perhaps only, way to resolve unemployment and poverty and the number one issue to be tackled. Little thought is given to ways of distributing the globe's resources other than through the market economy and the individual job. Creating more jobs in an unfettered manner and without determining their effect on the environment will simply exacerbate the environmental crisis. This single-minded method of decision making and problem resolution is a perilous situation and will need to change if we are to sustain human life on this planet over the long term.

***

The challenge to human society today is to change not only the parameters for decision making, but also the deeply ingrained fundamental, social, and psychological bases on which decisions are formulated. This change requires an adjustment to the social values with which humans construct a social and psychological identity. Politicians will make decisions based on the present values of society, so the transition being suggested in this book will need to be society-wide and not exclusively focused on the decision makers. Furthermore, a change of this magnitude will not likely be generated by politicians. In fact, for change of this scale to be achieved, it will require a significant groundswell on the part of the public. It will also require a crucial change in social values. This new way of thinking will fundamentally alter the basis on which societies function. It may also incorporate some of the best practices that are found sporadically throughout the world today.

Social values need to be separated into two levels. The first set of values comprises those unique to individual culture and that are usually based on religious practice, language, and symbols. The traditions in food and clothing, etc., comprise this category. These give flavour to life and to community identity. The second set of values, and of primary concern in this book, is those that provide personal and social identity to individuals and have an impact on how society is organized and how the physical environment is viewed and exploited. Most of these values are tied directly to our belief system. These values are largely constructed from the job one holds, the money one makes, and the things one accumulates throughout life. The dominant organizational system that describes the present era we live in is generally referred to as the capitalist system, although how that term has been operationalized has changed considerably through time. Although it may vary slightly in its execution throughout the globe, essentially the world works on this model. It is arguable that the values that underpin capitalism and describe our present worldwide civilization will need alteration if we are to survive the environmental and social problems that confront us today and into the future. Whether or not society has the political will and capacity to alter our beliefs to the extent necessary to save the planet is yet to be determined, however.

Repertoires of values that comprise the capitalist system and constitute our current social organizing structure are based on the territorial imperative and on the exclusive ownership of property. Further, they demarcate one's social position in the world and provide testament to whether or not one has achieved success as an individual in society. Success in achieving these values provides one with power within the group. Those with wealth, and the power that gravitates to them through that wealth, encourage some individuals to overexploit the world's resources and allow only minimal access to those same resources by others who don't possess the same level of means. The wealthy, whether individuals in society or the nation-state itself, continue to increase their wealth at the expense of all others and to the detriment of the planet's environment. The present and historical patterns in this regard may be shifting slightly. China and other parts of Asia are gaining wealth and power, perhaps at the expense of the United States, and other developed countries. Although this pattern may seem like a major change in the system, only time will tell whether the magnitude of this change will be significant. Regardless of the outcome, this change may only determine who holds power and not in how power and wealth are used and shared across the globe. The change that seems to be taking place at the moment appears simply to be an alteration in location and not in the behaviour that is needed to secure the planet's survival. The world was witness to a similar change when global domination shifted from the United Kingdom to America at the end of the second war, and this did not alter the structure of the economic system but simply its location. What is really required at this point in human development is a fundamental shift in the underlying system, the culture that supports it, and the prevailing concepts of power and wealth.

Under the present social system, decisions regarding access to resources are not dependent on equity, but on financial power. Some argue that this state of affairs is the natural order of things and fundamental to human nature and, hence, consistent with biological determinism. The same type of argument for maintaining the status quo was made in the days of slavery and feudalism. The human community moved away from those solidly held views and transitioned to a new way of thinking that did not embrace such values. It is now time for a similar and dramatic change to our present system in the face of the colossal social and environmental problems faced by today's society and raised in this book.

***

The capitalist system that dominates Western culture today is based on the values of material consumption and accumulation of wealth and property. Western capitalist culture favours the rich and powerful over the middle class and the poor. This class-based society has created a celebrity culture that extols the virtues of the wealthy and the famous. We now have many politicians running for office, not because of their skill in public policy or administration, but because of their celebrity. These values provide the fundamental framework for human relations. Western culture is now distorted, with the majority of citizens looking from the outside in, and wanting in, and those on the inside wanting to maintain their position to the exclusion of those outside that inner circle. Both the formal and informal economic systems are geared toward and built upon maximizing the attainment and increasing the wealth and fame at the individual level. These individualistic values not only have practical value in everyday life, but they have taken on deeply held symbolic meaning both at the psychological and social levels. They form part of our cultural imperative and will require great attention if they are to be altered significantly and placed in proper perspective. Much of the rational underpinnings for these cultural practices are constructed on false consciousness, as described in Chapter 3.

From the psychological social perspective, material accumulation and consumption are measures of individual success and are the primary ingredients for determining purpose and self-worth for many in society. The human community has become mesmerized and captured by the imperative of consumption and accumulation. Capitalist regimes have spent a great deal of effort in creating sophisticated apparatus in the form of multibillion-dollar marketing campaigns to forcefully and relentlessly reinforce the importance of material accumulation and consumption to individual self-worth and dignity. Much of the focus on consumption can be attributable to our prehistoric past and our biological predisposition for survival, even though continued existence based on securing the basics such as food in this day and age is not in question for most of us.

Although one could argue that there may be nothing inherently wrong with the capitalist version of human culture in and of itself, the negative effect that it has had on the environment and its inability to provide all individuals on the planet with sufficient material accumulation and consumption demonstrates that this way of life has become extremely exaggerated and is not sustainable over the long term. Pundits on numerous occasions have mused, somewhat with tongue in cheek, that at some point in the not too distant future one person will wind up owning everything if our present system is allowed to continue uninterrupted to its natural conclusion. A new social organizing system that takes us back to focusing on the important biological needs of humans such as clean air, water, and uncontaminated land on which to grow food is paramount.

What might replace the values of consumption and accumulation that could provide purpose to life and individual self-worth and secure a sustainable environment on which we all critically depend for survival? This book offers the values of aesthetic consumption and accomplishment as an alternative or replacement for the present social markers in society. A later chapter in this book will provide more detail on this alternative.

***

There has been great debate and antagonism between the positions taken by those who embrace the biological perspective and those who hold the cultural deterministic view of basic human motivation. In the end it will likely prove to be a blending of the two that provides the answer to what motivates human behaviour. Although the importance of the role of culture in society is clearly understood by many of us, it may be important to reintroduce and rethink the biological component of human behaviour given the rapid generation of new information on genetics and neurobiology.

Neuroscience has made vast strides in providing new insight on the role of biology in human behaviour. The mapping of the genome is contributing greatly to the nature/nurture debate. New thinking suggests that culture may now be changing biology through the environmental/cultural influence on brain development as indicated by early childhood brain mapping. As McNamara (2004) suggests

> There is a period of time in early childhood . . . during which the cultural environment shapes the interneuronal connections in those parts of the CNS that are integral to the preconscious process for creating meaning out

of experience ... The human brain is biologically moulded in childhood by the process of neurological pruning or acculturation, to create particular kinds of meanings out of particular kinds of experience. That is why we can define culture as sets of shared meanings and values.

(p. 55)

Biology and culture may no longer be thought of as mutually exclusive or antagonistic ideas, but forces that influence and shape one another. As Galbraith (1965) commented when delivering the Massey Lectures on CBC Radio back in 1965, "if there is no margin to spare, there is no margin for risk" (p. 8), meaning that if one is born into a culture of deprivation, the portion of the brain devoted to maintaining life at that basic level is likely larger than those born into an affluent situation and who experience different realities. For those in poverty, the brain is likely to take on attributes for focusing on what has worked successfully for their survival in the past, and they may not be willing to take chances on new ideas in order to attempt a better life, although one may be offered such an alternative. It may be safer to stay on social assistance than take a chance at jumping out of poverty by trying something new but with great consequences if the attempt fails. This Catch-22 may at least partially explain intergenerational poverty, and is a concept that is greatly misunderstood by those who are born affluent.

The issue of biological and environmental influences as motivating forces in human culture may be reengaging as possible explanations for why humans act as they do. Biological, as well as cultural, forces must be part of the analysis when we consider social problems and their elimination through social policy. Culture and its backward-looking view may now be as much a hindrance as it was once considered to be the major contributor to human survival and development. Because of new developments in gene mapping and neuroscience, biology is reemerging as a respectable perspective on human behaviour, where it was once considered to be passé, even injurious, to uncovering the truth about the formation of poverty in society. Society needs to take into account both the biological and cultural forces as it proceeds to rectify the problems that are the subject of this book.

References

Blackmore, S. (1999). *The Meme Machine.* New York: Oxford University Press.
Dawkins, R. (2004). *The Ancestors Tale: A Pilgrimage to the Dawn of Life.* London, UK: Phoenix.
Galbraith, J. K. (1965). *The Undeveloped County (in, The Lost Massey Lectures).* Toronto, Ontario: House of Anansi Press.
McNamara, T. (2004). *Evolution, Culture and Consciousness: The Discovery of the Preconscious Mind.* Dallas: University Press of America.

5 Planning Theory in Social Policy Development

Planning theory provides the framework for undertaking social policy development. It is a tool that is as fundamental to the policy maker as a theorem is to the mathematician or a blueprint is to the builder. For the nonacademic reader, don't let the word 'theory' put you off. There is nothing more practical than theory. Theory acts as a guide to the process of policy building. Theories provide a blueprint or a road map for explaining how things in the real world should or are expected to work. Theories are useful for tentatively explaining the world as we experience it, and we can decide whether or not those theories need alteration or complete rejection in favour of developing new theories that better explain reality over time and as we gain new knowledge and understanding. Without theories as guideposts, we are simply left to experience the world without explanation or ability to make cognitive sense of it.

This chapter is hierarchical in its presentation, with the more general and abstract theories examined early in the chapter, and the detailed and specific ideas left for later in the discussion. The initial and grandest theories provide a foundation for those that come after. So, theories build on theories, from the grand explanation down to the on-the-ground concepts that provide guideposts to planners. It is important to use theoretical approaches that are compatible and consistent with one another, providing consistency from beginning to end. It is also important to emphasize that formulating policy on any of the theories found at the beginning of the chapter will dictate what is possible and consistent when selecting the more practical planning approaches later in the planning process. The presentation of theories in this chapter should be thought of as a funnel, with the large general theories at the top and the more specific and operational suppositions at the end of the chapter. This arrangement is offered in order to present a logical progression of useful ideas that create the basis on which social policy can be established. It is a person's theory of society that dictates for him or her what social interventions should be eventually considered by the policy maker in addressing the social inadequacies in society that need attention. For some, intervention in the social structure is seen as social engineering and to be minimized, at best, or avoided altogether. For others, intervention is seen as the way to create a modern civilization. It is important to know what theories manifest themselves in the planning process and what outcomes these differing views of the world have on social construction. Providing an understanding of these machinations is the aim of this chapter.

All modern and developing countries, including those that embrace the ideas contained in the Keynesian state (KS) (Keynes, 1964), base policy formulation on theoretical ideas about how the state and economy operate. Many of these operational notions are ingrained in us by the culture in which we live and the worldviews and myths transmitted by our society largely, but not exclusively, through the media. These ideas centre on the notion that humans intervene in both the social and ecological systems that provide the environment in which they live. What are often in dispute are the amounts of intervention that are appropriate and the nature of that intervention in the social policy formulation process. It is thought that manipulation and intervention in the social or ecological system can enhance conditions of life. Whether or not this general concept is true, humans intervene consistently in all aspects of life, especially in the environmental and social systems, so the question of whether or not intervention in these systems is a good idea or not is not debated here, but the reality of intervention is simply taken for granted. What is of importance to this discussion is to examine a repertoire of available fundamental theories that society can utilize in the process of social policy formation, many of which will lead in different directions. Understanding where theory leads in practice is essential to decision making.

Perhaps the most fundamental theory in this regard emanates from the central concept of the Keynesian state (KS). Many of the fundamental principles that are commonly found in the day-to-day operation of society are contained in the theory of Keynesian economics. Although it is true that most states that operate on these principles construct a customized version of the KS, the fundamental principles of the theory can be found in each society's unique system of beliefs. The application of theory when it comes to state construction is a matter of interpretation rather than inflexible implementation of a rigid system of thinking, although some participants in the process may suffer from dogmatism.

One of the major objectives of the KS is to smooth out the business cycle so that the boom and bust periods that often occur naturally are flattened out, allowing for a more stable economic cycle. In addition to attempting to stimulate a faltering economy, the KS puts in place programs that provide a soft landing for those who are negatively affected by a downturn in the economy and endure a subsequent loss of their means of life support through unemployment. Keynes provided council to the Roosevelt plan that put the unemployed back to work in the depression of the 1930s and helped to deliver the United States from the morass experienced throughout the depression. To this end, KS societies attempt to anticipate changes to the economy and plan their monetary and fiscal policies in accordance with those anticipations. The KS system is based on the philosophy contained in logical positivism, which values rationality based on research and observation of the conditions in society, particularly focusing on the ebb and flow of the economy. The central idea of the KS is that when the economy is on a downward trend, governments need to prime the economic pump by injecting capital into the market through government programs, often social programs that stimulate private spending. And when the economy overheats, governments need to increase interest rates to borrowers to reduce spending in order to cool the economy and hence avoid unwarranted hyperinflation. In those heated-up periods, KS theory suggests that governments need to pay off their accumulated debt, which will give them room to act the next time pump priming is required. This is often where the system breaks down because governments often do not engage sufficiently in debt and deficit reduction when it is most appropriate, but prefer to continue growing government program spending or, more likely, to provide tax cuts with an eye on the next election.

There are those who do not hold to Keynes' philosophy and argue that attempting to manipulate the economic system in this fashion is not helpful and may in fact hurt the natural functioning of the market over the long term (Hayek, 2007). It is easy to see from this discussion what the implications of adopting the KS system—or not—are when selecting approaches to planning social policy. Those who abide by Keynes' ideas see the need and economic practicality for increasing social programs during hard times. Those who do not embrace Keynesian theory think that this type of intervention simply prolongs the agony of the economic downturn because the natural functioning of the market is prevented from operating as it should and is slow to self-correct. Those who follow the primacy of the market would tend to do little, if any, social planning during market downturns, but would rather rely totally on the machinations of the market to dictate social conditions instead. This book sees the importance of the Keynesian approach to social development, and, therefore, the remainder of this chapter is based on the workings of that fundamental concept.

Although all of this sounds perfectly logical, there are some additional theoretical viewpoints, on which approaches to decision making and planning depend, even in such a tightly structured theoretical system as the KS. Approaches to planning are based on theoretical foundations, each of which lead the planner—and consequently the plan—in quite different directions depending on which worldview and set of theories form the basis for planning and development. It is important and necessary to sort out these theoretical approaches in order to understand their implications to the planning process. Figure 5.1 provides a graphic display of the important domains of theory that affect social policy planning and development.

As conceptualized here, the worldview one holds dictates whether one believes in and can support intervention in the human system by public institutions in order to promote such things as equity and equality (limited inequality) for all citizens, particularly as they relate to social services. Those who embrace the social welfare agenda, for example, will have no reservation for endorsing high public institutional involvement in satisfying the basic needs of its citizens. At the other end of the spectrum are those whose worldview holds that the marketplace is the natural and paramount forum for satisfying basic human needs, and they will tend to be closer to the corporatist end of

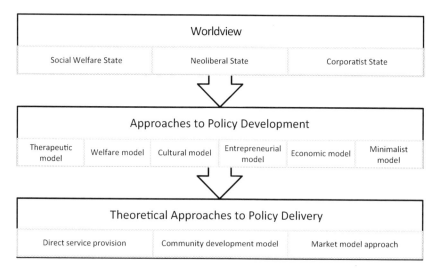

Figure 5.1 Domains of Social Policy Theory

Note: The approaches to policy development in this figure are based on those presented by Theo Beckers in "Integrating leisure policies in advanced societies: The squaring of the circle," Conference proceedings, *Cities for the Future*. Den Haag: Stiching Recreate, 1989.

the continuum. These are competing notions about how the world best operates and one's ideas about how to build civilization for the future. The commitment to one of the three worldview models will dictate what approach to service development is likely to be preferred. For example, if the welfare state is chosen as the most appropriate path for developing a social policy agenda, then the therapeutic, welfare, or cultural model (as opposed to entrepreneurial, economic, or minimalist model—for definitions of each of these models see endnote)[1] of social policy development is the appropriate format for proceeding with the task. On the other hand, if the corporatist state seems more suitable, then the market model of service development is likely to be selected as the framework on which action is based. This approach would minimize public institutional involvement in social policy development and provision in favour of the private marketplace. Service delivery follows vertically in Figure 5.1. For example, if the cultural model was selected for service development, then the community development approach would likely be the best fit for delivering that policy to the public. More will be said about the community development approach to policy delivery later in this book.

***

It is quite normal for participants in any decision-making process to hold differing theoretical approaches that are inspired by their personal philosophical, ideological predispositions, and mental constructs. Most of us approach life with a set of firmly held suppositions that have been formed throughout the course of early life through the socialization process that indoctrinates us into the ways of our particular society. These suppositions guide how we approach everyday life, including the principles we hold dear, our notions of the social order, and our ideas about planning in society. Without consciously thinking about them, we approach any task, including decision making, with the philosophical and ideological underpinnings that provide a basic framework for how we think about the order of the world and how it works. Additionally, it is thought that most of us operate on a default system—that is, we have a preset way of dealing with problems regardless of their origin and makeup. Although this may work for us some of the time, it is generally thought that the approach to resolving a social issue should be constructed on the context and nuances of the problem rather than simply by utilizing a predetermined ideological approach. Each situation to be addressed deserves a thorough and complete diagnosis before a policy plan is constructed to address that problem. This would provide a solid basis on which the best approach to resolving a particular problem could eventually be found.

John Friedmann proposes a continuum of planning approaches, and each stage on the continuum rests on a very different set of assumptions and is contingent upon a unique set of circumstances the planner is attempting to ameliorate. In his scheme Friedmann (1987) offers six theories that lay out his major approaches to planning. He contends that when dealing with a problem, social planners rely on one or a combination of these approaches either consciously, according to what they perceive to be the best approach to resolving the issue at hand, or simply out of inclination and without forethought or diagnosis of the context of the problem. Of course, this book values the former approach over the latter. It is suggested here that the selection of an approach to problem resolution is best served by problem diagnosis and analysis and not simply through social convention or ideology. It is best if the selection of the general approach is based on the nature and context of the problem to be resolved. This method of implementing theory is often referred to as the 'contingent'[2] approach to leadership.

Friedmann's (1987) fundamental theoretical approaches to policy development are described as social reform, policy analysis, social learning, and social mobilization. I have added a fifth approach, which I have called radical planning. Although Friedmann talks about radical planning he includes it in the social mobilization framework, whereas I prefer to set it out as a separate category on its own. The radical planning approach is the extreme form of social mobilization and may involve drastic action and is only appropriate in limited but critical circumstances. What follows is a brief description of Friedmann's categories. For a more detailed description I recommend Friedmann's original treatise on the subject which can be found in his book, *Planning in the Public Domain: From Knowledge to Action*.

According to Friedmann, social reform is a top-down activity constructed on the principles of scientific rationality, scientific management, and public regulation. It is based on the belief that, without state intervention and control, the market economy would produce inefficiency, waste, and injustice. This type of planning is directed from the top by management and subject experts. According to this model, the expert undertakes scientific analysis of the situation under investigation, develops comprehensive plans of action based on this analysis, and implements those plans. This is often achieved without widespread citizen participation in the process or any attention given to the public's day-to-day aspirations. It is based on the premise that those in charge of policy setting are in the best position to appreciate the particulars of the situation and possess sufficient understanding of all the relevant issues to address the problem adequately. In most cases, this approach is ideologically driven by the political elite in society rather than purely analytical. Often this planning approach is designed as a vehicle for implementing a predetermined resolution to the issue that is based solely in ideology or the mindset of those holding power. Policy analysis, another of Friedmann's general planning distinctions, relies on the top-down model of development, much like the social reform model. However, this model is more science based and brings together three academic fields: systems engineering and quantitative modeling, management science and general systems theory, and political and administrative science. The emphasis in this approach is placed on the analysis of data and not necessarily on the meaning and realities of the issue faced by the people it affects. Policy analysis, the second basic approach in Friedmann's scheme, uses the language of systems theory, using such terms as 'steady-state', 'feedback', and 'boundaries'. The approach is very much driven by technical expertise, and there is little room for public consultation or input, let alone control. This approach is basically left in the hands of the expert and relies on research and the interpretation of those data it produces to direct decision making. This model relies heavily on the notion that data can provide an answer to the problem and there is no need for political discourse in problem resolution. Many politicians like this approach because they can obfuscate responsibility by pointing to the data for dictating their actions and decisions, particularly when the decisions they take are not well received by their constituents.

Social reform, and to a lesser extent policy analysis, are often the planning models of choice for national governments who wish to be prescriptive in addressing what they understand to be local or regional issues. National governments often develop social policies as a response to individual and local problems without meaningful input from those most affected by the situation, the citizens themselves. They are often surprised when local people reject their proposed solutions, and perhaps, even the description of the problem itself. The theoretical approaches presented so far are top down, even in instances where decision makers attempt to garner some input from those affected. Usually their idea of garnering input in these approaches is disingenuous and an attempt to get agreement for the plan that is constructed a priori, rather than for gaining insight and different perspectives to the problems and solutions presented. Citizen participation in these approaches to planning rarely gets any more sophisticated than soliciting respondents' answers to closed-ended questionnaires. It might be more accurate to classify them as 'sales or marketing' approaches rather than planning theories. Usually, citizen input in this format simply seeks the uncritical acceptance of the plan by the local people. Citizen input in this instance becomes salesmanship by the proponent of the policy. Although the critique of the first two theories of planning and decision making presented earlier may seem overly harsh, they are still two very legitimate theories if used in the right circumstances and are the preferred models of planning in some contexts. Why they have engendered a bad reputation is because they are often used inappropriately and in contexts that warrant a more participatory approach. As a matter of fact, they are often offered as participation when they are not truly intended for that purpose.

The social learning model represents a drastic departure from the two previously outlined theories. Its approach is learner centred rather than top-down. It links collectively constructed knowledge to action and recognizes the political realities when solving social problems, including those of social development. Perceptions of reality are not limited to those constructed by the experts, but are as numerous as the number of participants in the planning process: no single agent has the exclusive right to represent reality. This approach, unlike the first two, is based on commonly held values and not solely on science or technique. Its most determining characteristic is its dependence on transformative practices originating within civil society. Stankey, McCool, Clark, and Brown (1999, p. 443) set out what they believe to be the fundamental characteristics of the social learning model:

1 It provides opportunities for interaction and deliberation.
2 It is inherently political, in that it involves questions of the nature and distribution of values.
3 It represents all interests who ultimately hold veto power in the discussion and decisions.
4 It integrates perspectives, knowledge, and interests.
5 It honours a wide conception of relevant knowledge, admitting both the formal knowledge of science and the experiential or personal knowledge held by citizens.
6 It is centred on a task-oriented action group—a dynamic, interactive group focused on an issue.
7 It involves a decision that feeds back into the learning process. Indeed, the fundamental purpose is to build learning among group participants in a way that facilitates action.

The social learning model recognizes the legitimacy of personal knowledge in the decision-making system. People live in unique circumstances, and each society possesses special knowledge about the environment around which it is constructed. This knowledge may not only be legitimized in the planning process, but may, in fact, be made primary in it. Although local knowledge is given precedence in this form of decision making, it may be constructed on both positivistic and interpretive research as well. What is unique about the use of research in this approach is that it is not seen as making a decision about the situation at hand, but the results of research may be used by those engaged in the process to interpret their reality and to make decisions based on that interpretation.

Social mobilization, according to Friedmann, extends the basic philosophy of social learning into the realm of action. It is constructed from the three great oppositional movements of history: utopianism, anarchism, and historical materialism—or Marxism. It developed as a countermovement to social reform, so it is revolutionary in spirit. Its perspective is that of the victims and the underclass in society. Its purpose is the political practice of human liberation. This model views the role of the individual and the community in the problem-solving process as dominant and sovereign.

Social learning and social mobilization are bottom-up approaches to planning and decision making that place as much, or more, value on the psychological and social growth of the citizens involved in the process or project as they do on the resolution of a particular problem. Those engaged in this type of approach have faith that if the process is correct, the outcome will also be appropriate. These approaches consider problem identification to be the prerogative of the group or community involved and the solution of problems as a vehicle for capacity building within the community. The whole process is seen as an individual and collective learning experience, which will carry over to other projects in the community.

Lastly, Friedmann identifies radical planning, not as a separate general planning theory as mentioned previously, but as an extension of the social mobilization model. As stated earlier, I believe this category is sufficiently unique to require that it be set out as a theory of planning on its own. In this model, planning focuses on the structural problems of society and provides a critical interpretation of existing reality. Radical planning attempts to chart the future course of a problem and then acts to alter it. The act itself may take the form of social disobedience and be temporarily disruptive to social functioning. It elaborates conceptions of a preferred outcome based on emancipatory practice. Perhaps its most outstanding feature is that it suggests the best strategy for overcoming the resistance of an entrenched, established power structure. Radical planning is an amalgam of analysis, social vision, and strategic thinking. Radical planning involves designing social actions with the explicit aim of emancipating a group of people from a clearly identified oppressive social or political force. The radical approach is usually the approach of last resort and occurs when all else fails and when citizens have become frustrated by their inability to resolve problems by other, more conventional means. The most recent demonstration of this approach at work can be found in the Occupy and, the so-called Arab Spring movements.

Any one of these planning approaches may have more appeal than the others to a particular planner. However, adopting a single approach and applying it to all social problems is not an appropriate practice. The nature and context of a given problem are the criteria on which one of Friedmann's overall approaches should be selected. That said, when a community is the subject of concern, it is likely that the social learning and social mobilization strategies will have some role to play in the planning process.

It is not hard to match up Friedmann's macro approaches to planning with the worldview perspectives, the theoretical approaches to policy development, and the various approaches to policy delivery, as laid out in Figure 5.1. It is important to understand that these contrasting types and various levels of policy and planning tools are associated and fit best with certain parts of the larger set of theories described in Figure 5.1. If these levels of theory are not matched carefully, policy development and planning activities may be fraught with severe difficulties, including intragroup dissension, and any chance for success in the policy process may be limited.

***

The difficulty in social policy formation is that all problems, particularly the problems with which social planning deals, are variable in their construction and require quite different approaches to their resolution. Some of these theories may be unfamiliar to many participants in the planning process. As a consequence, the first activity of the planning group is to diagnose the problem and determine its genesis and nature before focusing on the possible approaches to its resolution. All members of the planning group must agree to the basic approach that is taken to problem definition and resolution; otherwise, irresolvable conflict will arise throughout the activity, leading to a contentious outcome. It is quite imaginable that people who have differing worldviews will also define the problem they are facing quite differently. This difference is often why planning exercises not only fail, but result in frustrating experiences for those directly involved in the planning activity. Selecting the wrong approach to planning can also cause the wrong solution to the problem to emerge. It can be like pounding a round peg into a square hole, as the saying goes. Additionally, philosophical and ideological underpinnings may cause participants in the process to define the problem differently. For example, those who come to view the world with a capitalist perspective may define a problem from a lack of growth perspective. Someone leaning more to the left of the political spectrum may consider the problem to be one of distribution of output and not solely a growth issue. If the planning group is made up of members holding each of these viewpoints, it is important to identify these positions so that a process can be put in place to resolve, rather than ignore, these differences and to make sure they do not interfere with the successful outcome of the project. To allow them to remain subterranean or unidentified will only lead to continuous conflict without the participants involved in the process understanding what is causing the impasse.

This potential difficulty points out that the planning process needs to incorporate members who possess great skill in group dynamics and group work in addition to general planning skills or content knowledge of the subject under review. Self-reflection by the planning group and review of the issues that arise throughout the process are mandatory components of any planning activity if the group is to keep on track and avoid any unidentified group dynamic problems that may emerge throughout the process and interfere with the progress of the plan.

***

So what is the social policy planner to make of all of these theories as he or she moves forward in constructing a plan? As mentioned earlier in this chapter, theories are intended to guide the planning process and to offer some coordination of its activities. Theory will also help those in the process understand what type of research and citizen participation activities are legitimate, and perhaps essential, in plan construction. At the very least, each participant in the process should understand the basis on which he or she is acting. This understanding will rationalize the discussion so that everyone in the process will recognize on what basis the process may move forward. It is also imperative that the principals understand that what they can offer to participants in the process is dependent on what theoretical approach has been engaged. For example, a planning process that is based in the social reform model cannot offer participants control of the process, given that the politicians will decide what direction the policy will take in the final analysis. The social reform model is limited to offering participants input for consideration before the final decision is reached by the decision makers, but nothing beyond that. On the other hand, the social mobilization model is likely best used in situations where the planner can have some confidence that he or she can leave complete control over policy decisions to the participants in the planning process.

***

Theory provides a structure to the policy development process. By understanding and identifying the limitations of the theory chosen, all who participate in, or are affected by, the outcome of the process will understand on what basis the result was reached. They will also be able to appropriately organize themselves to participate in the policy formulation process.

So, with the discussion of the various theories on which social policy formulation is constructed now concluded, we can turn our attention to the most apparent social problems facing society and in need of our attention. The next chapter begins that examination with a focus on poverty.

Notes

1. The **therapeutic model** regards local government's provision of services as primarily a tool for service development for special populations such as individuals with disabilities.

   The **welfare model** focuses on a local government that operates under a traditional social welfare policy and provides specialized services to counteract gaps in provision by the commercial or voluntary sector (typically associated with disadvantaged groups or those least able to pay);

   The **cultural model** views social services as an integral part of an autonomous cultural policy such that experiences, provided by the public sector, are expressions of the prevailing societal and community culture.

   The **entrepreneurial model** suggests that local government should engage in the provision of social services and programs that generate profits, which in turn can be used to subsidise activities that are traditionally not self-supporting, but are socially desirable.

   The **economic model** sees service provision on the part of local government as a vehicle for attracting outside investment and industry into the community, thereby producing economic benefits to the community as a whole.

   The **minimalist model**, as the term implies, demands the least service provision possible on the part of local government as it becomes primarily the responsibility of the commercial or volunteer sector.

2. In this theory of leadership, the person in the group who possesses the most appropriate and best skills for the task at hand assumes leadership. This leadership position may be short lived as the situation changes and leadership is shared with others in the group.

References

Friedmann, J. (1987). *Planning in the Public Domain: From Knowledge to Action*. Princeton: Princeton University Press.

Hayek, F. (2007). *The Road to Serfdom* (Vol. 2). Chicago: University of Chicago Press.

Keynes, J. M. (1964). *The General Theory of Employment, Interest and Money*. New York: Harcourt Brace Jovanovich.

Stankey, G. H., McCool, S. F., Clark, R. N., & Brown, P. J. (1999). *Institutional and Organizational Challenges to Managing Natural Resources for Recreation: A Social Learning Model* (Vols. Leisure Studies: Prospects for the Twenty-first Century). (E. Jackson & T. L. Burton, Eds.) Pennsylvania: Venture Publishing.

Part II

6 Poverty and Marginalization in the Keynesian State

It is often claimed that a critical measure of a civilized society is how it treats its minorities, including their marginalized and financially disadvantaged citizens. Although it can be argued that social progress has been made on some issues such as gender equality and race discrimination, it has fallen behind on other measures such as poverty. It is evident that at least one marginalized group, those suffering from poverty, have not made much, if any, progress in overcoming their situation since the end of World War Two, and their condition continues to deteriorate. In Canada, it is claimed that 4.8 million (14.7 percent), or one in seven, people live in poverty (Canada Without Poverty, n.d.). The United States is similar, with 46.2 million, or 14.5 percent, Americans poverty stricken (United States Census Bureau, 2013). In the United Kingdom (Office for National Statistics, 2013) data suggest that almost a third (33 percent) of the population experienced poverty in at least one year between 2010 and 2013, equivalent to approximately 19.3 million people. In contrast, across the European Union (EU) as a whole, a quarter (25 percent) of the population found themselves in poverty at least once during that period, with a slightly larger proportion of people in the United Kingdom experiencing poverty at least once over those four years.

Poverty in both the developed and in many parts of the developing world is not being eradicated in spite of continuing economic growth and governments' regular rhetorical commitments about reducing its prevalence. Although some progress in gross domestic product (GDP) has been made in many parts of the developing world such as China, India, and Brazil, considerable inequality within these countries persists.

Much of this chapter enunciates the nuances of poverty throughout the world and therefore, it is important to begin this discussion by providing a basic definition of the subject. This is not a simple task because poverty, like beauty, is said to be in the eye of the beholder and is defined differently throughout the world by diverse cultures. Suffice it to say that the basic concept of poverty is defined as the lack of sufficient resources to command and consume a minimum standard of calories, which leaves the individual underfed and undernourished. It is also defined by the lack of other bare necessities that sustain life, such as housing and healthcare. Relative definitions of poverty suggest that poverty is defined and measured by the standard accumulation of goods and resources to which an average person in any given society expects to access by virtue of being a citizen of that society. Reid proposed a definition of relative poverty when giving evidence to Senate hearings on poverty (The Senate Standing Committee on Agriculture and Forestry, 2006).

> I have come to the conclusion that individuals evaluate their station within the social order in which they live and whether or not they command sufficient resources to meet the minimum requirements of life based on their society's set of social standards and values. Poverty is a contested concept, and it is not an absolute variable from my point of view. It is something that is society-defined and society-driven.
>
> (p. 5)

Poverty in this definition is self-referential—that is, it is self-defined and if someone feels that he or she is poverty stricken when comparing his or her life's circumstances to others and finds it decidedly inadequate, this person is said to be experiencing poverty. Although this definition is operative in many societies, it is fraught with obvious difficulties. The most contentious of these is that many individuals will want to compare themselves to the most affluent members of their society. In order to overcome this objection, people must compare their circumstances with the norm of society. Often this can be done by the use of the statistical calculations such as the Low Income Cut Off measure provided by Statistics Canada or other such national formulas. That said, there is also some virtue in making a simple comparison within neighbourhoods and communities. This method is often the most natural judgment that individuals make.

Poverty, regardless of whether one embraces the basic or relative measurement, seems to be worsening given that much of the growth in the economy is being consumed by fewer and fewer people, particularly in the developed world, leaving an ever-growing poor population and a widening of the income gap between those who have access to resources and those who don't. Some predictions have suggested that in a decade or so the poor population in the United States will be as visible as it is today in many of the Third World countries across the globe. So the issue of poverty is as much about the unequal distribution of resources as it is about the ability of populations to consume sufficient calories to maintain life, although that level of poverty continues to exist as well.

A large measure of social policy is about reducing or eradicating poverty, either in attempting to diminish its consequences on those who find themselves experiencing its ravishes or in attempting to protect the general population from falling into it. Poverty is viewed as either a system problem, in that the economy is unable to supply a means for making a living to those unemployed and marginalized by the market system, or an individual problem whereby those in poverty may lack the skills to find a job or are simply thought to be lacking the motivation for work. In the latter case, the poor and those on social assistance are often characterized by society as social deviants or the undeserving poor and a drag on the economy. One of the objectives of this book is to expose the false consciousness notion of poverty that denigrates those experiencing it and to provide a more realistic picture of its true structure.

Poverty engenders an emotional response by those in the general population who are confronted by it. Many people experience negative emotions when confronted on the street by the homeless or by those asking for a handout. Of course, some are saddened by these manifestations of poverty and see it as a failure of society, but those on the other end of the spectrum believe that those in this condition should be dealt with harshly and as minor criminals. There are notions that the deserving poor in society should be supported by the public purse and the undeserving poor, who are considered to be among the free riders in society, deserve to live marginalized lives. Governments continually attempt to motivate the unemployed to engage in work and become self-sufficient and, hence, off the public social assistance system. But I hasten to remind the reader that getting someone off the welfare roll is not the same goal as reducing or eradicating their poverty. Governments, however, seem to embrace the notion that if you are not on the government system then you don't suffer from poverty, which, of course, we know is not the case at all.

One of the fastest-growing poorer segments of the population is the working poor. This is the result of the concept of labour flexibility, which is code for reducing wages in the name of becoming competitive in the global labour market. Since the globalization of the financial and manufacturing system, we seem to be in a race to the bottom when it comes to compensating those who work on the floor of those industries. If workers are not willing to, or can't, work at the bottom of the wage scale, those industries simply move off shore and locate where workers are willing to work for less.

Increased productivity in the workplace no longer depends on labour input as much as it does on technological innovation. Technology often replaces highly skilled and highly paid jobs, leaving the lower-paying ones. When the fruits of increased technology are employed to create additional jobs, those jobs are frequently found in the service sector and at the low end of the income scale. These jobs often compound the problem by locking people into wage rates that cannot meet their minimum living requirements. Unions, which have traditionally negotiated living wages for their works, are increasingly under attack by business and some governments citing competitive disadvantage in the global economy and a barrier to continued economic prosperity. This may be another example of false consciousness.

Governments need to focus on the issue of poverty and not simply concentrate their attention on reducing the number of people engaged in the social assistance system. This change in attitude is particularly important at a time when a large number of people are taking more than their fair share from the economic system and are miserly in their support for those who have fallen on hard times. This book focuses on closing the gap between those who exploit society by taking the majority of resources out of the system and those who receive less than an adequate amount of those same resources. Merit in light of what benefits society receives from work needs to be explored, and suggestions for what effort and contributions society should reward, and in what quantities, requires rethinking. The social organizational structure that maintains the status quo or ideas about what should replace it are presented and discussed in detail later in this volume.

Capitalist countries of the West have attempted to address the issue of poverty through growing the economy, suggesting that if the general economy does well, so will those at the low end of the economic scale. Society has attempted to convince the poor that they, too, will raise their future standard of living through the progress of the market economy. At least a century of this rhetoric has proven this dogma to be ineffective. In fact, it has now proven itself not to work at all, based on the fact that poverty has not been eradicated but continues to grow for many in the affluent countries. How long can this dream of a better economic life be pushed off? As a consequence of the lack of progress on this issue, social policy aimed at maintaining individual welfare over the short term has become a permanent reality for many, not a method for dealing effectively with a temporary situation.

In difficult economic times, increased social spending is an absolute necessity in order to deflect increasing poverty. But for some affluent countries, the social budget is increasingly seen as a target for reducing government deficits that have grown large due to reduced revenues through self-imposed deterioration of the tax base. And, although governments struggle to remain financially viable, the general wealth of most Western countries continues to grow. The prevailing ideology at the present is to cut spending on social programs in order to reduce deficits and taxes. The maintenance of the poor is often seen to be an impediment to reducing government debt and reducing taxes. The affluent members of society often view themselves as victims when their taxes are used to support what they consider to be the undeserving poor. This so-called crisis is the direct result of the lack of political will in providing sufficient funding for state functioning and the public enterprise. Ironically, the lack of political will to deal effectively with poverty comes at a time when most countries are increasing their overall general wealth and affluence. The matter appears to some to be an ideological problem, and hence, a distribution issue, not a difficulty in growing the so-called 'financial pie'.

***

Poverty is best understood when it is considered within a context. It may be starker but no less complicated in the developing world than it is in the more affluent countries across the globe. In developing countries, poverty is widespread throughout the population and affects society more deeply than in the developed world. This fact should not lead to the conclusion that poverty in the West is less devastating to those suffering the condition than it is for residents in the less privileged areas of the globe. It is true, however, that the structure and root causes of poverty in the two spheres are quite different, and each situation needs to be explained separately.

In most Western countries the theory of the Keynesian State (KS) has been implemented to address poverty within the larger context of the capitalist economic system. The origin of the welfare state was dramatically different for many of the countries in the developed world than those in the developing countries. In the West, there are some basic principles on which the well-known model for economic progress—the KS—was constructed. It is worth reviewing some of those ideas, remembering that they may not apply to all developed Western countries beyond the English-speaking orb. Canada, Britain, and the United States will be examined here in some detail for the light they shed on social policy development, particularly policies that attempt to positively affect poverty and that may also impinge on climate change and other forms of environmental degradation. Although countries such as France, Germany, and the Scandinavian countries, among others, also boast a highly sophisticated social welfare system, the particulars of their origins are different than for the English-speaking countries. An important point to remember is that a fundamental concern of the KS is with generating constant growth in the economy. The KS approach to the economy is more favourable to workers in that it encourages government stimulus during recessions, unlike the approach offered by Hayek (Wapshott, 1983) and other conservative thinkers, which simply lets the market correct on its own and without government intervention. Each approach, however, relies on generating growth, thereby supporting material consumption and accumulation. Consumption has been fundamental to our version of capitalism and, as it turns out, has been extremely detrimental to the environment and left a large segment of the world's population in poverty.

Although Canada, Britain, and the United States are all more or less considered welfare states, each came by that designation differently in order to accomplish somewhat similar but slightly different goals. What they had in common was the overwhelming devastation wrought by poverty during the beginnings of the Industrial Revolution in the United Kingdom and the Great Depression in North America and the mass populations it affected severely. In the United Kingdom, it was displacement and poverty caused by the birthplace of industry and the industrial city that led to the early beginnings of the welfare state. In Canada, the origin of the welfare state can be attributed mainly to the social devastation, particularly the lack of access to healthcare, made overwhelmingly noticeable by the depression. In the United States the demoralizing poverty experienced by farmers, caused by the Dust Bowl in the early 1930s and the subsequent depression, provided motivation for the creation of what eventually became known as the 'New Deal'; the U.S. version of the welfare state. Despite the different motivations for action in each country and the magnitude of the measures taken by all of them, their effort produced similar results in each state. The beginning of social policy in the non-English-speaking countries of Europe was different in each case. In France, one might trace the beginnings of social welfare policy to the French Revolution where, unfortunately, the goal of poverty alleviation and equality for all citizens got lost in the bloody search and punishment of the aristocratic class, which had trodden on the peasant population for centuries. Germany, on the other hand, had a meagre and short experimentation with social policy under the Kaiser in the early 1920s through experimentation with pensions for the elderly. This experiment with social policy was interrupted by the Nazi regime and World War Two.

Until these varied experiments with poverty alleviation through the development of social policy, governments acted passively in dealing with social ills. Much of the thought on poverty at that time was based on a misreading of Darwinian's theory of evolution, which left individuals on their own and without support. Those in power, on the other hand, routinely viewed poverty as a social crime. Spencerism misrepresented Darwin and his notion of the 'survival of the fittest'. Spencer's interpretation of Darwin's theory legitimized governments' nonresponse to the descent of individuals into poverty, as it was seen to be in keeping with the natural order. In Britain, the United States, and Canada, it took the insightful philosophy of economist John Maynard Keynes during the Great Depression to legitimize active government intervention into the market system through fiscal pump priming by way of government funded make-work and other social programs. These actions by government encouraged employment and its consequential stimulative effect on the economy, generally. Keynes' strategy focused on getting the economy rolling after a protracted period of depression, and by so doing, alleviated abject poverty for many citizens. The consequence of this basic action legitimized the role of government in monetary and fiscal policy and the function of government in attempting to level out the boom and bust cycles of the market. And, when leveling out is not possible, then to at least provide a basic social service floor through which no citizen is allowed to fall. Additionally, governments became engaged in providing basic services to the less fortunate, either directly or indirectly, and in so doing, moved Western nations beyond the reliance on the charity model of social service delivery and toward a formal government social policy and interventionist role. Whereas the Keynesian revolution provided a rationale and a framework for the social welfare state, each country had its own unique experience and activists who shaped it.

***

In Canada, the origins of the social welfare state began by providing meagre unemployment insurance benefits to persons who found themselves out of work, and hence without income, due to of the vagaries of the market economy. However, the origin of the welfare state in Canada is usually attributed to the thinking of the province of Saskatchewan, which produced the first government-funded Medicare system in North America. Saskatchewan is traditionally one of Canada's smallest and poorest agriculturally based provinces and is often cited as providing the spirit for developing Canada's welfare state. Tommy Douglas stands out as the champion of healthcare policy in Canada. The election of Douglas as premier of Saskatchewan, and eventually the leader of the Co-operative Commonwealth Federation (CCF) party (the forerunner of the New Democratic Party), led to Saskatchewan becoming the first province in Canada to tackle the devastating inequality in the healthcare system, which was functionally controlled and administered solely by the medical profession. Douglas fought a pitched battle with the doctors of the province who threatened to strike the system if the provincial government instituted what physicians saw as a socialized medical system. Douglas was labeled a communist by the medical profession and other far-right opponents. In spite of the campaign of fear waged by the doctors of the province, Douglas's administration won out and introduced the first government-funded medical system in North America. It wasn't long after that battle that the federal Liberal government under the direction of Prime Minister Mackenzie King introduced the same basic measures for all of Canada's citizens. No longer would a citizen of Canada go bankrupt as a result of being stricken by a catastrophic disease or, worse yet, die because he or she couldn't afford treatment. The spirit of collectiveness that Douglas demonstrated eventually carried over into other social policy areas, such as unemployment insurance and pensions. The welfare state in Canada was shaped by a number of government social policies spurred on by the original success of the transformation of the health policy in Saskatchewan. The more notable policies adopted in Canada that shaped the welfare state in its formation stage are listed in Table 6.1.

Tommy Douglas is credited as the initiator of the welfare state in Canada, as was William Beverage in Britain and his ground-breaking report in 1942 on the social welfare needs of the British population. Canada developed its own comprehensive proposal, outlining a set of needs, policies, and suggested remedies in the form of the federal government–sponsored Marsh Report (Marsh, 1943).

Table 6.1 The Basic Welfare State in Canada

Act	Date
Unemployment Insurance Act	1956
Saskatchewan's Medical Care Act	1961
National Medical Insurance Program	1964
National Housing Act	1964
Canada (Quebec) Pension Plan	1965
Guaranteed Income Supplement	1965
Canada Assistance Plan	1966
Established Programs Financing Act	1967

Source: A. Moscovitch: Welfare State.

Many of the programs and legislation that are contained in Table 6.1 were first outlined in the Marsh Report.

From the time these social policies first appeared, many revisions to them have been undertaken. These adjustments have been made based on the ideological worldview of the government in power at the time and the social and economic environment in which they found themselves. Those on the left of the political spectrum view social policies as an important component of a civilized society. Those on the right see the same policies as an impediment to the proper functioning of the market and a full employment economy. Regardless of which ideology is in power at any given time, and in spite of the many adjustments to these pieces of legislation throughout the decades, they have survived in some form or another and have shaped economic and social relations in this and other Western countries for over half a century.

Until recently, most of the policies and programs implementing the welfare state have been enriched by most Western nations. That is not the case at present, however. As we move toward a more conservative and individualistic society, many of the programs outlined earlier are continually being eroded, and some are in jeopardy for their very existence. There continues to be a strong push from the right of the political spectrum to privatize many of the services and programs that are contained in Canada's social policies, and the defenders of public social policy are ever vigilant to maintain the historic gains made. Canada is not alone in this social policy retrenchment. The United States and many other countries throughout the globe are also experiencing such pressure. As a most recent example of this deterioration, the federal government of Canada has increased the retirement age and eligibility for receiving Old Age Security from 65 to 67 years old. The U.S. Congress continues to question the viability of the meagre entitlement programs available to its poorest citizens. So the attack on the welfare state is ever present.

***

The origins and motivations for the U.S. version of the welfare state are found in the Great Depression of the 1930s. The initial impetus for this movement is attributed to the extreme difficulties experienced by the farm population as a result of the Dust Bowl. As Arthur Schlesinger, Jr. (1958) suggests,

> [F]arm prices had fallen more than 50 per cent; and the parity ratio—the ratio of prices received by farmers to the prices they paid—had plummeted from 89 in 1929 down to 55 in 1932 ... the seething violence in the farm belt over the winter—the grim mobs gathered to stop foreclosures, the pickets along the highways to prevent produce from being moved to town—made it clear that patience was running out.
>
> (p. 27)

What subsequently became known as The First New Deal began with the introduction of the Agricultural Adjustment Act of 1933.

> The Agricultural Adjustment Act was an omnibus (Bill) which gave farmers . . . their three main demands . . . protection against the ruinous effect on prices of their surplus crop, inflated currency with which to pay their debts, and cheap credit.
> (Keller, 1963, p. 25)

General unemployment relief was the second issue to be dealt with by Roosevelt and his New Deal. The Roosevelt administration basically provided a three-pronged approach to the devastation of the Great Depression: (1) the Civil Conservation Corps that provided a quarter of a million make-work jobs at barely subsistence wages in the national forests; (2) the creation of the Federal Emergency Relief Administration, which provided grants to states for direct emergency relief to the poor; and (3) the development of the National Industrial Recovery Act that provided employment through public infrastructure and building construction. All of this was meant to be short term until the economy recovered. During this interval it was thought that private enterprise and industry could gear up to once again be solely responsible for generating advances in the economy and supply employment and decent wages to all. This philosophy was quite different from Canada's. The action taken by the American government was in support of the private marketplace. Canada, on the other hand, was constructing a mixed economy where government was seen as a permanent partner in the economic system. We can see the same influences at work today as both countries debate their social welfare policies. And, whereas President Obama has managed to reform the healthcare system in the United States and win healthcare coverage for the majority of, if not all, U.S. citizens, health insurance has mainly been left to private enterprise to supply, unlike the Canadian and British model that pays for healthcare directly through the government treasury. In spite of this small win, the Republican Party in the United States continues to try to unravel these modest gains in hopes of reprivatizing the entire system. The fundamental difference in the U.S. system, when compared with Canada and Britain, is that healthcare in the United States seems to be considered a privilege and purchased. In Canada and Britain, it is seen as a right and publicly funded. This basic difference in spirit may carry over to other social policies as well.

Subsequent to the main contributions of Roosevelt's government cited earlier, the United States also introduced some other direct measures. The Tennessee Valley Authority, for example, was created to allow government to engage in providing citizens with electric hydro from the great waterways of the country rather than turning that function solely over to the private sector. The Securities Act of 1934 was intended to protect the public from fraud and misrepresentation by large corporations—or anyone else for that matter.

The Glass-Stiegel Banking Act was likewise introduced to prevent abuses in the mostly regional and private banking system.[1] The National Labor Board was established at that time to give more power to labour, but this institution was hotly contested by big businesses, who felt that they could better control labour and their representation if left to do it on their own. In addition to providing labour with more power, the National Labor Board was developed as a watchdog on private corporations and mandated to provide mediation, conciliation, and arbitration during violent disputes between corporations and labour. Perhaps the most notable acts affecting the largest number of people was the Civil Works Administration and, like the National Reclamation Act, resulted in 40 million people being put to work. All of these measures were intended essentially to put money in the hands of the masses so that they could spend for basic goods and services, thereby supporting or propping up the private economy. These measures were never intended to develop a systematic welfare state with government legitimized as a permanent player in the economic system, unlike in Canada and Britain, where government was always seen as a permanent player in the system, even if it was to be a junior partner or service provider of last resort.

***

The impetus for the British experience can be traced back to World War Two, when William Beverage (1942) was first asked by the British government of the day in 1941 to examine the insurance needs of the British public and become "chairman of a committee to consider social insurance and allied subjects" (Beveridge, 1954, p. 101). It would be almost twenty years later, however, before any comprehensive introduction of his ideas in legislation was attempted by the then prime minister of Great Britain, Lloyd George. In the meantime, competition among the various political parties raged, each generating their policy positions on publicly funded social insurance schemes, which mainly centred on pensions for those of retirement age (70 years) and for widows and orphans. In some respects, this was motivated by a realization that war would soon end and there would be a major transition of manpower from the war effort to civilian life. The first task Beverage asked his committee members to complete was an inventory of all the various and sundry government programs that existed. Although there were not many at the time, some programs would need to be incorporated into any new scheme that might emerge from the committee's deliberations. Perhaps more important, these various schemes and programs needed to be coordinated and organized into a comprehensive package that could address a host of individual needs and attend to families' difficulties. Additionally, there were anomalies with the benefits individuals were entitled to, based on the affluence of their employer and the solvency of the private insurance companies at the time.

Beverage also set out to answer a question put to him earlier in the century that asked why, with so much wealth, is there so much poverty—a question that needs to be addressed again today. His reply to this question is to be found in a document titled "The Scale of Insurance Benefits and the Problem of Poverty", released in 1942. The report concluded that distribution of wealth was the problem and not the ability of society to grow the economy or produce sufficient goods. He concluded that the solution to this problem was social insurance. Beverage's original concept calls for workers and employers to contribute to social programs through taxation to a fund that could be tapped during times of difficulty or in retirement. The report was submitted to the government in November 1942. The plan focused basically on issues of poverty, such as pensions and children's allowances; however, it also noted that:

> The Security Plan is only one step of many that have to be taken. To get the New Britain of all our desires, we must deal with Want but with four other giant evils;-with Disease (that is the purpose of the Health Service), with Ignorance (dealing with that means more and better schools), with Squalor (curing that means better planning of towns and country-side and more and better houses), with Idleness, that is to say unemployment.
> (Beveridge, 1954, p. 115)

There seemed to be great support in Britain for social reform as part and parcel of the war effort. The time seemed to be right for this type of initiative. Beverage's work marks a departure from the government's fixation only on unemployment and widened the scope to poverty in general. The extent of his vision would broaden the scope of social policy to include poverty among the elderly and widows in addition to other sectors of the population. The basic principles of the Beverage Report, which later provided the foundation for the social security scheme that the British enjoy today are (1) compensation for industrial injury financed by the individual, the company, and the state; (2) the unification of numerous departments dealing with social insurance; (3) ensuring that all benefits and contributions would be at a flat rate and that rate should be standardized for different kinds of social need; (4) the establishment of categories of individuals to ensure that each person would receive benefits accordingly to their category (e.g., workers, pensioners, housewives, etc.); (5) that the whole insurance system should be based on a means-tested public assistance scheme that would address absolute poverty; and (6) social insurance would cover the whole population and not just those in need.

The last and perhaps the most difficult questions Beverage had to answer were related to financing such a social insurance scheme. For the answer to those questions Beverage was able to discuss his ideas with John Maynard Keynes. Keynes was also employed by the government to work out questions of finance generally, and he and Beverage collaborated on the question of social insurance. Keynes looked at this question not in isolation to the larger issues he was considering, but as part of the whole matter of government finance and national fiscal health, and hence, the term Keynesian state was born.

The tabling of the Beverage Report laid the foundation for the social welfare state in Britain and its subsequent adoption elsewhere around the globe. Although it had its critics, mainly among business and the right wing of society, it has been in existence in Britain since the early 1940s. As in other jurisdictions, the ideas contained in the Beverage Report have been under attack in recent days. Certainly, the idea of public enterprise and government intervention into the economic system has been questioned by the recent conservative government in Britain as well as in other social welfare states around the world.

Keynes and the other generators of the welfare state in the countries mentioned earlier attempted to make life more pleasant for those in need and to fight the ravishes of poverty. It is important to point out that all of these schemes were laid out within the parameters of the capitalist system and relied on economic growth, largely through the exploitation of the environment. Of course, back in the days of Roosevelt, Beverage, and Marsh, concern for the environment was not a consideration. In fact, the environment was seen as a commodity to be dominated or overcome in the service of humankind and not necessarily conserved.

The deterioration in social circumstances of those living in poverty produces similar results in most parts of the developing world. Countries such as China and other southeastern countries are becoming increasingly affluent, but they, too, are having difficulty in raising the general standard of living for their poorest citizens, although they enjoy positive international balance of trade accounts and increasing economic development in the region. The struggle for more equitable distribution of wealth in this fast-growing part of the globe continues as the world witnesses the transference of economic dominance from West to East.

***

Poverty is discussed but little understood; in fact, it is surrounded and characterized by many myths. The face of poverty in the developed and developing world has some similarities but also many differences. Poverty takes on many shapes and forms and may be seen and felt differently depending on the society in which it is experienced. In Canada, Britain, and the United States, the official unemployment rate fluctuates somewhere between 4 and 7 percent. In the Scandinavian countries it runs a little less. Some, but not all, of this poverty can be explained by the lack of employment and stagnation of wages over the last few decades. There is an increasing population of low-paid employed workers, mainly but not exclusively working in the service sector, who are said to constitute a growing group of citizens classified as the working poor. Historically, unemployment rates fluctuate in accordance with the business cycle, but today's poverty may be more structural given the jobless recovery we have been experiencing since the last recession.

The reported unemployment rate may simply represent the tip of the iceberg, with many of the casualties of unemployment not counted in the statistics because these individuals have lapsed from the official unemployment system. They have given up looking for work and are, therefore, no longer considered part of the labour force. Government statistics on unemployment only count those individuals who are looking for work and exclude discouraged workers who have dropped out of the labour market. Often these workers return to the labour market and begin seeking work only when the economy appears to be picking up. They are then returned to the unemployment statistics. Although working, there are many people at the bottom of the employment scale who remain in poverty because of low wages. Describing poverty participation rates as simply those without work or income is not a very sophisticated method of study and it excludes many people who deserve inclusion in the analysis.

The picture of who lives in poverty is varied, with some living in extended and persistent destitution, and others experiencing short episodes of impoverishment. Although some individuals are chronically unemployed and without any means of income beyond the social wage, others are known as the 'working poor' and often hold down numerous jobs but still are not able to make ends meet and rise above the national poverty level. Others are persons with severe social, psychological, or physical disabilities who suffer from insurmountable barriers to education and other deficiencies because of personal circumstances. If these difficulties were rectified, they may eventually become able to earn a decent living. Many of those who find themselves in this economic circumstance also suffer from poverty-related issues such as lack of healthcare or proper nutrition. So, many of the issues social policy deals with fundamentally stem from, or contribute to, poverty. Pay rates and poverty seem to be tied directly to education, with those at the top of the pay scale highly educated and trained and those at the bottom with little skill or education. Although this state has traditionally been the case, well-educated people are now experiencing difficulty finding suitable employment. Education may no longer be the powerful force for avoiding poverty it once was.

The assessment of poverty in less developed countries, particularly in regions such as Africa, is altogether a more dramatic story. If poverty visits an individual in a developing country, there are usually few to no social supports to assist that individual unless a Western-based or domestic nongovernmental organization (NGO) is operating a charitable effort in their vicinity. Developing countries often possess a communal or extended family ethic that attempts to reduce the impact of poverty on any individual in the family or community. That said, it is often the case that the entire community is in the same deprived situation, so collective action may not result in a positive outcome in these circumstances. It used to be said that the rural poor could always find work in the city as a method of finding their way out of poverty, but that may no longer be the case given the oversaturation of people in the cities. So poverty is also increasing in the cities, as well as rural areas, and the social policies to address it are inadequate, perpetuating the poverty of the rural poor who are attempting to escape those conditions by migrating to urban centres.

Poverty in cities has now grown to match or exceed that found in the countryside in many developing countries. The explosion of what is termed 'squatting' by individuals in overcrowded shantytowns, where housing is often made from cardboard or previously discarded sheaths of tin or fiberglass, can be observed in many developing countries' cities. This is often the face of poverty in the developing world. More recently we have seen a massive migration of people out of war-torn regions such as Syria and Afghanistan and flooding into Europe, which is increasing the size and complexity of poverty as well. It has become clear that the largest single group in Western society that faces poverty is recent immigrants.

Rural Canada and other Western countries also have been losing populations as the family farm has given way to the factory farm. In spite of the rural exodus to the urban setting, poverty continues to exist in the countryside, but is often less visible than in the city. As the interim report of the Canadian Senate Standing Committee on Agriculture and Forestry studying poverty (2006, p. v) suggests,

> The rural poor are, in many ways, invisible. They don't beg for change. They don't congregate in downtown cores. They rarely line up at homeless shelters because, with few exceptions, there are none. They rarely go to the local employment insurance office because the local employment insurance office is not so local anymore. They rarely complain about their plight because that is just not the way things are done in rural Canada.

***

In previous decades in Canada, a high proportion of older adults were at risk of poverty. However, as a result of the introduction of public pensions, that picture has changed substantially. In Canada and some of the other Western countries, poverty rates among the elderly are now below the rate for other population sectors. As late as 1980, the poverty rate for the elderly was slightly above that for the population as a whole in the United States, Germany, Norway, and Finland. Fifteen years later, poverty among the elderly was slightly below the average in all of the countries studied (with the exception of the United States).

In Canada nearly 15 percent of elderly single individuals live in poverty (Canada Without Poverty, n.d.). That said, the Canadian government has become concerned that seniors once again may be in jeopardy of falling into poverty. The government has recently convened meetings with the provincial finance ministers to consider making adjustments to the Canada Pension Plan and the Old Age Security system that would avoid this eventuality.

By 1995, poverty had turned into a risk for young adults in all countries, with poverty rates increasing for those eighteen to thirty years of age or younger. What seems to be on the rise are young families experiencing poverty, so much so, that most advanced countries are implementing school breakfast programs because officials see hunger on the rise in many school-aged children. It is estimated that one in five children is now in poverty and, in some jurisdictions such as First Nations communities in Canada, that average is exceeded dramatically. Perhaps the greatest poverty crisis lies in immigrant populations in many of the developed world countries, including Canada. These are often the same people who are attempting to escape poverty in their homeland.

***

Determining what constitutes poverty has been an obscure and highly contested debate. Essentially, and at the very macro level, poverty is viewed in two distinct ways. Poverty can be classified as abject or relative in form. In many of the African countries, abject poverty is viewed as the lack of sufficient calories to sustain life. Second, and perhaps more applicable to the developed world, poverty is a relative matter, although abject poverty also continues to exist. Relative poverty is judged in relation to the mores or standards of life that define the referent society. That is not to say that absolute poverty does not exist in developed countries as it does in the developing world. Absolute poverty is a fact in most, if not all, of the developed world countries, but the type of poverty endured by many in the affluent world is relative by nature.

Relative poverty in Canada and the United States is a culturally, socially, and politically constructed concept. The definition of poverty is derived in a political context that often places limitations on the definition. That is to say that individuals evaluate their station within the social order in which they live and whether or not they command sufficient resources to meet the requirements of life based on their society's set of social standards and values. One's personal experience when evaluating the idea of poverty is germane to its eventual definition. Poverty, then, is a highly contested concept. Certainly, Canadian citizens have a different concept of what constitutes poverty in Canada versus those in many African countries, for example.

A number of thoughts and issues need to be raised that have an influence on how society views poverty today and what might be done about it in the future. Figure 6.1 may not represent an exhaustive catalogue of concerns or ultimate solutions to the problem of rural poverty, but it does, I think, present a number of the issues and ideas that need to penetrate the discourse in order to first come to understand the nature of the phenomenon and then to eventually achieve the elimination of poverty.

***

Poverty is not purely an economic condition. There are psychological and social elements of poverty that may be as important to confront as the provision of an adequate income if poverty is to be eradicated entirely. As Gilbert (2002, p. 67) tells us: "The socially excluded are usually poor, but they suffer from more than just a shortage of money; they endure multiple deprivations, the cumulative impact of which leaves them detached from the mainstream of society". Figure 6.1 presents the basic elements that can define poverty.

90 Part II

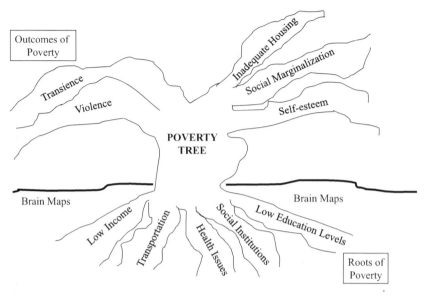

Figure 6.1 Roots and Outcomes of Poverty

There are thought to be many roots for poverty creation in addition to the pure lack of income that is often the sole focus in combating its debilitating effects. There are also many outcomes of poverty beyond simply the material ones such as hunger and the lack of the ability to acquire possessions. Figure 6.1 sets out some of the major roots and outcomes of poverty.

Although I have attempted to differentiate between the root causes and outcomes of poverty, there may be specific instances where an outcome as I have identified it here can, in fact, be a root cause for someone experiencing poverty. I would concede that it is situational and determined by circumstances, and the root causes shown here may be outcomes in some other situation. I acknowledge that cause and effect are not clearly established, but I think the division in Figure 6.1 is a generally useful idea when attempting to explain poverty. All too often those in power focus on symptoms when they should be addressing root causes, and become frustrated when the problem doesn't get resolved through their efforts. Fundamentally, poverty should be seen and treated like a system and not as an individual variable such as income.

Poverty in Figure 6.1 is depicted as a tree. Below ground, the roots of poverty are identified as low income as well as the other variables listed. Lack of transportation is a contributor to poverty, especially for the rural poor, but it is also a concern for poor urbanites. The cost of public transportation, even when it is available, or the cost of such commodities as an automobile or petrol for travelling to work if the employer is a distance away is often prohibitive.

Health concerns are also a major factor, particularly mental health problems that are of a psychological or social nature and often so debilitating it makes earning a living in the market economy almost, if not absolutely, impossible for the afflicted person. Many state-sponsored work and job training programs are founded on the assumption that mental stability is assured, which is not always the case. In the fight against poverty, often what is needed in the first instance are psychological or social therapy programs before job skill training can be useful.

Low education levels also make working in a highly technological society difficult, if not impossible. There are fewer and fewer low-skilled jobs in our highly technological and knowledge-based work environment. In fact, the manufacturing workplace needs fewer and fewer workers and relies more and more on technology. In instances where low-skilled workers are needed, these enterprises and jobs are being consistently transferred to the developing world where labour is cheaper and environmental laws less strict. It is increasingly evident that in the developed world economy the once-dominant manufacturing activity is being replaced with financial and service-sector jobs, as was the case when manufacturing replaced agriculture as the major employer decades ago. As a result, the 'new economy' is now very much built on a highly educated and, it would appear, reduced, workforce. Lack of education, then, is a major contributor to poverty in the developed world. What is often left for the low-skilled person without education are low-paying service-sector jobs which frequently assign those employed in that sector to the working-poor stratum of society.

Social institutions that have been constructed to address poverty in an agriculture or manufacturing dominated world no longer have relevance in a highly technological environment. This is particularly the case where the 'new economy' no longer needs as many people in the production process as it did historically. Full employment no longer means that all willing workers are gainfully engaged in work in the market economy or possess a paid job. What it has come to mean is that a goodly number of willing workers are unemployed at any given time, usually in the neighbourhood of 6 to 8 percent in Canada, and perhaps more numerous in other jurisdictions. As a consequence, social policies, and the institutions that have been constructed to administer them, are in need of renovation at the least, and maybe total replacement in order to make them relevant to the new reality. The construction of policies and the replacement of present institutions in favour of new structures to deal effectively with the root causes of poverty and their outcomes will be addressed in greater depth later in this work.

As depicted in Figure 6.1, poverty, regardless of its motivations, leads to consequences and poor outcomes for individuals trapped in it and for society generally. Transience in search of work creates instability in other areas, as well as the general upheaval to the personal stability that it produces. Lack of consistency in learning in school for children in poverty-stricken homes is certainly one of the largest instabilities produced by constantly moving in search of work. Instability in housing also causes transience, a main outcome of poverty.

Although not all families in poverty experience violence, many do. It often comes in the form of intrafamily violence produced by the constant and unrelenting pressures and stresses on those in poverty. Not possessing sufficient food or finances that provide for the routine necessities of life, such as stable housing, supplies for schooling, or adequate clothing, are also causes of intrafamily violence. Additionally, people experiencing poverty are often forced to live in neighbourhoods that are inadequately serviced and becoming derelict because of insufficient funds for maintenance and upkeep. Many of these neighbourhoods are grounds for violent crime and other illicit activities. The neglect of low-income neighbourhoods and the people in them is familiar to many cities throughout the world. Most affluent neighbourhoods in New Orleans, for example, have been reconstructed and brought back to life post Katrina. The same cannot be said for some of the poorer and mainly black sections of that city. It is well documented that violent crime is routinely greater in low-income areas than in the more affluent parts of cities.

Poverty often leads to social marginalization. Those experiencing poverty are frequently excluded from engaging in social and recreational programs that are otherwise available to mainstream society. As Taylor and Frisby (2010, p. 36) suggest, "citizens living on low income are systematically excluded from participating in activities in their own communities by the very public institutions that have mandates for including them".

Two single-parent social assistance recipients and participants in a recent research project conducted by Golden (2008) were unable to join and take advantage of a group known as 'Parents without Partners' because of their destitution. Parents without Partners is a group of single parents who meet regularly to discuss common issues and create social events for themselves. Golden's research project provided resources for these women to join the Parent without Partners group, and it became immediately clear exactly how important this activity was to the social functioning of these women, both from a psychological and social perspective. Most importantly, their self-esteem seemed to be positively affected through social participation. The factors outlined in Figure 6.1 and discussed earlier often lead to poor self-esteem for those living in poverty. Self-esteem may be the most critical, negative element produced by the turmoil of poverty and needs special attention by the institutions that have been created to address this issue. Unfortunately, many of society's institutions established to address poverty have a negative effect on self-esteem rather than strengthening it. Even today, people on social assistance are often made to feel inferior or less than adequate when they are in contact with the social welfare system. Many of the negative stereotypes about the poor are reinforced by government agencies that are mandated to serve that sector of society.

There are volumes written about self-esteem generally, so a short discussion pertaining to poverty-induced issues of self-esteem will suffice here. There are some unique features with poverty-induced low self-esteem. Perhaps the greatest locus for the lack of this critical element is the amount of negative feedback those in poverty receive from society generally, and from their peers particularly, although their poverty may be through no fault of their own. Poverty is often viewed by the general public as individually created and a character flaw of those experiencing the phenomenon, and not as a general failing of the social system. Society constantly tells those in poverty they are the masters of their own fate and in poverty because of their own personal inadequacies. It became apparent throughout the research project by Golden, referred to earlier, that those in poverty came to believe this constant message. They, too, began to see themselves as undeserving members of society that need to be punished and looked down upon by others for their inadequacies.

Following from the discussion earlier, social policy needs to be comprehensive and address all the variables identified in Figure 6.1, and not just with income, if it is to successfully address the poverty issue. Governments tend to take a simplistic approach to the subject of poverty reduction and only make efforts at its eradication by providing job skill training and by providing short-term subsistence income. The discussion earlier makes it clear that poverty is a result of many more variables producing considerable negative outcomes, which all need to be addressed in a systematic and comprehensive way. The days of viewing poverty as simply a matter of income are gone. All of the variables outlined in this chapter, both root and outcome, need social policy attention if the general condition of poverty is to be addressed adequately

In addition to the social and psychological variables that are outlined in Figure 6.1, it may be time to include discussion on the biological factors that can affect poverty. This has been a taboo subject in the past because many in society have used this area of enquiry inappropriately and as an avenue for blaming the victim of poverty for his or her plight and to dismiss the role the social environment plays. The issue of eugenics and other biologically based evils practiced by societies throughout history has discredited this line of enquiry. Although it is not in the purview of this book to provide a detailed discussion on the potential role biology may play in poverty creation and retention, the recent work in neuroscience and genetics opens up some interesting prospects for this study and should be pursued in the future. Certainly brain-imaging technology opens this area up for important research. We know that the first few years of life and the social environment to which we are subjected are important to brain mapping. Brain mapping may have a lot to say about how we interpret the world in later life, and early brain development may have something important to contribute to explaining poverty's continued prevalence in society and to refining the definition of that state.

***

Poverty has both a horizontal and a vertical dimension to it. It is vertical in terms of sector-specific collapse in the economy in a defined geographical area and horizontal in that it is class based, perhaps even with the potential of creating a permanent underclass. In Canada, for example, the forestry sector, which dominates many of the communities found in northern Ontario, has been depressed for a number of years, even for decades and, as a consequence, entire populations may find themselves in poverty through no fault of their own. Whole sectors of the economy can be affected by technological innovation and global trade agreements leading to changed circumstances in regions of a country that rely on single industries. And, there are families in pockets throughout the country that experience generational poverty regardless of where they live and what economic activity is going on around them. They simply cannot take advantage of the positive environment in which they are immersed for whatever reason, be it the lack of appropriate skills, psychological health, or other social problems. These personal and social conditions can account for discovering pockets of poor citizens in areas where a booming economy exists.

A complicating factor masking the complete understanding of poverty, in addition to the horizontal and vertical nature of the condition, is the invisibility and mobility of the poor. Traditional rural dwellers and cultures from various parts of the world demand that families, including the poor, deal with difficulties independently on their own. The notion that accepting charity is a personal failing runs deep. Hard times have been taken for granted in many rural areas in Canada and the Western world, and it is left to individual families to deal with it, usually on their own. That is not to refute the caring and compassionate nature of these communities. If discovered, great care and compassion are extended to the needy, but it is the discovery of that need that is often difficult and complex.

Rural citizens, particularly single people, often migrate to urban centres to escape the stigma of poverty. It is in the cities where services for the poor are usually much better developed and where anonymity can be achieved as well. These two factors often entice the rural poor to migrate to urban centres when they can. That being said, there is an emerging trend in the rural/urban fringe where some urbanites in need of social housing are being offered rural accommodation in under-subscribed rural social housing stock, reversing the migration pattern. In the case that I am most familiar with, the housing stock was originally built to house local senior citizens but was not taken up sufficiently, leaving dwellings for other uses such as housing the urban poor who are willing to migrate. This has accommodated such a small number of the urban poor, however, that it has not made a dent in fixing either the poverty problem or increasing the use of surplus housing. Additionally, the social and psychological complications produced by this reverse migration on both the migrants and the community are yet to be determined, but all indications are that it has its downside in terms of psychological integration into the host community. Quite often the basic social services that many poor families require are not found in a number of these rural communities, which adds to their burden. At the very least, there are issues with the social and psychological integration of the newcomers into the social life of the community. There is often accompanying depression by those who move because of the loss of family and friends from the old location.

***

The poor in Canada or other Western nations should not be considered to be a homogeneous population in either condition or in need. There is a continuum of poverty, and at each pole on the continuum there are different prospects for dealing with that state, with or without long-term government or NGO intervention. There are poverty-stricken individuals who are in that position temporarily and, given a small change in the economic environment, will be back into the labour force and be out of poverty within a short time. On the other end of the continuum are those who are dealing with severe social or psychological problems and who are not ready for employment skill training but are in need of social skill development and mental health attention before employment training can be appropriate or effective. Unfortunately, most governments are prepared to provide employment skill training, but not address the social and psychological problems that are often pervasive for those at the most difficult end of the continuum.

***

Poverty has been a difficult condition for governments around the world to define and eliminate. Much of this difficulty lies in the politics of the subject. If governments define it, then their constituents will expect them to eradicate it, and many governments have different priorities and do not possess the political will to address this issue adequately. There are also worldview issues such as those presented in Chapters 2 and 3 that inhibit governments' willingness to define poverty, let alone eradicate it. There are some efforts made to describe it, but no definition exists on which all governments and agencies can agree. What has often been the focus of discussion is a classification system of poverty that essentially provides four distinct, pragmatic conceptualizations.

The Basic Needs approach provides a typical and minimal definition of poverty. This definition focuses on measuring the minimum consumption (as opposed to income) necessary to sustain physical well-being. In some developing societies it is simply a matter of caloric consumption. In the developed world it usually focuses on estimating the cost of basic shelter (low-cost apartments), clothing, and dietary needs (enough calories to avoid hunger). In this view, a family is poor if its before-tax income is insufficient to pay for a defined basket of 'basic needs' items. What constitutes this basket of goods is determined by an outside agent such as the United Nations or some other national or international agency. In Canada, Statistics Canada provides the Low-Income Cut-Off (LICO) as one method for measuring poverty. Statistics Canada sets its low-income threshold at 20 percentage points above the average proportion of income spent by families on food, shelter, and clothing. If the family's income falls below this threshold, Statistics Canada classifies the family as 'low-income'. For example, if an average family of four spent 43 percent of its after-tax income on food, shelter, and clothing, adding 20 percentage points implies a LICO after-tax threshold equal to 63 percent of after-tax income devoted to food, shelter, and clothing. The Low-Income Measure (LIM), on the other hand, identifies low income as those families that have an after-tax income lower than 50 percent of the median income for families in the target population in any given year. The Market Basket Measure of Poverty was developed by Human Resources Development Canada. This measure of poverty is based on the estimated cost of purchasing a basket of goods and services deemed to represent the standard of consumption for a reference family of two adults and two children. This basket of goods includes the costs of food, clothing, shelter, transportation, and other goods and services that are determined to be essential for different regions across the country.

Each of these methods has adherents. The right side of the spectrum would favour the basic needs approach to poverty definition, and the other end of the range would favour the low-income measure, using the 60 percent median income level of the population as the measuring statistic. This is the statistic and method the Organisation for Economic Co-operation and Development (OECD) uses to calculate poverty. There is a wide variation in the numbers of people designated in poverty based on these differing measures.

***

A complicating factor in contemplating definitions of poverty and associated concepts is how society determines economic progress. Most governments make a basic connection between how well they are doing financially and what measures they have taken to reduce poverty. Most, if not all, countries calculate their economic progress through measuring their GDP. This measurement simply sums all economic activity in the economy for a country in any given year. This calculation does not discriminate between those economic activities that add to the general well-being of the population and those that are responsible for illness or those that have a psychologically depressing effect on a community or nation. The GDP measure simply does not discriminate or place a moral value on the activities that generate economic activity. For example, the activity of the tobacco industry is seen as a positive and on the plus side of the ledger when measuring the GDP. Even the economic activity that is stimulated through the health sector to deal with the health effects of smoking is seen as contributing to the GDP positively. It could almost be seen as double counting. This method of calculating how a country is doing does not seem appropriate when one considers the implications of this method on those experiencing poverty, particularly when poverty is defined to be a larger condition than simply the lack of income as outlined earlier in this chapter.

Poverty and Marginalization   97

In addition to the problem created by nondiscrimination among those economic activities that may have positive or negative effects on the well-being of the population are the misleading conclusions that are often drawn by using the GDP as a measure of how well individuals in the population are doing. The GDP is a measure that describes how the overall economy is doing, but not necessarily the individuals within it. GDP is an indicator that relies on the average, or mean, to estimate the aggregate economic activity of an economy, but it is not a description of individual circumstances within that economy. Although the GDP may be increasing dramatically, indicating a healthy economy generally, these increased resources may not be equally shared among the population of that country, therefore providing no tangible benefit to those in poverty. In fact, using the relative definition of poverty as described earlier, those in poverty may consider themselves to be left increasingly behind in spite of an increasing GDP. So, although some may be doing exceptionally well, others may get left even further behind and in greater relative poverty. Here are what those advocating the Canadian Index of Wellbeing (CIW; 2009, p. 2) as an alternative or additional measure to the GDP have to say about the GDP:

> Over the years, the very high profile and oft-cited Gross Domestic Product (GDP) has emerged as a surrogate for wellbeing. When Canada's GDP is growing rapidly, we are said to be "doing well". When it is going down, we are said to be "doing poorly". That's a problem. The GDP was never intended or designed to be used for that purpose. It is simply a measure of national income. Even its inventor, Simon Kusnetz, said that "The welfare of a nation can scarcely be inferred from a measurement of national income as defined by the GDP." Its objective is, by definition, to measure the value of all goods and services produced in a country in a given year. For this reason, it misses out on capturing many things that really matter to the quality of life of Canadians.

When examining poverty, there is need not only to discriminate between the economic activities that are adding positively to the well-being of individuals and subtract those that are having a negative effect, but also to consider distributional effects of the activity. One of the most recent attempts to calculate this measure is the newly created Canadian Index of Wellbeing (see, How are Canadians really doing? The first report of the Index of Wellbeing, June 10, 2009). Early in their report they set out what they think should be included in the discussion of well-being for any given population:

> The CIW is a new way of measuring wellbeing. It will provide unique insights into the quality of life of Canadians—overall, and in specific areas that matter: our standard of living, our health, the quality of our environment, our education and skill levels, the way we use our time, the vitality of our communities, our participation in the democratic process, and the state of our arts, culture and recreation. In short, the CIW is the only

national index that measures wellbeing in Canada across a wide spectrum of domains. The CIW goes beyond conventional silos and shines a spotlight on the interconnections among these important areas: for example, how changes in income and education are linked to changes in health.

(Candian Index of Wellbeing, 2009, p. 1)

And they go on to say to imagine an index that:

distinguishes between good things like health and clean air, and bad things like sickness and pollution; promotes volunteer work and unpaid caregiving as social goods, and overwork and stress as social deficits; puts a value on educational achievement, early childhood learning, economic and personal security, a clean environment, and social and health equity; and, values a better balance between investment in health promotion and spending on illness treatment.

(Candian Index of Wellbeing, 2009, p. 2)

If the items listed by the CIW in the quote earlier constitute well-being for the general population, then lack of any of those indicators must also influence the definition of poverty. This will provide a more sophisticated and accurate measure of poverty and will generally be used throughout this book when discussing poverty. Indeed, these measures need to be the heart and backbone, perhaps the sum total, of the social policy debate generally. An additional feature of the CIW concept is not only the identification of indictors, but also their linking across domains. Not only are the vertical links important, but the horizontal links are as well, so social policy needs to be linked with environmental policy. In fact, this book does not separate the two. Environmental policy is seen as part and parcel of social policy. All of these policy domains are said to constitute the life-world. The idea of wellness as a replacement for the notions of poverty and welfare will be discussed in more depth in later chapters of this book.

Note

1 Incidentally, this act was repealed by the Reagan government, and many argue that this allowed banks and other financial institutions to produce subprime mortgages that were so ruinous to the economy and led to the most recent meltdown of the financial system in the United States.

References

Beverage, W. (1942). *Scale of Insurance Benefits and the Problem of Poverty.* London: Queens Printer.

Beveridge, J. (1954). *Beveridge and His Plan.* London: Hodder & Stoughton.

Canada Without Poverty. (n.d.). Retrieved from http:/www.cwp-csp/poverty/just-the-facts/

Candian Index of Wellbeing. (2009). *How Are Canadians Really Doing: The Report of the Index of Wellbeing.* Waterloo, Ontario, Canada: Canadian Index of Wellbeing.

Gilbert, N. (2002). *Dimensions of Social Welfare Policy.* Boston: Allyn and Bacon.

Golden, L. (2008). *Rural Poverty, Serious Leisure and Social Integration (Unpublished PhD Dissertation).* Guelph, Ontario, Canada: University of Guelph.

Keller, M. (1963). *The New Deal: What Was It?* New York: Holt Reinhart & Winston.

Marsh, L. C. (1943). *Report on Social Security for Canada.* Ottawa: Edmund Coulter.

Office for National Statistics. (2013). Retrieved from Persistent Poverty in the UK and the EU, 2008–2013: www.ons.gov.uk/ons/rel/household-income/persistent-poverty-in-the-uk-and-eu/2008–2013/persistent-poverty-in-the-uk-and-eu—2008–2013.html

Schlesinger, A. M. (1958). *The Age of Roosevelt: The Coming of the New Deal.* Cambridge: Houghton Mifflin Company.

The Senate Standing Committee on Agriculture and Forestry. (2006). *Understanding Freefall: The Challenge of the Rural Poor (Interim Report).* Ottawa: Senate of Canada.

Taylor, J., & Frisby, W. (2010). Addressing Inadequate Leisure Access Policies through Citizen Engagement. In H. Mair, S. M. Arai, & D. G. Reid (Eds.), *Decentering Work: Critical Perspectives on Leisure, Social Policy, and Human Development* (pp. 35–58). Calgary: Universitry of Calgary Press.

United States Census Bureau. (2013). Retrieved from www.census.gov/hhes/www/poverty/about/overview/index.htm

Wapshott, N. (1983). *The Clash That Defined Modern Economics.* New York: W.W. Norton & Company.

7 Beyond Poverty
Major Areas for Active Social Policy

Although I consider poverty a key issue to be addressed through social policy, there are other issues of importance that affect the entire population and, therefore, need to be made part of the social policy discourse. In some cases these themes manifest themselves because of poverty or, in other instances, are the cause of it. Although many of these additional themes are directly related to poverty, they can also stand on their own and constitute concerns that society wants to address as separate public questions. Many of these domains affect the entire population of a society and they possess attributes that, if treated or enhanced, would constitute a desired benefit to the general public. These actions can be remedial or developmental in nature. They are remedial in that the policy attempts to overcome a noticeable inadequacy that impairs the functioning of an individual or group in society. Some of the measures taken up by social policy are developmental in that their adoption will lead to the general enhancement of social performance and add to civil enrichment; however, their absence will not impair present social functioning. These remedial and developmental areas of concern can be classified in many ways, but they will be categorized here as healthcare, housing and homelessness, education, justice, and democracy. This chapter will address each of these issues individually and relationally where appropriate. Each has an institutional component to it in addition to its substance, which also needs to be made part of the discussion. Each of these subjects could form a volume on their own so they are briefly introduced in this book to provide the reader with a framework for understanding more broadly the field of social policy.

***

Apart from poverty, healthcare constitutes the greatest challenge today for most countries throughout the world. Although it is often related to poverty, particularly in the developing world, healthcare has a universal component to it, as well as a very personal and individual perspective. Perhaps the most recent example of those interconnections across the globe is the rise of the Ebola crisis. Because of the accessibility and proliferation of transportation throughout the globe, communicable diseases such as Ebola can infect distant populations overnight. The world experienced a rapid transmission of such a deadly disease with the advent of the HIV/AIDS epidemic in the 1980s. Diseases such as HIV/AIDS and Ebola spread quickly in the absence of an initial vigorous medical response. The disease spreads rapidly among the local population of the infected country and beyond.

There are numerous reasons why healthcare remains a problem for many countries. In some of the largest countries in the developed world, such as the United States, the politicians can't decide whether healthcare should be an entitlement, and therefore a right of citizenship, or a commodity to be sold on the open market. In other countries, healthcare budgets that reside in the public sphere are a huge drain on finite resources that are under pressure for allocation to other competing purposes. In the less developed world it is often a matter of the pure lack of resources that determines what is provided by the public or private system. An enormous problem for some developing countries throughout the world is that many healthcare workers are being trained in the developed world and being enticed to stay after training by these same countries and not returning to their homeland, therefore creating a 'brain drain' in the health field. This adds to an already bleak healthcare picture in many countries throughout the world

The challenges presented to populations and governments around the world have changed throughout the decades. Although some diseases have been reduced or eradicated and become less problematic, others have become more prominent. For example, in the Western world, the infectious diseases of polio and tuberculosis were rampant during the 1940s and '50s and great attention was paid to their elimination. In both cases, these efforts were quite successful. Later on in the 1980s and '90s, the focus shifted to noninfectious diseases such as cancer and cardiovascular illness. In the developing world such problems as malaria, traditionally, and more recently, HIV/AIDS and Ebola, have demanded the majority of attention. What may be different today than in the past is the speed of change in the mutation of these diseases, thereby providing resistance to eradication. In addition to the magnitude and speed of mutation occurring within most of these diseases are the mobility of populations and the rapid spread of many of these infections worldwide. Diseases that are controlled through antibiotics have become resistant to those medicines, causing their re-emergence.

As mentioned previously, Western government public health departments and organizations have been dedicated to the eradication of infectious diseases such as tuberculosis and polio. Much of this effort has been quite successful. In places such as Africa, cholera and other waterborne diseases have commanded attention, and some progress has been made in afflicted countries. Diseases such as malaria and other illnesses spread by insects persist in spite of great effort by in-country governments and world health organizations to address these blights. HIV/AIDS and Ebola are rampant at the moment and of great concern around the world. Progress is being made on these critical diseases.

What may be different today than in the past is the worldwide attention and organization brought to bear on the issue of health and healthcare. The World Health Organization (WHO) has been created by the United Nations to provide leadership in tackling the many public health questions that affect the world's populations. Their present focus is multifaceted. The most fundamental problems associated with nutrition and water remains a priority. The subthemes in these categories are caloric balance in nutrition and eradication of micronutrients that inflict many of the wells, streams, rivers, and lakes that provide drinking water to much of the world's poor. These issues are not exclusive to the developing world. For decades many of the streams and rivers in the developed world have been subjected to farmland chemical run-off that contains many of the super nutrients that are used in fertilizers in an attempt to make the land more productive. These super-nutrients have been responsible for the increase in algae in the reservoirs of drinking water that service large populations. The additional difficulty of antibiotics being injected into cattle to help them resist disease and finding their way into drinking water contributes to the problem of poor health for the populations that depend on streams and groundwater for drinking and cooking.

Chronic disease is also a focus for the WHO and other international and domestic health organizations. Cardiovascular, respiratory problems, and cancer formulate the diseases that deservedly attract most attention. Great amounts of financial resources have been devoted in the West toward this concern. Technology and treatment regimens have made dramatic advances in this area of healthcare. Recent success through advances in medicines and technologies is one reason, among others, why healthcare costs in the developed world have risen so dramatically over the last few years. The fact that most of us are living longer is also a contributing factor. Individuals in the later stages of their lives use the healthcare system more and incur the greatest costs than other sectors of the population. The increasing costs of healthcare are an organizational problem, and not necessarily one of funding. In the near- and long-term future, governments of all stripes will need to dramatically overhaul primary healthcare in order to provide adequate care to their citizens more effectively and at a cost they and society can afford. In the near future the social policy domain will need to organize a wide-ranging debate on what the public healthcare system should encompass and determine what resources the population is willing to dedicate to this function.

Maternal health is another major focus for the worldwide health organizations. Even though there has been great advance in this area in the developed world, childbirth still represents one of the greatest threats to a mother's health and life in the developing countries. Disease prevention programs and screening for disease in mothers and children take up most of the effort in this domain. Nutrition for both mothers and children is also of primary concern. This is often not as much a medical problem as one of economics and finance and the many crop failures due to droughts that occur regularly around the globe.

Finally, great concern remains for communicable diseases. Where we once thought that most of these diseases had been eradicated, some old ones are back and new ones are on the horizon. The swell in the population worldwide and the increase in the mobility of people are possible explanations for why these previously thought to be eradicated diseases are back on the scene. Air travel makes trekking to the farthest reaches of the globe possible for many of us and, as a consequence, we are confronted by diseases that we have no immunity against and carry them great distances back to our home countries. The numbers of migrants is up, and in spite of great medical surveillance, disease is being transported. Increasing failure to vaccinate children in the developed world as well as in the developing regions of the globe is also contributing to the reappearance of diseases such as measles, particularly in the developed world. Lack of vaccination in the developing world is a matter of finance and organization. In the developed world, resistance to having one's children vaccinated is built on unfounded fear that it can cause other more serious afflictions. In addition to a lackadaisical attitude toward vaccinations is the problem of the increasing resistance to antibiotics. We now have super-bugs that are resistant to our repertoire of antibiotics for fighting most infectious diseases. These super-bugs provide great challenges to the medical system when they invade the healthcare infrastructure.

Tuberculosis (TB) has not been heard from for over half a century in the developed world, but is now back and of great concern in some quarters. The return of TB is often attributed to the increase in homelessness and the overcrowding in shelters, where many people in poverty find themselves each night. TB is an airborne disease and flourishes in crowded conditions. Diseases such as the avian flu and other potential pandemics are a threat to all civilizations as well. Although the concern is real, there have been recent instances where governments have been overzealous when a potential threat appeared on the horizon but did not materialize. Severe acute respiratory syndrome (SARS) comes to mind in this regard. What was thought to have great potential to reach worldwide epidemic proportions turned out to be overestimated and less perilous than first thought. Countries such as Canada took extreme measures to combat this potential epidemic, perhaps theoretically appropriate, but resulted in great skepticism among the public when the predicted consequences did not materialize. What was learned from this event was that the world's public health authorities have not learned how to determine risk accurately. Preparing for the worst scenario is not only expensive but causes great skepticism among the general populace when the threat does not materialize, and may cause them to act inappropriately when the real event surfaces. Governments and health organizations will need to determine methods for diagnosing threats accurately and react appropriately so people do not become indifferent to their warnings and programs.

Finally in the category of health, the prevention of disease through vaccine is a high priority for public health institutions. This program extends to the HIV/AIDS problem as well. The recent success with regard to genome mapping holds great promise for taking healthcare to the next level of effectiveness. It is likely that in the not too distant future society will not only be able to determine the probability of diseases for each individual because of their genetic history, but also provide a genetic treatment for those diseases. This advance will increase the need to determine ethical and judicial parameters in order to reduce the risk of discrimination by institutions such as insurance companies that may refuse insurance coverage to those who might possess a certain gene. It could also lead to the inappropriate genetic manipulation of fetuses. These and other moral issues will require great debate among the population before we jump headlong into this new frontier.

The prospect of these great future advances in medicine provokes many philosophical questions for both individuals and society and for social policy formulation generally. Among the most pressing of those questions is the issue of resource allocation. We may be able to construct knowledge and invent technologies to address many of the diseases outlined earlier. A question of whether or not society will want to commit to underwriting the enormous costs that many of these treatments may potentially demand will need to be resolved. In Canada, present governments are contributing an increase of approximately 6 percent to healthcare budgets annually. The question of how long this can be sustained will need to be answered soon. That is not to suggest that this amount cannot be sustained, but it needs to be made a priority of society if there is consensus to do so.

Beyond the issue of financing, there are many more pressing philosophical questions that need to be addressed, such as: Do I want to know what may bring an end to my life and when that may occur? What about the issue of artificial human life? Although it may be potentially plausible to produce such individuals at present or in the near future, society has not yet had a wide-ranging debate about the desirability and consequences of this possibility. These are important social policy questions that need to be addressed by society, and the sooner the better.

***

A pressing concern in the healthcare and social policy debate is the area of mental health. Governments of all stripes have not grappled sufficiently with this issue. Over the eighteenth, nineteenth, and early parts of the twentieth century, the mentally ill were treated as curiosities and not to be understood as people suffering from a disease until the advent of psychiatry and psychoanalysis. Freud and his contemporaries began to explain mental disease from a scientific perspective, which eventually overshadowed the mystical explanation. Institutionalizing mentally ill individuals was the method of choice for initially protecting the public from them, and then later on as a location where treatment, no matter how primitive, could be administered. Given the advent of effective psychoanalysis and chemical treatments, public policy in the 1970s recommended deinstitutionalization, returning those of no danger to themselves or to society back to their community as a more humane way of treating mental illness. It was felt that drug and psychotherapy treatments are more humane and sophisticated than the primitive methods of electric shock, lobotomies, and cold baths and could be administered in the community in a more humane way. It was generally felt that an enlightened public policy would support deinstitutionalization of the mentally ill and be in favour of treating this disease at the community level.

On the surface this approach seemed like a civilized way to provide for people experiencing mental illness. What was not considered by those in charge of implementing this policy were the adequate resources required to support people who had limited capability of functioning in the community. Many quasi-functioning patients were returned to the community and they wound up on the streets due to the lack of government commitment to providing adequate resources, including money and the professional personnel required to successfully care for these individuals. Advocates for the homeless and street people, who often wind up being incarcerated, will testify that many of their clients would otherwise be institutionalized in mental hospitals if they were once again made available. Although deinstitutionalization seemed like a good idea, it was not made fully functional because of the lack of funding for care and treatment at the community level and was, therefore, destined to fail as a social policy. It is now understood that deinstitutionalization is a good idea, but it must be accompanied by adequate resources to make it work successfully—a policy not yet embraced by many governments.

***

The issue of public vs. private provision of healthcare is constantly being debated and is an issue that never seems to get resolved. During the recent debate on healthcare in the United States, public provision was on the agenda in the early stages of the discussion, but was not much in evidence when the legislation was finally passed. The issue of government involvement in any sphere of life is a sensitive issue in the United States, and it became a flash point again in the recent healthcare debate. In many other English-speaking countries, there has been a steady erosion of the public system over time. Great Britain, although maintaining a public system, allows a growing parallel private system to run alongside it. There will always be some differences in how each country designs and implements health policy, but it is becoming increasingly clear that governments will need to play a central role in its provision as the supply of this service becomes more sophisticated and costly as a result of the development of complex technological treatments.

In Canada, the public/private debate is perpetually with us. There are those among us who dislike our so-called socialized medical system. It is a misnomer to suggest that Canada has a socialized medical system, however. This is a fundamental point that is often misunderstood by critics from within and outside the country. What Canada has constructed is a single-payer system, and the payer happens to be the provincial government with funding assistance from the federal government. All medical practitioners who participate in the Canadian system are private practitioners who are paid by the government for their services but are not limited in any other significant way by the payer. Patients in this system, as in the privately funded systems, choose their medical practitioners and are not subjected to dictates in this regard by the government bureaucracy. A healthcare practitioner cannot partially opt out of the system and remain partially in it. They are either in or out, and that is the determining criteria for participation.

There are those who argue that a health system can be more efficient if it is placed in the private marketplace. Efficient, in this case, needs to be defined, however. Efficiency can be perceived in a number of ways. First, those who are sick can be eliminated from their plan thereby reducing costs, and until the most recent reforms were enacted, we saw that practice occurring in the U.S. system. In the United States, many people were denied private insurance because of pre-existing conditions. Not so today. Also, many people were denied continued insurance coverage by their private provider after they were sick and their initial cost for treatment was paid by the insurer. This practice leaves many ill people very vulnerable. Again, the question of whether healthcare is a right of citizenship or a commodity to be bought and sold in the marketplace must be squarely faced by politicians and policy makers. It is increasingly becoming apparent that the continued development of healthcare demands more state involvement in the process, both from a regulatory and supply perspective.

Essentially there are two methods for rationing healthcare. The first is to ration by price. The second is to ration by time. Private systems are apt to ration by price, which tends to eliminate the poor from the system. In such cases, those outside the private system often have only walk-in clinics or hospital emergency services available to them, but these clinics don't provide continuous coverage that a family practitioner would offer. Additionally, more resources tend to be devoted to administering the private system than in the public system. Healthcare in the previously privatized system in the United States cost twice as much per person as it did in the government-sponsored single-payer system in Canada. In the United States approximately 30 percent of the healthcare budget is absorbed by administration, whereas the Canadian healthcare system allocates approximately 17 percent to that function. It will be interesting to see what proportion of the budget gets allocated to administration in the new U.S. system.

Rationing healthcare by time, the mechanism of rationing in the public system, tends to make wait times for surgeries, particularly elective surgeries, and other procedures longer than in the private system. Often, a combination of approaches is tried by various governments, but they usually contain weaknesses that become apparent as time goes on because of that blending. For example, it is often asked: Why not operate a two-tier system that allows for a private system to operate alongside a public system, thereby accommodating those who want and can pay for a private system and those who need the public system given their resources? In some ways this plan, it is thought, would reduce the wait times in the public system. It is argued by supporters of the public approach that those who can afford to participate in the private system will, over time, object to providing resources to a public system from which they receive little, or no, direct benefit. As a result of this lack of support for the public system, the quality of healthcare becomes threatened as fewer resources are made available. It also becomes an equality issue. Those who can afford it get better care in the private system than those who must remain in the public system. This has been precisely the criticism of those critical of the British arrangement.

The preferred policy option on this issue often comes down to a very fundamental philosophical perspective: how one determines the best option between public and private service provision depends on whether one sees healthcare as a right or a privilege. If it is viewed as a privilege, then private health insurance is seen to be the preferred option. If, on the other hand, healthcare is viewed as a human right, then public provision tends to be the preferred alternative.

***

The responsibility for housing in the developed world rests mainly in the domain of the private sector. That is not to suggest, however, that there is no role for public institutions and the volunteer sector. In most jurisdictions, governments are heavily involved in housing provision by providing cash incentives to builders and tax encouragements for construction of affordable housing. In Canada a government institution also provides mortgage insurance. In addition, some housing is built by local governments for those at the low end of the income continuum, usually under the rubric of affordable housing. The municipal role in housing is often financially supported by provincial governments through targeted program funding. Providing accommodation for the homeless is a government responsibility at all levels if and when it gets attended to.

In most, if not all jurisdictions, the use of land on which housing gets built is controlled by legislation. In Canada, for example, each province administers a planning act that lays out where different types of development can occur through land use policies and procedures. Social policy related to housing often gets introduced through such acts of parliaments as well. Again in Canada, the responsibility for housing, especially public housing, is shared between the federal and provincial governments. Many housing-related policies are found in the National Housing Act of 1944 (National Housing Act, 1944), and now the Canada Housing and Mortgage Corporation (Canada Housing and Mortgage Corporation Act, 1985) which promotes affordable housing and choice. At the national level, such areas as mortgage insurance, housing research, funding for social housing, national building codes, and so on are responsibilities shared between the federal government and the provinces. The federal government of Canada is also responsible for housing on First Nations reservations even though they are physically located throughout the provinces and across the country. Housing is such a major issue, particularly affordable housing, that all of the provincial governments in Canada, as well as the private sector, are heavily engaged in housing development. Many provincial governments also extend to municipalities some responsibility for public housing. Greater involvement by municipalities in housing is an increasing trend. Public housing is often meager in its supply and generates many other social problems because of its inadequate provision.

Housing policy is an issue that is locally specific and, therefore, it is difficult to generalize standards across single jurisdictions, let alone between and among nations. The best that can be said with regard to standardized housing policies for low-income individuals is that it is generally felt that housing for those on the margins is constantly on the periphery of the political agenda and never addressed satisfactorily.

Housing for the homeless is a major problem in most countries. The very depth of homelessness is not always easy to identify and measure. Those living on the streets of many of our cities across the world are hard to locate because of their transience. Increasingly it is recognized that homelessness may go beyond the mere lack of shelter but also take into account its general adequacy. Homelessness and the risk of homelessness has been defined and categorized by Mah and Desantis (2000). They see three categories of homelessness: literal homelessness, where individuals live rough on the street; hidden homelessness, where those without their own abode live in illegal or temporary accommodation such as makeshift squats or abandoned buildings; and those who are at imminent risk of becoming homeless. This latter category may be composed of those who live in unsafe housing conditions or inhabit accommodation that is unaffordable or in overcrowded facilities, perhaps with other families, and those whose accommodation is badly suited to their needs. In this category may be people who are placed in hospital rather than in long-term care facilities or in group homes that are geared specifically for their individual needs.

In addition to the homelessness continuum outlined earlier, there is a typology of the likely candidates for homelessness. There is the 'one-time homelessness', which is usually the result of an unexpected event such as a natural disaster or family breakdown. Episodic homelessness is characterized as periods of housing stability interspersed with periods where housing is not available. These episodic events can be caused by the temporary loss of a job or unexpected expenditure such as a healthcare bill or the repair of an automobile. Persistent homelessness, on the other hand, is the most difficult category to overcome. This situation is often defined as being homeless for longer than one year, or when a person is cycling in and out of hospital for physical or mental health difficulties, thereby causing them to change locations regularly in accordance with the state of their condition. Young people often find themselves in this category because they may have been forced to leave their familial home due to some type of physical, mental, or sexual abuse and rarely have sufficient resources even to acquire state-sponsored housing.

People who find themselves persistently homeless often develop special skills that allow them to survive. They are likely to be extensive users of hostels and other volunteer services that provide overnight accommodation in the urban core. Because this type of homelessness is quite apparent in the urban environment, one should not assume that homelessness does not occur in the rural setting, even though they may be without the types of emergency shelters found in cities. It is true that many homeless people migrate to urban areas where they can remain anonymous and where services are more abundant. Homelessness in rural areas is a reality, however, although it is mostly hidden. It is mainly of the variety where multiple families live together in unsuitable accommodation and where homeless individuals rotate through friends who provide them with a place to stay on a short-term basis.

As government budgets at all levels become increasingly constrained, public housing, especially for the poor, has become neglected. It is often the case that the poor and marginalized have little political cache, so issues such as housing that are vital to their welfare get pushed to the margins when public priorities are established. It should also be reiterated that when the policy of decommissioning mental health institutions and asylums became the politically correct thing to do and their patients were reintroduced to community living, great stress was placed on the public housing stock in most communities. No one argues with the philosophy behind such a change in mental health policy. What made life difficult in this regard was that the corresponding resources to assist people experiencing this problem at the community level were not forthcoming. As a consequence, public housing for these and other people in need did not materialize, so most countries have seen a dramatic increase of people living rough on the streets, in temporary shelters, or at risk of becoming homeless.

In Canada, most provincial governments have tried to deal with homelessness and other housing problems by introducing different pieces of legislation. In Ontario, for example, various acts related to housing have been created by the provincial government, such as the Residential Tenancy Act (Ministry of Municipal Affairs and Housing, 2006) whose aim is to generate a rental housing system that protects tenants, helps landlords, and promotes investment in Ontario's rental housing market, and the Housing Services Act (Ministry of Municipal Affairs and Housing, 2011), which sets out the standards for social housing in the province and how Ontario will transfer administration of provincial social housing programs to municipalities. Although these pieces of legislation are specific to Ontario, they are typical of the types of legislation that are found in most developed countries, and particularly in the English-speaking world that tries to address homelessness in a consistent manner.

***

Regardless of what country one is examining, there are some fundamental principles that housing and homelessness policies must embrace as general guidelines. Fundamentally, social policy and planning must be instituted at the local level, whether that be in the community or neighbourhood. This approach needs to be supported by senior-level governments through national policies and strategies that include the transfer of adequate resources to the local level in order to get the job done. However, as a fundamental principle, those who will eventually be the recipients of such policy must be actively engaged in its development. This means that those at the local level must have control of the policies that are enacted for their communities and that affect their lives directly. This fundamental principle does not only apply to housing planning and policy making, but to social policy construction generally. Senior-level governments need to be active participants in the eventual provision of housing. Local jurisdictions must have the discretionary powers for planning, including strategies for involving citizens in the planning process, allocating resources, maintaining quality assurance, and ultimately service delivery itself. This task goes beyond just the physical construction of abodes and includes connecting households with vital community services that can speak to their emotional as well as their physical needs and to assist households at risk to seek and maintain suitable housing over the long-term. All too often, families at risk are continually moving from one accommodation to another because they are regularly placed in unsatisfactory and substandard conditions that cause them to continually seek new space. The general rule of thumb is that housing should not exceed 30 percent of a family's gross income. When that limit is exceeded, the risk for homelessness increases dramatically.

Like many other social issues there are barriers to permanently solving the housing problem. Perhaps the greatest constraint lies in the complexity of the issue. People suffering from homelessness or from being underhoused, usually, but not necessarily, have additional social and psychological problems that affect their lives. Lack of housing may be an outcome of those compounding conditions. If that is the case, then these other social and psychological issues need to be addressed in tandem with the housing question.

Because of the complexity of the problem and the sometimes difficult lifestyles of those involved, politicians and the general public tend to blame the person experiencing homelessness for his or her situation rather than addressing the problem systematically and structurally. There have been instances in many developed countries where homelessness has been made a quasi-illegal offence and where municipalities have enacted by-laws to sweep the homeless off the street and into jail. This is often done through the rationale and rubric of not wanting the homeless to freeze to death during episodes of cold weather. Although there may be some weak logic in this explanation, simply sweeping them up and off the street for one or two nights will not go any distance in solving the problem permanently.

In addition to setting in motion policies and plans to technically solve the housing problem, there is need to develop and implement education programs to inform the public and their politicians about the extent and nuance of the

Beyond Poverty   111

problem confronting society. This education program should emphasize that housing the homeless is an investment with future financial returns and savings attached to it, and not simply an expenditure of public funds. This strategy may generate sufficient empathy and motivation to get public support for resolving the problem on a consistent and permanent basis. Continued research to better understand the problem in the first instance is also required. Until the general public subscribes to the importance of solving this issue, no conclusive action will be taken to permanently eradicate the problem.

Finally, resources need to be dedicated to generating planning expertise specifically focused on this social problem. The problem of homelessness is usually delegated to planning or other human service departments as an addition to their main mandate, rather than their primary focus. This is not sufficient to address this issue decisively, and we have witnessed the absurd wheel-spinning and lack of success this approach has produced. As a first start, the Housing Stability System created by the regional municipality of Waterloo in Ontario, Canada (Waterloo Region, 2007), is a cutting-edge conceptual system that may provide a framework for solving the housing and homelessness crisis, and a variation of their approach that responds to local cultural nuances could be adopted by many jurisdictions across the world.

Fundamentally, Figure 7.1 embraces housing from a holistic perspective rather than simply looking at it from a single viewpoint. In addition to the strict bricks-and-mortar approach to housing, the Housing Stability System

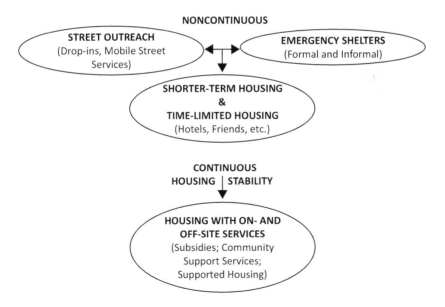

Figure 7.1 The Homelessness Crisis

(see Region of Waterloo, 2007) includes other social and psychological services that are often required by the homeless in order to make long-term housing successful in addition to providing a dwelling.

***

Education at all levels is prominent in the social policy field. In most, if not all, developed countries' education is supplied by the state. Additionally, and becoming more prevalent, are private schools that charge tuition to their patrons. Most, but not all, of these private schools are established by nongovernmental organizations (NGOs) that have a social or religious mission and operate at a break-even fiscal bottom line or with a small profit. Whether public or private, the state sets the curriculum and the academic parameters on which the school operates. Also, there are often other requirements instituted by governments for students such as a minimum school-leaving age and a mandatory requirement to enroll until that age is reached. There are provisions in most developed countries for families to home-school their children, but they, too, are subject to state standards, and students must meet evaluation criteria also set by the state. In many of the home-school cases, the state provides the curriculum and study materials. In most developed countries today, education at both the primary and secondary level is one of the social policies that have been universally applied and, for the most part, provision has been adequate. There are certainly discrepancies in the level of provision among and between school jurisdictions, however. It is not infrequent that schools in poorer neighbourhoods receive fewer resources and attain lower achievement scores than in more affluent areas. Often, resource allocation is built on achievement levels so those that start with more often end up with more.

The education provision we see in most developed countries may not be at the same level for many developing countries, where education facilities and programs are severely lacking. Universality has not always been the case historically, but since the emancipation of women and the black population in the United States and in other countries, accessibility for all has been achieved in the education sphere. There are still too many places in the world today that value male but not female education, so there is still work to do on that front.

In Canada, adequate state-supplied universal education has not always been a reality. During the nineteenth and early twentieth centuries, remote areas were difficult, if not impossible, to reach from an educational perspective. As a result, residential schools, mostly for aboriginal populations, were established by many religious orders at the request of the Canadian government. Scores of these schools practiced cultural genocide in order to eradicate what were then thought to be undesirable and primitive languages and religions practiced by aboriginal people. These culture genocidal practices have resulted in long-standing psychological damage to a number of those subjected to residential schools, and Canadian aboriginal populations continue to suffer from it today.

The damage has only been recently acknowledged by the government and the offending religious orders, and they are now in the process of making restitution to their victims. Recently the prime minister of Canada acknowledged this dark era in Canada's history and made a formal and blanket apology in the House of Commons to the First Nations People for this perversion.

Many developing countries have not yet reached the standards of education that the developed world has achieved and, therefore, schooling is still not accessible to many segments of the population, particularly for women or those living in remote areas. In some of the more fundamentalist Muslim countries such as Afghanistan, there is still resistance to the concept of universal education—again, particularly for women—but that resistance is slowly being overcome. In some regions of Pakistan, education is controlled by the Muslim fundamentalist clerics, and it is almost exclusively focused on religious studies and the principles outlined in the Koran rather than providing a general academic-oriented education. That problem aside, developing countries are attempting to provide universal primary education to most, if not all, of their population, but a great deal of effort is still required to achieve this goal.

Although universal education is becoming the norm across the world, there are many problems facing its adoption and implementation. Historically, education has been devoted to the maintenance and reification of the social status quo, and it has been only recently where women and girls, for example, have been encouraged to participate in general education. And, although girls and women have come closer to achieving equality in education, many jurisdictions are finding that their male population in ever-increasing numbers is leaving school before secondary school graduation. The increasing male dropout rate in many North American jurisdictions is quite noticeable, and this is occurring at a time when advanced education is required to participate in the knowledge and information-based economy. Attention is only now being given to this important issue, and it will take considerable effort and research to understand and effectively address this rising phenomenon.

Like many other social services, funding for education is not growing fast enough to fix the problems in the system. Funding for education is drying up because of the deficits incurred by governments at all levels and their need to bring national debt into balance. The lack of funding increase is being justified by reduced enrolments that are also a recent phenomenon, particularly in the developed world where the birth rate has been declining for decades. Given the perceived pronounced change in the global economic condition, it would seem that education will need to play an even more prominent role in social development in all parts of the world in the future. Given the transition of the world economy from a labour-intensive enterprise to a knowledge-based economy, countries that have led in the past will need to retool for the future, and it is the education system that will provide the basis for that retooling. Like housing, the homeless society needs to begin to view education, both formal and informal, as an investment in the future, not as a drain on the public purse. If the notions of the new economy contained in this book are adopted by society, educating individuals to live in this new reality will become even more important in the future.

***

Justice and democracy are extremely important subjects in the social policy discussion. Most Western societies have been building a just and democratic society since the end of World War Two. The ideas of justice and democracy, and how they get established within and by society, reveal the fundamental values held by that social order. How a society views the idea of justice and democracy provides the foundation on which all other social policies are constructed. Western society has always prided itself in its expression of a just and democratic society, but those concepts may now be showing signs of deterioration in the face of the so-called terrorism threat. All Western countries appear willing to reduce individual freedoms and undermine justice for the contrived necessity of carrying out 'a war on terrorism'. Imprisonment without full disclosure of either the charges or evidence against the detainee to the detainee, their legal representative, or the public, is now a reality in many Western developed nations. This is done under the rubric of homeland and national security. The justice and democratic portfolio needs to be highly scrutinized, and public debate on this issue is sufficiently urgent that it should head the list of issues for a national public discussion. Although the United States has led in reducing civil liberties in favour of attacking so-called terrorism, Canada has moved substantially in this direction as well; however, it appears that the new government is willing to soften some of the draconian provisions in the law.

Justice and democracy are under attack in the Western world from specific sectors within their own boundaries. Although we often think that democracy is under threat in Muslim countries by the fundamentalists, the same phenomena is apparent in the United States as well. Chris Hedges, in a book titled *American Fascists: The Christian Right and the War on America*, has made a strong case that the Christian Right, particularly those known as Dominionists, who are striving to make America solely a Christian nation, are making strides in achieving their primary goal. Hedges makes the case that a liberal democracy such as the United States that prides itself on the fundamental value of tolerance for all ways of life will eventually be subdued and subjugated by those who preach intolerance as in the case of the Christian Right. As Hedges (Hedges, 2001, p. 75) suggests, "This is the genius of totalitarian movements. They convince the masses to agitate for their own incarceration." In addition to this pathological religious zealousness and intolerance for all other ways of life, many of these sects do not believe in social programs or social policy at all. In fact, many of this persuasion believe in limited government and accept as true that those on the top of the economic ladder are put there by God and those at the bottom are also placed there by the deity. Social policy will also need to champion individual rights and freedoms that are the bulwark of a democratic and just society.

Although the forgoing issue is in urgent need of discussion and resolution, justice and democracy take a very different form for the majority of people. The democracy and justice policy arena, more often than not, gets played out at the local level where decisions that touch on everyday life are made. Although this subject is dealt with in more detail in a later chapter in this book, it is important to raise here the idea of citizen and local community involvement as a critical social space for achieving justice and democracy in both the developing and developed world.

Beyond the basic conditions of human rights, issues of justice and democracy often focus on the twin subjects of equality and equity. Equality is defined here as the conditions and obligations that are extended to each citizen in society. Equality is an intuitive idea that a society establishes and holds as a guiding principle and one that defines citizenship. Once established, usually in the form of a constitution or in legislation, this notion is extended to all people in the system without exception (perhaps excluding those who are incarcerated by the state), and its implementation is guarded judiciously by the governance structure and the rule of law in society.

Equity, on the other hand, sets out what a society determines to be a tolerable range of difference on any variable that is extended to those in society as a right. This idea often comes in play when a society considers the distribution of resources that are available to it, or in the opportunity for each citizen to participate in the financial benefits and conditions of society. Most societies in the developed world have set a minimum level of resources for each individual in the system, below which no one is allowed to fall. The realization of this principle usually results in social welfare policy. Most societies strive to make some level of opportunity available to all citizens in their society. The issues to which equality and equity are extended are a matter of considerable debate in most nations. Disagreement on which of these variables should be adopted by society cause civil strife and even revolutions in rare cases. Most politicians view democracy as the ability of political parties to contest elections every four years or so, but justice and democracy go much deeper than that. In the larger perspective, notions of justice and democracy extend to the ability of people to organize themselves into interest groups and express their desires and dislikes in the public arena and demonstrate their importance for adoption by the governance structure.

Related to the overarching issues of social justice and democracy outlined earlier are those of power. It is the issue of power where social justice gets resolved or distorted. Historically there have been many social arenas where power has been an issue. Gender inequality has been a major focus in the twentieth and, so far, in the twenty-first century, and although considerable advances have been achieved by women in the developed world, the same progress is still lacking in other parts of the globe. In addition to women's continuing struggle for equality, the issue of gay, lesbian, bisexual, transsexual, and transgender persons is still unresolved even in the most enlightened countries. Although marriage is now being extended to gays and lesbians in most developed countries, this is not the case in the developing world where homosexuality is still seen as a crime punishable by death in some instances. In many developed countries gay and lesbian people are often under physical attack and in fear for their lives when out in public.

Lack of power for those who are marginalized for whatever reason and for those in poverty is still a pervasive issue throughout society. These populations often do not have sufficient voice to influence the system commensurate to their numbers in society. The issues of aboriginal people that continue to keep them out of the mainstream of society are not sufficiently recognized. This continues to marginalize them in society, and First Nations people do not receive status equal to other groups in the Canadian democratic process, although the newly elected government has made verbal and budgetary commitments to rectify the situation. Such major issues as land claims and self-governance remain unresolved for this group of people. Not achieving resolution of these important issues continues their oppression in society—a long-standing neglect.

In addition to the major power issues outlined earlier, there are others of a more unique nature, mostly experienced by youth. Recently the problem of bullying has surfaced, and society is just now becoming aware of its ramifications on individuals and on the learning process in the education system. Bullying, we have come to understand, has negatively affected individuals to the extent that their education has been interrupted, and some youth have been so profoundly affected that they have attempted suicide, and some have been successful. Bullying in the modern context not only manifests itself in the physical realm, but also on social media as well. Associated with bullying is the general issue of security for youth. Some of our cities' streets are not sufficiently safe to allow children to travel on their own to or from school or to other social events. The paranoid society, perhaps justly, has cast a dampening effect on the idea of community and the safety of all in it, especially for children, who are seen to be the most vulnerable and at risk.

European and North American society can take some pride in the advances made against racism over the last century or two; however, discrimination, prejudice, and intolerance are still issues in society, although they may be operating at a subliminal level. This last decade has witnessed some highly publicized shootings of black youths by the police, which appear to be motivated by prejudice and racism. Slavery has not been completely eradicated, and human trafficking, much of it leading to enslaved prostitution, is still rampant. Social policy will need to address these issues in addition to those that have greater visibility on the social and political radar already.

References

Canada Housing and Mortgage Corporation Act. (1985). Retrieved from http://laws-lois.justice.gc.ca/eng/acts/C-7/FullText.html

Hedges, C. (2001). *American Fascists: The Christian Right and the War on America.* New York: Free Press.

Mah, J., & Desantis, G. (2000). *So What's in the Middle? A Brief Report on the Middle of the Housing Continuum in Cambridge.* Cambridge: Social Planning Council of Cambridge and North Dumfries.

Ministry of Municipal Affairs and Housing. (2006). *Residential Tenancy Act.* Toronto: Province of Ontario.

Ministry of Municipal Affairs and Housing. (2011). *Housing Services Act.* Toronto: Province of Ontario.

National Housing Act. (1944). Retrieved from www.cmhc-schl.gc.ca/en/corp/about/hi/index.cfm

Waterloo Region. (2007). *All Roads Lead to Home: A Homelessness to Housing Stability Strategy for Waterloo Region.* Retrieved from Stability.asp http://communityservices.regionofwaterloo.ca/en/communityProgramsSupports/resources/HHSS.pdf

8 Social Policy in the Developing World

The origin of social policy formation in the developing world is dramatically different than in the affluent countries of the West. Perhaps the most telling reason for this difference is that many developing countries are not constructed on Keynesian principles. In most developing countries, ideas about providing care stress community and family over state intervention. Whether this is by necessity or by choice is not completely understood. Most of these countries were traditionally nonmoney economies and were not founded on capitalist principles. A number of them entered the modern era as colonies of European nations and therefore did not develop a tradition of social welfare based on any notion of equality. Further, the colonials did not appear to be concerned about the internal economy or social conditions of the countries they occupied. The colonized countries were seen as peripheral to the homeland and were there only to supply the colonizer with natural riches through cheap or slave labour. The role of the colony at that time was to serve the occupying country by providing cheap raw materials and even cheaper labour for mining and the extraction of their natural resources. These raw materials were shipped back to the colonizing country or for trading with their trading partners. Little thought by the occupiers was given to the welfare of the aboriginal population; in fact, many of the local inhabitants were not seen as human or, if they were, they were believed to be a substandard and primitive people in comparison to the European colonizers. Servitude and slavery were thought to be legitimate and condoned in many parts of the world at that period in history. Only when it suited the colonizer were social programs, mainly healthcare, provided to the locals. This was not necessarily done in the spirit of benevolence but so those in servitude could be productive in their work for their colonial masters. Social policy was mostly provided by benevolent nongovernmental organizations (NGOs), particularly Christian organizations, who were just as interested in saving souls as they were in providing a better standard of living to the native population.

Provision of social policy in much of the developing world takes the form of the charity model of social development. It depends exclusively on the compassion of private, volunteer service institutions and the dedication of the people that comprise their membership. This model is an important component, perhaps the dominant part, of social policy in a great many parts of the developing countries today, particularly in Africa. Large nongovernmental institutions such as World Vision and other such organizations are thriving worldwide associations that supply a great deal of the social programs that fight poverty and provide healthcare and education throughout many parts of the world. Modern Christian-based NGOs that are in the business of saving souls have often rightfully subordinated this part of their mandate to provide social policy. Of course, many believe this is a demonstration of their Christian principles.

Inhibiting social development in the less developed world today is the corruption that was inherited from the colonial masters and continues to exist in the present system and culture. Unfortunately many of the former colonies, particularly in Africa, suffer from a colonial hangover, in that the present-day indigenous rulers often emulate the administration of absolute power and the corrupt practices of the former colonizer. And, like former colonizers, they do not understand when it is time to give up power to other legitimate contenders and different methods of governing. Much of this negative practice was well learned from the previous colonial governors.

An additional problem inhibiting social policy development in the developing world are the unnatural boundaries thrust upon many of these countries by Europeans and other powerful actors from across the globe. The countries of Africa, for example, were the creation of the European countries that colonized them, giving them artificial borders in the process. These borders reflected the struggle between and among the colonizers for the land and respective resources they contained, but had little or no significance to aboriginal populations themselves. The states of the Middle East and North Africa were created by the United States, France, and Britain. The countries of North Africa and the Middle East essentially became the spoils of war at the end of World War One. The African nations and some of the Asian countries were configured sometime earlier. These unnatural configurations placed cultures and societies together that were not necessarily compatible but enclosed by political boundaries that suited the powerful nations that subjugated them. As a consequence many of these countries continue to experience protracted conflicts inhibiting the development of unified social policies that would benefit their people today.

Given the rise of China on the world economic scene, Africa may be in a state of quasi-recolonization. China is pouring vast amounts of money into the African continent in search for the great quantities of resources they need to fuel their growing economy. Whether or not Africans will be the direct beneficiaries of this newfound wealth-creating activity is yet to be determined, but given the state of fragmented, and often corrupt, governments on this continent, concern needs to be expressed given historical patterns. This problem may not only apply to African countries but to other parts of the developing world as well.

Democracy, however that is defined, has had a hard time establishing roots in many parts of the developing world, particularly in African countries that find themselves continually in unstable economic circumstances. Much of what stands for social policy in these countries today is constructed on the charity model of social welfare provision, as discussed previously. A great deal of social development and welfare policy in the developing world is provided by international NGOs or by offshore government-sponsored institutions such as the World Bank or International Monetary Fund (IMF) and not the country's government. Social services in many of these countries are meagre and in many cases do not provide what most would consider the barest measure. First and foremost the social services that are provided are usually focused solely on relief from the prospect of starvation. In some cases, and when the imminent threat of starvation has been reduced, these expatriate institutions turn their efforts toward community economic development activity and local capacity building in hopes of establishing a basic economy at the local level. What is often standard thinking in the NGO community, and I think rightfully so, is that economic development activities cannot be accomplished on an empty stomach, so attention must first be given to addressing the lack of nutrition and issues of starvation. It seems that in some parts of the world we rarely seem to get past this first stage.

What is the root cause for the lack of development in many of these countries? No doubt there are a plethora of reasons that keep many developing nations in poverty. If we use Africa as an example, it could be argued that the inability to construct a middle class is one of, if not the main cause, of this dilemma. When one examines the Gini coefficient[1] for the African continent there is a striking lack of separation between the rich and poor which may seem like a good thing on the surface but upon greater scrutiny can be argued to simply represent the lack of a significant upper class and a complete lack of a middle class. The one exception is in South Africa where the Gini coefficient is high and emulates the developed world. The low coefficients in the rest of Africa would be considered a good result in the affluent countries of Europe and North America because it would signify that all of the wealth is not going to the upper income class. In Africa the opposite is true, in that most people are poor and there is, with little exception, the lack of a substantial middle economic class. There are a few rich and the many poor but not much of a middle class, and it is the middle class that constitute the majority of consumers in most societies and, consequently, are the main drivers of a consumer-based economy.

The picture of poverty in the developing world is changing. On some measures poverty is actually reducing in many parts of the developing world. China, India, South Africa, and Brazil are good examples where gross domestic product (GDP) is rising. Whether or not all citizens in these countries are benefiting from this GDP growth and their general quality of life is improving is questionable, however. A measurement that does not use the mean as the measuring statistic might provide a more accurate picture, but the GDP uses the mean and is the traditional measure for estimating the progress of a country. A more useful and accurate measurement statistic would be the median, which might provide a better indication of how well an individual in any given society is doing at any point in time, no matter how well the country is advancing as a whole. A comprehensive measure that includes a number of variables such as in the Canadian Index of Wellbeing (Canadian Index of Wellbeing, 2009) is a good example of a comprehensive estimate of how an individual is doing in any given economy. Many countries are now looking at this measure as a model for estimating progress in alleviating poverty and promoting well-being and, hopefully, it will become a standard measure across the globe in due course.

The overall trend in the numbers of people who are economically poor in the developing regions of the world seems to be on the decline, or at least not getting worse. "According to the most recent estimates, in 2012, 12.7 percent of the world's population lived at or below $1.90 US, a day. That's down from 37 percent in 1990 and 44 percent in 1981" (World Bank, 2015). That said, trends only tell the historical picture, and there is no guarantee that the positive trend reported earlier for 2012 will continue into the future, given the frailness of many of these economies. There are too many uncertain variables such as the price and availability of oil and other important commodities on which much of the developing economies depend to be certain about their future progress in reducing poverty. It would appear, however, that East Asia and the Pacific, along with South Asia, are developing their economies rapidly and have had record GDP growth over the last decade (see United Nations, Department of Economic and Social Affairs Report, Rethinking Poverty, 2009), although the economy of China now seems to be slowing down. Whether or not this trend will continue or whether all people in these countries will benefit directly from their rising GDP is yet to be determined. Most of the other regions in the estimates available seem to be holding their own or losing ground only slightly, with the exception of sub-Saharan Africa. Sub-Saharan Africa not only remains problematic but is actually increasing its share of people who are living on less than $1.25 U.S. per day. It is estimated that in sub-Saharan Africa 388.7 million (World Bank, 2015) continue to live in poverty. For whatever reason, sub-Saharan Africa does not seem to be able to increase its economic position in the world in spite of the vast amounts of aid that have been poured into that area for over a half century and the increased extraction of its natural resources by China and other countries.

The increased wealth creation experienced in some of the former colonial countries throughout the world is not being distributed to the entire population anywhere close to equally. According to the World Bank, South Africa, for example, projects a Gini coefficient of 65 in 2011 (a low Gini coefficient indicates a more equal distribution, with 0 corresponding to complete equality; a higher Gini coefficient indicates more unequal distribution, with 100 corresponding to complete inequality). South Africa's Gini coefficient is higher than most of those in the developed countries. The United States' Gini coefficient was 40.5 in 2010 and the largest among the affluent countries. Canada's was 33.7 in 2010 (World Bank, 2015).

***

Poverty is often considered to be solely a function of income or lack thereof. Research (Golden, 2008) has clearly shown that not to be the case. Most definitions of poverty suggest that it is a function of deprivation of many variables, including health, education, social exclusion, and the lack of access to participation in decision making in one's community and society, in addition to income. The United Nations provides a definition of poverty. In their words:

> Poverty has various manifestations, including lack of income and productive resources sufficient to ensure livelihoods; hunger and malnutrition; ill health; limited or lack of education and other basic services; increased morbidity and mortality from illness; homelessness and inadequate housing; unsafe environments; and social discrimination and exclusion. It is also characterized by a lack of participation in decision-making and in civil, social and cultural life.
> (United Nations, Department of Economic and Social Affairs, 2006)

Interestingly, and given the description of poverty earlier, many of those who live in the less developed world would not see themselves in relative poverty when they measure their existence against their neighbour, but certainly would if they were to compare their standard of life against most of the populations of the developed world. Nevertheless, they do feel the searing grip of absolute poverty—even those who might live slightly above a starvation existence. That, of course, points up the inadequacy of using numbers such as $1.25 U.S. per day to define absolute poverty. Can there be much difference between $1.25 and $1.50 per day to define the basic existence of a person? Thinking of these numbers as a definitive measure of poverty is totally inadequate, and society must think of it in different terms in the future. Perhaps in the future we will define poverty for the entire globe by the standards of the most affluent countries. Only then will we incorporate some notion of justice in the definition of poverty.

Absolute poverty exists in the developed world, but relative poverty provides a better indication of this condition. There is little absolute poverty in mainstream society in the developed world. That is not to say that there are no pockets of absolute poverty in the developed countries because there certainly are, but they are not large in comparison to the developing world. In Canada this absolute poverty definition would apply, although not exclusively, to much of the aboriginal population, particularly those in the northern part of the country. Many First Nation individuals and reservation communities would fit the definition of absolute poverty were it not for government intervention. What makes poverty in First Nations communities complicated is their reliance on hunting and gathering. If a person is well fed and housed through the use of natural materials, can we really say he or she is experiencing poverty because this person doesn't command $1.25 per day U.S.? Many First Nations people living off reservations would be slightly above the absolute definition, but not necessarily comfortably so.

An example of absolute poverty is clearly visible in certain neighbourhoods in the urban environment in the United States. It is estimated that up to 50 percent of Americans are dependent on food stamps for their existence. This suggests that absolute poverty exists and without assistance from the food stamp program, the lives of many American citizens would be in peril.

In developing countries, poverty is more often than not absolute. Purely and simply, the lack of sufficient resources to provide enough calories to sustain life over the short and long term, access to adequate shelter, and the ownership of a minimum set of personal belongings place them in this category. When seen as a lack of sufficient calories, poverty is not only absolute but catastrophic. Something needs to be done given that the increase in population is mainly going to take place in the developing part of the world where poverty may already be rampant. A report titled "Rethinking Poverty" (United Nations, Department of Economic and Social Affairs, 2009, p. 15) suggests:

> By 2050, the world's population is projected to surpass 9 billion, with developing countries accounting for most of the 2.3 billion increase. The population of the developing world is expected to rise from 5.6 billion in 2009 to 7.9 billion in 2050. In contrast, the population of the developed regions is expected to increase slightly, from 1.23 billion to 1.28 billion (United Nations, Department of Economics and Social Affairs, Population Division, 2009). The continued rapid increase in the population of developing countries highlights the importance of having appropriate policies designed to promote the sustained economic growth and structural transformation of their economies so as to ensure durable poverty reduction.

The world's leaders set out to eliminate world poverty at the Rio summit in 2005 in a proclamation called the Millennium Goals. What became clear is that it would take Herculean effort to bring the African countries out of absolute poverty as defined by $1.25 U.S. a day. Nineteen of the twenty-nine sub-Saharan African countries have half of their population living in absolute poverty.

Observers of the continuing economic struggle in sub-Saharan Africa will not be surprised to hear that none of these countries have reached the targets of poverty reduction set for them by the Millennium Goals. Sub-Saharan Africa only reduced the number of people living on less than $1.25 per day from 56 percent in 1990 to 48 percent in 2010 (United Nations, 2014). Poverty is still pervasive in Africa, but there may be some progress in other parts of the world. Worldwide poverty had decreased in developing countries from 47 percent in 1990 to 14 percent in 2015 (World Bank, 2015), a considerable achievement. However, this is not so considerable when you look at the dollar amounts as previously indicated that define poverty. There is no doubt that the measure of $1.25 U.S. per day, or even $1.90 per day, that is used by so-called progressives is a realistic number on which to assign poverty or not. This measure is clearly inadequate on all counts. Notwithstanding the criticism earlier, $1.25 is the measure that all of the international organizations use for defining absolute poverty.

Issues such as health and education are not contained in the definition of absolute poverty, but suffice it to say that these are critical concerns that belong in any social policy that is designed to maintain or enhance life. Many of the subject domains cited earlier have been dealt with separately in this chapter, but it needs to be recognized that many of these entities are related and affect one another and need to be attacked comprehensively. Cholera, for example, is often the result of the lack of clean water and poor animal husbandry practices. To fight the disease medically without attacking the other contributing factors such as upgrading agricultural practices and water purification systems is a fruitless task. Although it may deal with the symptoms and save some lives in the process, it doesn't address the root problem, the lack of education, and increasing sources of clean drinking water.

Social services in most developing countries have the additional mandate for healthcare and education, as well as the provision of some basic services such as water procurement, housing, and rudimentary economic development. Much of this service provision takes the form of community and capacity development. The dilemma, of course, is at what point an NGO turns its attention away from crisis intervention and toward the more long-term goals of capacity and community development in hopes that people and communities will become self-sufficient from a basic survival point of view. Obviously the answer is to do both, but from a logistical and financial perspective, that multifaceted approach may prove to be difficult, if not impossible, to achieve.

***

Many national governments in developing countries do not have adequate resources to address issues of poverty on their own. Often a distinguishing feature of social provision in developing countries lies beyond national or local government activity and rests with NGOs and global organizations, particularly those from the developed world. As a consequence, global institutions such as the World Bank and IMF have a great deal of sway in matters that affect social provision and state policy. As a consequence, developing countries are left vulnerable to the ideological and theoretical whims of the countries that dominate these global institutions by virtue of the power of their funding. 'Structural Adjustment Programs' (SAPs), forced on many developing world countries in the 1990s, is an example of such practice. The IMF and World Bank embraced a philosophy that featured private enterprise over communal or government ownership of resources and enterprises. In order for many of the developing countries to secure loans from these global institutions, they were forced to sell their state-owned enterprises and resources to the private sector, most of which were offshore, multinational, foreign-owned companies. In the agriculture area this condemned many individuals to increased poverty and put whole communities on the verge of starvation. Many of those affected were people reliant on subsistence communal farming for their very survival. As an additional consequence of SAPs, the affected country was unable to protect their fledgling industries through subsidies or tariffs until they were sufficiently solid to play successfully in the international market. Shortly after initial implementation, the devastating outcome of SAPs soon became apparent to even the most ardent supporter of the free enterprise model, and these draconian practices were soon abandoned or severely modified. That said, many lives were put in jeopardy until this folly was reversed.

Social policy in the developing world suffers greatly from the issues outlined earlier. Advancement in this area of society is not progressing sufficiently in order for these countries to catch up to the developed world, which seems to be the long-term goal. The fact that many of these poorer countries have not achieve the Millennium Goals, as laid out by the Rio summit, is testament to the increasing disparity between the affluent West and the poorer countries of the globe. As bleak as the picture appears in some parts of the globe, countries such as China and South Korea are demonstrating that progress can be made. Perhaps a good first step in any reconstruction effort would be for the affluent countries of the West to forgive repayment of the loans they have provided over the years and which keep many of these countries in searing poverty. This would at least provide a clean slate for many of these struggling countries and a solid starting point for future development.

Note

1 The Gini coefficient is a standardized measure that measures the distance between the richer and poorer members of a society. The measure is standardized so that countries or regions within a country can compare themselves with others.

References

Canadian Index of Wellbeing. (2009). *How Are Canadians Really Doing: The Report of the Index of Wellbeing.* Waterloo, Ontario, Canada: Canadian Index of Wellbeing.

Golden, L. (2008). *Rural Poverty, Serious Leisure and Social Integration (Unpublished Doctoral Dissertation).* Guelph, Ontario, Canada: University of Guelph.

United Nations. (2014). *The Millennium Development Goals Report 2014.* New York: United Nations.

United Nations, Department of Economic and Social Affairs. (2006). *World Summit for Social Development Programme of Action, Resolution 1, Annex II Para. 19.* Retrieved from www.un.org/en/development/desa/index.html

United Nations, Department of Economic and Social Affairs. (2009). *Rethinking Poverty: Report on the World Social Situation 2010.* New York: United Nations.

World Bank. (2015). Retrieved from www.worldbank.org/en/topic/poverty/overview

9　Community Building

Most discussions on the subject of social policy identify democracy as a vital part of the social development universe. Identifying how democracy is enhanced or achieved is often neglected, beyond simply stating that it is important and part of the formal political process. There are many venues for engaging the populace at both the national and local levels in the development and provision of social policy, thereby strengthening the democratic foundation. The recent advancement of social media in political campaigns by all parties demonstrates clearly the developing and deepening relationship between those who govern and those who are governed. Public involvement in governance does not just happen at election time any longer, but is an ongoing dialogue given the widespread use of social media. Public involvement in the social policy development process is a rich venue for advancing democracy and in creating a sense of inclusion in community and national development.

Conceivably, citizen engagement can occur at many levels, including at the international, national, and local levels. It is most likely that beyond voting for national representatives or in belonging to a political party, most of us engage with democracy at the community or local level through many different types of activity. It is in communities where our lives are lived and the provision of much social policy gets played out. National governments develop macro social policies such as healthcare, social assistance, and housing, but it is usually the local government that implements those policies through on-the-ground resources and programs for citizens. The local community is the ground where social policy gets delivered. Additionally, discussions about the adequacy of social policy and the required changes to it should be generated at the community level, if policy and social service provision is to be bottom up and not top down or hierarchically driven. It is in the community where human needs are identified and ideas about how to satisfy those needs are best determined.

Regardless of the level at which social policy is engaged, fundamental to its essence is the notion of social justice as was alluded to in the last chapter. Social policy is essentially devoted to providing the basic necessities of life to those without means to function adequately and to seek social justice in a society that often differentiates its citizens by wealth. Social policy intercedes where social, physical, and psychological harm is perpetuated by a system that neglects many members of society and showers its riches on the few. Although many argue that the 'invisible hand of the market' automatically corrects imbalances in the fiscal and monetary system, years of experience would suggest otherwise. Social policy, usually the responsibility of government, is required to correct that imbalance and through policy, attempts to reduce unacceptable inequality within and among societies. The idea is that social justice corrects for imbalances, not only in the fiscal functioning of society, but also in other important domains of life such as healthcare, education, and human rights. Through these policies and programs social inclusion and democracy are enhanced.

***

The ideas of community development (CD), capacity building (CB), and social capital (SC) are the major components of community building and should be viewed as a system and not as individual, isolated, separate entities operating independently. Taken together they collectively express the major elements needed for building communities. Figure 9.1 provides a graphic representation of this notion.

As this figure suggests, building community requires agreeing to a process for conducting activity, a set of skills to apply to the task, and the communication between and among all groups in the community so that all actors in the system are working together to complete the mission, whatever that undertaking may be.

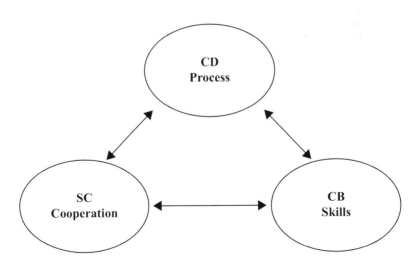

Figure 9.1 Three Major Components to Community Building

The focus on community development (CD) has become a major mechanism for applying the notions of democracy and social justice at the local level. In addition to the responsibility of government to act in creating social policy, civic institutions in most developed societies have become features on the landscape for policy development and delivery as well. Whether or not this has always been in the best interests of society is a matter of debate, but it is a reality nonetheless. It is generally thought that the creation and delivery of social policy is a partnership between governments and civil society. The balance in that relationship is always a concern and needs to be constantly monitored, debated, and adjusted. Governments often want civic institutions to assume as much social policy delivery as possible so they can reduce their effort.

Community development has many nuanced definitions, all of which take a slightly different tack to its expression. The two largest differentiations inside the notion of CD is the concept that views it as primarily product centred with a tangible goal such as creating a new locally provided service, or second, as a process focused on informal experiential education whose chief objective is for local people to take control of their existence individually and collectively, with the aim of determining their own destiny rather than having it dictated by some outside force. It is this last definition on which this chapter and the general philosophy of this book are built. Reid and van Dreunen (1966, p. 49) provide an overarching definition of community development and describe it as

> a process for empowerment and transformation. The focus on Community Development is to identify and resolve problems of a social, physical, or political nature that exist in a community in such a way that these conditions are changed or improved from the perspective of the community members. The goals of Community Development are self-help, community capacity building, and integration.

The values expressed by the concept of CD are mostly articulated at the local level. The basic philosophy contained in this general concept is not limited to community or local undertakings, however. CD expresses a set of values, skills, and processes that can be applied to an action that goes beyond the local and extends into the national and international arenas as well. CD is an expression of the human aspiration of inclusion, as well as social and individual development, in the politics and policies that affect living conditions and life experiences. Community development is as much a philosophical concept as it is a tangible activity. It is viewed as a process as much, or perhaps more, than it is a product. In a number of cases, CD is seen as individual and collective self-help aimed at producing community autonomy through informal education, collective strategizing, and action.

***

Community development can be incorporated within the notion of 'alternative development'. Friedmann (1995, p. 31) suggests that alternative development "involves a process of social and political empowerment whose long-term objective is to rebalance the structure of power in society by making state action more accountable, strengthening the powers of civil society in the management of its own affairs". Our present-day politicians have the propensity to believe that citizens are quite satisfied to vote every four years or so and then leave the governing of the nation, including the development of social policy, to them. This way of governing may make life easy for the politician, but does little to enhance the social solidarity of their constituent communities, increasing a sense of power among the citizenry, or in strengthening democracy generally. Since the advent of social media, modern political parties see the value of engaging citizens throughout their mandate dialoguing about their ongoing activities, and not just at election time. Political parties that neglect to engage their citizenry at this level do so at their own peril.

Citizen groups often spring up as either single-issue-oriented associations, and hence short lived, or as permanently established groups with a mandate to interact with politicians and public decision makers over the long term. Often these groups have competing agendas and may not desire the same outcome on a particular issue. It needs to be recognized that geographic communities contain multiple policy communities within them, and one should not assume that a geographic community is homogeneous and speaks with one voice. It is often the case that those who populate a community on an issue may wind up in opposing camps on a different question. This at times leads to frustration on the part of officials because it necessitates diligence in communicating widely on every issue of importance and not falling into the trap of making assumptions from earlier discussions, decisions, debates, or votes. Additionally, it is important to note that geography cannot always be used as a method for identifying community. There are many 'communities of interest' that have no natural geographic boundaries but are composed of people from across the globe who share a special interest. These groupings also define community. These types of communities have multiplied since the advent of the internet and social media. Community development is a fluid process producing communities of interest with varying degrees of permanency. This fluidity at the community level provides a rich basis for understanding the development and practice of democracy.

There are many distinct ways to define community development. Sanders (1970) provided the seminal work on this subject when he identified four basic approaches to community development. Community development as *a program* views citizen engagement as a strategy to achieve a predetermined goal. In this approach people are invited into the process as long as they subscribe to the articulated goal vocalized by the power structure or interest group in charge. Often environmental groups act in this way. It is frequently said that to achieve a sustainable environment you have to first get people to accept the underlying goals and subsequent program as conceived by a particular knowledgeable group. So the goal becomes set, and community development becomes a matter of convincing citizens of the worthiness of the goal and motivating them to become involved in achieving it. Community development as *a method* is not too dissimilar from the previous approach, but the emphasis here is on developing unique ways to involve the public in goal achievement. These methods may, in fact, be created by the advocates. It may be demonstrations, sit-ins, or less invasive activities that are emphasized, but citizens are engaged in selecting the method of achieving the goal and not necessarily in other aspects of the process that are of concern to community development in its purest form. Community development as *a process* embraces the idea of self-help. In this approach, the process begins with problem identification. Citizens are actively engaged in this part of the activity, as well as in later stages, such as in creating strategies and implementing projects. This approach recognizes that the participants will be the ones who live with the results of any outcomes that are produced by the action, so community members are engaged initially in problem identification and continuing through to the decision-making stage. A strong feature of this approach to CD is the objective of individual growth and personal development of the participants and the community engaged in the process. These objectives are as important as achieving a tangible product goal. This approach to CD is as much concerned with developing capacity in the community to resolve present and future issues as it is with achieving some singular external objective. It embraces the idea that communities can be actively engaged in solving their own problems and, although outside assistance may be required, it is not the overall driving or dominant force in the decision-making and development process. This is likely the purest form of citizen participation and the one most closely aligned to the ideals of pure community development. Community development as *a movement* is not too dissimilar from the process approach, but perhaps puts more emphasis on values and ideological concerns. The basic issue on which the movement is developed is ideological in nature, so citizens are attracted to the movement as a matter of principle and not something they will need to spend considerable time defining. This suggests that the exterior goal to be achieved is more important than individual growth and development, which also is likely to occur, but is not of foremost concern as it is in the process approach outlined earlier.

What all of these different approaches to community development have in common are varying degrees of commitment and engagement with indigenous problem identification, levels of participation, the notion of self-help, and community control of the process. For it to be truly identified as pure CD, all of these aspects would need to be present in the process in some form or another. The process approach to CD embraces all of these principles to a larger degree than the other forms of CD.

A distinction must be made at this point between what has become known as community-based development (CBD) and community development (CD). These terms are often used interchangeably, which is not theoretically correct, and both are quite different in implementation and outcome. Community-based development is not necessarily bottom-up planning or development. It may be implemented from the top and may not involve many, if any, members of the community other than as service recipients. Often large NGOs that are not indigenous to or controlled by the community, but come from outside to deliver services at the community level, should not be automatically considered to adhere to CD principles. Service delivery that is not developed and controlled at the community level does not embrace the philosophical underpinnings of CD and should not be considered as such. The CBD approach to service delivery is most likely product centred, concerned mainly with service delivery and with little intereste in process goals that include enhancing skills or networks in the target community. After the implementation of the CBD approach, the community may be no further advanced in its capacity to create and deliver that service by itself in the future than it was initially. Although this is not inherently negative, given that it doesn't always matter how a particular service gets delivered in some instances, it must be remembered that this approach does not contain the elements of capacity building (CB) and social capital construction inherent in the CD approach. Knowing the difference between the two approaches is important when designing a social policy or community intervention.

***

The second concept vital to effective community building is social capital. Social capital brings into the idea of community building the amorphous and abstract but vital elements of norms, networks, and trust that facilitate cooperation within and between groups in the community. As in systems theory, it is the relationship among the parts that is often the critical factor in community building, and it is social capital in a community that can build those relationships. Relational variables permit or encourage multiple entities in the community to work together. As Coleman (1988) tells us, social capital consists of a social structure that facilitates the actions of players in that system. Without trust, norms, or networks built up to a substantial degree and operative in the community, success in solving community social issues such as poverty are less likely to occur than if those elements are present and well developed. Social capital can be recognized as operative when relations among people and groups change sufficiently to produce action. Community-building initiatives, even if they are community driven, have less of a chance of success if there is no social capital available to support those proposals. Part of the goal of community building is to develop social capital so the capacity to identify and solve community problems becomes greatly enhanced.

Capacity building (CB) in the community is the third major requirement of community building. The ideas contained in the notion of CD are as relevant today as they were in Sander's time—new words to express similar or related ideas have surfaced in the literature. Each of these new ideas has nuances that, in my view, help to explain or enlarge the original notion of community building. One of those concepts is capacity building (CB), which suggests that communities need a set of practical skills in order to engage in community building successfully. Expertise in areas such as community self-diagnosis, networking, organizing, leadership, group work skills, and problem solving are the main proficiencies that will enable a community to effectively engage in a CB and, hence, social policy development. These and other context-specific skills that are identified by those undertaking the task constitute the areas for skill development that is important in building capacity in the community in order to carry out social policy development. There is a deep and wide literature on the subject of capacity building and social policy planners, and the CD practitioner would be well served to become fluent in that literature, if not so already.

Reid and Muruvi (2011, pp. 27–29) provide a more detailed list of skills (see Appendix at the end of this chapter) than those presented earlier that could be required at any given time when engaged in a community-building project. According to them these skills relate to the major issues of governance, capacity to plan and implement projects, skills related to engaging and facilitating other sectors of the community in the process, planning skills, and determining sustainability of the project over the long-term. Muruvi's (2011) research to identify these skills as necessary components to community building was undertaken and completed in Ghana and First Nations communities in western Canada. However, they have application to other parts of the world as well. Many community projects start with the best of intentions and aspirations for the future but fail because of the lack of the required skills identified by Muruvi to carry out the process.

The difficulty with both the concepts of social capital and capacity building is that groups in society that are usually the recipients of social policy may be the least capable of generating and cultivating these elements on their own. Often groups that are targets for social policy rely on outsiders and professionals to initiate action in the pursuit of solving a particular social problem. This condition is often the result of top-down policy development and control that has been practiced for decades. It is also often the case that outside professionals and groups who are brought in in a top-down model do not have the time or the mandate to actively cultivate social capital or build capacity in the target community. This not only creates barriers to reducing the chances of effectiveness of the social policy, but also leaves the disadvantaged community fragmented and less than a cohesive unit. It is a remarkable circumstance when target groups take initiatives to create social policy or organize themselves in order to make demands of the power structure to satisfy some need or rectify an injustice. It is vital that governments and civil society alike devote resources to community workers and grant them the mandate for building capacity and social capital within disadvantaged groups. This would not only ensure more productive and appropriate social policy to address needs in the population, but also create communities that could effectively carry out their own initiatives to satisfy needs. This approach would also possess educational value, given that CD purports to enhance community and individual education as a goal. This is how democracy is built, which is one of the goals of social policy, but it is regularly, if not entirely, overlooked as an essential part of the process and why social policy is frequently left to be developed and implemented in a top-down fashion.

***

Professionals and academics readily admit that one of the negatives of CD is the time it takes to successfully complete a project. It certainly takes considerably less time and human resources for a professional to simply create a potential resolution to a community problem identified by him or her and implement that solution. However, a top-down approach usually has a smaller probability of long-term success due to the lack of commitment by community members, who might otherwise have an interest in the proposed action if they were actively engaged early in the process. As a long-term CD practitioner as well as an academic, I shudder to recount how much time and resources have been wasted by politicians and social policy planners who thought they could create and implement policies on their own initiative, bypassing the involvement of the community that was to be affected.

The description of the problem to be resolved would be conceivably different depending on who was involved in creating that definition. If the project has any chance of success, community members must be involved early in the process, which usually means their engagement at the problem recognition and definition stage and not solely at the end point, which is often the case. Professionals are likely to possess a technical understanding of the issue at hand, but not an emotional one. Obviously those who live with the problem every day will have a deeper and more personal understanding of the intricacies involved. Although a longer startup time may be considered to be a negative feature of CD, it will likely be more effective and, hence, less time consuming over the long run if the community is engaged extensively in the process. Community development stresses effectiveness over efficiency.

***

In a society that asks all of its citizens, including the more affluent, to contribute to social wellness through social policy and taxation, it is important to consider the notion of social solidarity. In addition to providing life-sustaining and enhancing programs to individuals, perhaps the greatest and most important outcome of social policy is in generating social solidarity among the population. In employing the term social solidarity, we are seeking emotional attachment of all members of society to the overall goals of that society and the mechanisms for reaching those objectives. This needs to be considered as a major aim of social policy practice, and it is often not considered in the equation sufficiently, perhaps not at all. The inclusion of citizens in social planning and development and its implementation provide an important venue for achieving social solidarity. A subtle but important ingredient to community development is the interaction of citizen's at all socioeconomic levels with one another to increase individual and social functioning. In this type of discourse, diverse communities get a glimpse of the different lifestyles that exist in their community and have the opportunity to come to understand values and life goals other than their own. The affluent need to understand that social policy contributes to social solidarity and maintains and enhances their way of life in addition to those it directly seeks to serve. On the other hand, those on the opposite end of the affluence continuum get a glimpse of the interests and perspectives of the affluent. It is through dialogue among all segments of the population where values are discussed and common ground agreed to. Social policy that is universally applied to the entire population, whether rich or poor, encourages the belief that we are in this life situation together, although we may have different lived realities. Because of these differences and the inadequacies in the social system, we need to create mechanisms to enhance all lives, not just the lives of the few. To do otherwise results in population separation, leading to ghettos and gated communities, much like we have done in the recent past. When we segregate ourselves in this manner, we can only expect to develop suspicions of one another, leading away from social solidarity. If we are to continue or enhance social functioning, all segments of the community will need to interact and develop positive relationships and not aggravate suspicions and stereotypes held by the other.

Societies that have a two- or multitiered set of social policies that apply to one or other of the classes promote divisiveness that results in the idea that the underclass are the problem and the upper class are being victimized by the marginalized. When some, usually affluent, individuals in society are not recipients of a basic social policy such as healthcare, for example, but buy their services from the private marketplace, there is no incentive for those individuals to see themselves as a part of general society. Further, they may not see any benefit for continuing to support the public system if they have no direct stake in it. Under this scenario those who receive social services provided by government are often viewed by the affluent as simply taking their resources from them undeservedly and without giving the contributor anything in return. In this way of thinking, the affluent often view themselves as being victimized by the poor. They believe they are supporting those who are largely considered undeserving. Class warfare is the inevitable result of such a basic differentiation, and it is the role of social policy to avert such outcomes and to create social solidarity within the population.

***

In addition to the philosophical foundations of citizen participation in the social policy and planning process, the issue of implementation must be addressed. Each of the foundational approaches to planning as proposed by Friedmann and discussed in Chapter 5 of this book possesses a corresponding citizen participation (CP) framework. As many authors (Arnstein, 1969) are quick to point out, citizen participation is not a single concept but a continuum from highly active and engaged public to mere tokenism or manipulation. Many of the points at the lower end of the continuum actually result in nonparticipation, although it gets expressed as a form of CP, beginning with manipulation that is devoted to attempting to persuade the public of the power structure's view of the problem and their strategies for its resolution. It is often viewed as therapy for the service target group by those in power. The continuum progresses, with each point on the scale increasing the value of the participant's position and weight in the process, leading to the end point where citizens are in complete control of the discussion and outcome of the activity. Again, a more complete description of these points on the scale can be found in other volumes, including the seminal work of Sherry Arnstein. Suffice it to say that Arnstein's model of citizen participation stretches from direct manipulation of the public, to informing the community of what is to be done, to consulting with them on an equal footing, to simple placation, to developing partnership, to delegating power to those interested in the project, and finally, to assigning complete control of the mission to participants in the process. The point to be made here is that citizen participation is not a singular idea but many distinct levels of engagement, each with different outcomes that need to be made apparent in the planning process and not left unidentified. If the level of expected participation is left ambiguous, people in the process will create different conceptions of what is intended and, therefore, are left with wide-ranging and dissimilar expectations as to how they and their input will be treated.

What is central to the success of engaging citizens in the process is a truthful and exact undertaking with regard to what is being offered to those invited to participate. It may be better to state that those in charge are willing to consult with the public but not leave the impression that they are offering control of the process when, in actuality, they are not. All too often, and in their exuberance, politicians and other decision makers offer considerably more in terms of citizen control of the process and its outcomes than they are able to provide in reality. There are many instances where planners and decision makers offer prospective participants in the activity control of the process and outcome, but in actual fact are unable to deliver on that high promise and actually make available much less. When there is great distance between what is offered and what actually takes place, participants in the process feel they have been betrayed and come away frustrated with the experience. It may be this shortcoming that has left many citizens disbelieving their leaders and skeptical of invitations to participate in community and social affairs.

Those initiating the planning and policy process must make a critical decision early in the effort with regard to what level of participation is required and acceptable. It must be determined what is desired by the exercise. Is it to manage or to stimulate change? If it is the former, then social reform or policy analysis with a corresponding CP approach that is situated at the lower end of Arnstein's model is the realistic option. If, on the other hand, the process calls for stimulating change, then in all likelihood a social learning or social mobilization approach is appropriate, with citizen participation located at the higher end of Arnstein's model—either a considerable amount of delegated power extended to the participants, or complete citizen control of the entire process.

Recent scholars have taken the concept of CP beyond Arnstein's original notion of citizen participation in the process of decision making to that of empowerment. Friedmann (1995, p. 33) sees "three types of power; social, political, and psychological, leading to empowerment". Social power includes access to information, knowledge, and skills. Political power is concerned with access to the decision-making system. Finally, and perhaps the most important of all three loci of power, is psychological power. As Friedmann (1995, p. 33) suggests, psychological power "is best described as an individual sense of potency. Where present, it is demonstrated in self-confident behaviour". Most often empowerment is achieved through actions taken and processes contained in the CD process, including the development of networks, trust, and norms, the elements that define social capital.

***

The role of the volunteer sector is a particularly important ingredient in the social policy development process. The volunteer sector not only delivers services, but it also provides an advocacy role in support of the disadvantaged and marginalized in society. Given the diminishing concern for the marginalized in society by governments, the advocacy role is a much-needed function at present. Not only can volunteer associations lobby governments on behalf of those in need, but they can also launch public relations activities to educate the public on the issues of concern and subsequent need for social policy. They often fill the role of liaison between those in need and the governance system.

The negative side to the increase in the proliferation of volunteer organizations and programs is the propensity for governments to abdicate their role in the social policy arena and leave more and more service delivery and funding to civic society and charitable institutions. Governments often see this sector of society as a replacement for their potential involvement. Government replacement in social policy was not the original intention of the volunteer sector nor its *raison d'être*. On the contrary, the intention of this sector is to provide service to disadvantaged groups and individuals until such time as the governments can enact policies and programs that will serve the public better and make volunteering redundant. Of course, this redundancy has not yet come about on most social issues, and the role of the volunteer sector has generally widened and deepened. This deepening and widening of their role is a demonstration of the ineffectiveness of the government sector in this policy field and some would say demonstrates their significant neglect of the poor and marginalized in society. The volunteer sector plays a much-needed role in the social policy arena. One must view their heightened responsibility with some concern, however. The volunteer sector will inevitably become stronger as governments retreat from the social policy domain. Some volunteer advocates are beginning to wonder out loud if they are doing a disservice to the poor by providing a partial service through their work and allowing governments to retreat from solving the problem of poverty comprehensively.

According to Arai (1996), the volunteer sector is where democracy gets played out for the majority of people. It often provides a practice space for developing and honing a sophisticated understanding of citizenship rights and responsibilities. It is where people who possess a concern for equity and social justice are able to express their disquiet or aspirations. Personal voice is often found through voluntary activity as is personal empowerment. Some individuals have launched a career through volunteering, particularly a political career. Volunteering is a place in civil society where networking and social capital are constructed. Finally, voluntary associations provide a space for people to mobilize for change in society through social policy advocacy. It is where people of like minds congregate and express their desires for democratic development and for creating a more just society.

Voluntary associations have been successful in fulfilling advocacy objectives throughout their existence. At times they have been so successful they have pushed governments to provide social policies that were not part of that political party's agenda or worldview. They have also been seen to be in opposition to the government in power in many cases. When that has happened, some governments have threatened to remove the association's tax exemption status, identifying them as a special-interest lobby group and not a voluntary association at all. On the other hand, and as argued earlier, governments are quite happy to have volunteer associations provide direct service to those that are in need because this allows them to reduce their role. But politicians often resent the volunteer sector's advocacy role and see it as a direct attack on their policies. The poor and marginalized are not a very valued constituency for many political parties, so when a party gains power they often neglect this particular segment of the population and don't like to be reminded of it.

***

The present trend today is toward developing partnerships between and among the voluntary, private, and government sectors. From a philosophical point of view, this may make sense. There is a great distance between a philosophical notion and practicality, however. The goals for each of these entities in society are quite different from one another, and because of that I, for one, am skeptical about the practicality of many of these partnerships. Certainly, if a private corporation has a philanthropic mandate and simply wants to partner because it provides the company with a favourable or enhanced image, then this may provide for a satisfactory partnership. If, on the other hand, the corporate entity is looking to gain profit from the activity, then one must be skeptical about this arrangement. Also, some dubious companies are looking to enhance their public image through partnering with a volunteer association and should not be given that opportunity. Corporations that are major polluters should not have the opportunity to be seen as good corporate citizens through partnerships with a socially oriented voluntary agency, for example.

Appendix

Accountability—linked to governance, seeks to establish to whom is the leadership answerable, if it is to the community, how is that achieved and if not why. **Agenda**—related to actionable things that the community has put down; what is on the community's short-term/long-term plans. **Community mobilization**—ability of community to come together to discuss, plan or implement issues of interest to the community as a whole; important to determine how, why, when community mobilizes and who mobilizes the community. **Community participation**—how the community engages in the development process, and strategies used to facilitate or promote community engagement, allow community voices to be heard, allow the community to make collective decisions. **Community reach**—relates to whether mobilization targets and manages to bring to the decision making table all segments of the community; are there any segments difficult to mobilize and why; are there marginalized segments of the community who are not participating? **Community utility**—extend of usefulness to the community of local institutions or organizations (or their functions/services), which are potential implementing agents or can provide leadership for community initiatives. **Conflict resolution**—a measure of ability to execute power, moderate disagreements and facilitate dialogue shown by potential leadership, which ensures norms and rules of community are followed, diverse opinions are respected and negotiations proceed peacefully. **Contact with external agencies**—an indicator of the ability to form partnerships which can help build capacity to plan and implement, and mobilize resources for development. **Continuity**—a measure of sustainability of community groups/organizations and their programs; assesses whether group functions are not impacted by changes such as in leadership. **Cooperation/collaboration**—an indicator of various community segments to work together for a common purpose; also a measure of ability of the community to form linkages and work with external partners. **Critical mass**—a certain threshold number of people or community groups that will enable the community to implement development programs/projects. **Decision making**—an indicator of strategy for participation; assesses how are decisions made, who makes decisions and what influence does the community have on final decisions that are made. **Delegated power**—one measure of how power is acquired; determines to whom the leadership is accountable. **Democracy**—a system of governing where the whole population participates mostly through representation; concerned with issues such as fairness and transparency. **Demonstrated competence**—an indicator of experience and assesses whether the community or community group/organization has skills that have actually been put into practice. **Developmental mandate**—a stated vision that includes development of the community, **Execution of power**—evidence of leadership using its legitimate power/authority to get things done. **Forming linkages**—evidence of partnering, collaborating or contacting external or internal groups to work together on issues of benefit to the community. **Gender equity**—a measure of whether participating enabling strategies specifically target inclusion of women or marginalized gender in the planning, implementation and other decision making processes. **History of sharing**—evidence of community solidarity and helping each other materially and socially; often closely linked to functioning of traditional leadership. **Inclusiveness**—openness of activities and processes in the community to all, a measure of strategy for participation **Leadership structure**—a measure of where power to lead, direct and facilitate community processes rests; who constitutes that power. **Legitimate authority**—power that is recognized by those who are being lead; assessment established where that power lies and why. **Longevity**—a measure of permanency and hence sustainability; establishes how long the group/organization with leadership potential has existed in the community. **Organizational structure**—how power or authority is distributed within institutions that provide leadership to the community, could be represented by executives of community groups, councils of traditional authority and so on. **Planning/implementing experience**—evidence of that the community has engaged in development activities before which suggests existence of skills to plan and implement development initiatives **Proven track record**—a measure of how well the community or community group has performed in the past in planning and implementing community development initiatives; can help assess gaps in capacity. **Resource mobilization**—evidence of or capacity to source resources, material, financial, human capacity to support community anti-poverty efforts. **Social cohesion**—a measure of how well the community works together as a unit, includes aspects of social solidarity, common identity and culture of helping each other. **Structural coherence**—the extent to which the leadership and organizational structures are aligned to the community boundaries or structure, includes issues of structural fragmentation. **System for checks and balances**—measure of the existence of structures to ensure power is executed openly, fairly and inclusively to prevent autocracy within the leadership. **Target setting**—evidence that community can set and work towards specific goals that can be used to assess progress; an indicator of capacity to plan and implement. **Technical expertise**—measure of the existence of specific skills within the community needed to undertake specific development initiatives. **Traditional authority**—a system of leadership often based on hereditary ties that goes back for generations, which works by using its power and legitimacy to enforce systems of values, norms and taboos that ensure the normal functioning of society. **Traditional belief system**—system of taboos and traditions which is used to govern people's behaviors, relationships to each other as well as the environment; may be used to regulate species of plants that can and cannot be used, who can access certain resources such as forest grooves and bodies of water and when, and what animals should or should not be hunted (see Reid & Muruvi, 2011).

References

Arai, S. M. (1996). Benefits of Citizen Participation in a Healthy Communities Initiative: Linking Community Development and Empowerment. *Journal of Applied Recreation Research, 21* (1), 25–44.

Arnstein, S. R. (1969). A Ladder of Citizen Participation. *American Institute of Planners Association Journal, 35* (4), 216–224.

Coleman, J. S. (1988). Social Capital in the Creation of Human Capital. *American Journal of Sociology, 94*, S95–S120.

Friedmann, J. (1995). *Empowerment: The Politics of Alternative Development.* Cambridge, MA: Blackwell Publishers Ltd.

Muruvi, W. (2011). *Assessing Community Conditions that Facilitate Implementation of Participatory Poverty Reduction Strategies (Unpublished MS.c. Thesis).* Guelph, Ontario, Canada: University of Guelph.

Reid, D. G., & Muruvi, W. (2011). *The Community Poverty Scan and Asset Based Approach to Poverty Reduction.* Guelph, Ontario, Canada: School of Rural Planning and Development, University of Guelph.

Reid, D. G., & van Dreunen, E. (1966). Leisure as a Social Transformation Mechanism in Community Development Practice. *Journal of Applied Recreation Research, 22* (1), 49–65.

Sanders, L. T. (1970). The Concept of Community Development. In J. Cary (Ed.), *Community Development as a Process* (pp. 9–31). Columbia, MO: University of Missouri.

10 The Role of Research in Social Policy Formation

This chapter selects and discusses the most appropriate macro instruments and research protocols available to social policy practitioners for the purpose of analyzing the requirements of a population and for constructing policy to address those needs. Research operates within the philosophy, theme, and spirit of the previous chapter on community development (CD) that favours public engagement in the problem-solving process, for not only present conditions, but in anticipation of future needs as well. This chapter provides a more detailed examination and explanation of the previous ideas, which set out community development as the primary mechanism for social development. Community development, as it is used here, is a philosophical approach to community building and social development. It stresses community engagement and social learning as much or more than achieving a tangible outcome the activity itself may produce. That said, the function of all social policy activity is to enhance social functioning, which in itself can be considered a tangible product. The alternative approach to CD in social policy development is direct service delivery, which is top down and excludes any meaningful involvement by the general public in determining what is in their best interests. The mere idea of social policy inherently includes some form of meaningful citizen involvement in the process.

The underlying principle in social policy research is its participatory nature involving large numbers of individuals and groups of people in the policy analysis and construction process. It is a matter of determining the future at the grassroots level collectively, rather than having the future determined by some distant or elite authority. It not only seeks information about the subject under review from the public, but also involves them in the design of the research project itself, in data collection, and in the interpretation of the results of data analysis. The intensity of participation in these aspects of research depends on the context in which the policy is being constructed and the level of decision making required. The initiating agent will often make a preliminary assessment of what type of participation is required for the project and implement a tentative involvement strategy until the situation warrants a change to that earlier decision. Consultation with others interested in the potential participation strategy is generally undertaken before the decision about the appropriate level of participation is finally concluded. Participation is likely to be fluid and will change many times during the course of the project. Skills in community organizing, group work, and communication, are necessary, fundamental requirements for conducting research and social impact assessments in social policy development.

***

There is often a debate in the social policy field as to whether or not there is a role for scientific research to play or whether policies should be built purely on individual and collective philosophy and belief. Given that much social policy is developed or delivered by nongovernmental organizations (NGOs), often religious-based groups, the foundation of social policy has not always been grounded in scientific data, but rather through ideology and personal commitment to some long-held conviction. Additionally, social policy has quite often followed the dictates of cultural relativism even when the culture misrepresents the aspirations and needs of large subgroups within that society. Sam Harris (Harris, 2010) in his book *The Moral Landscape* tells us that morals and values have a scientific basis although humans have always relied on myths and religion for the origin of their mores. He argues, for example, that morals and values can be constructed on the consequences or actions and outcomes dictated by those qualities. He would have us believe that any value or moral that leads to outcomes that enhance the well-being of a population and the globe, or the results of initiatives that lead to evil or bad effects can, or should, be determined by science. Here is what Harris (Harris, 2010, p. 64) has to say on the subject:

> [M]orality can be linked directly to facts about the happiness and suffering of conscious creatures. However, it is interesting to consider what would happen if we simply ignored this step and merely spoke about 'wellbeing.' What would our world be like if we ceased to worry about 'right' and 'wrong' or 'good' and 'evil, and simply acted so as to maximize wellbeing, our own and that of others? Would we lose anything important? And if important, wouldn't it be, by definition, a matter of someone's wellbeing?

In his scheme science, particularly but not exclusively social science, can answer questions about what ought to be initiated as much as determining what phenomena exist in the environment at the present moment. Physical and biological sciences that examine the state of the planet and other related matters can also lead to moral social statements and dictate values. Preserving the planet, and hence life, has to be considered a proper human value and moral question, regardless of the culture in question, its history, or origin. The engagement of science and scientific principles of enquiry bring into question the absolute faith many of us have had in the past in cultural relativism as the sole mechanism for settling questions of a moral and social nature. Given the present physical and social state of our societies' and their degradation over the last while, we need to inject a strong dose of realism into value clarification and development, and can no longer rely exclusively on the cultural relativism argument for setting society's social agenda. The outputs of research based on scientific principles and processes matter greatly in social policy development. Instituting individual and social well-being as a central marker for determining societal values seems to me like a reasonable place to start in determining social policy initiatives and the research that is carried out to support it.

In making the argument for the importance of realism in value determination and social morals through adoption of scientific principles, we must consider and reiterate what science portends to do. It must be remembered that science creates hypothesis, either inductively or deductively, and then tests those hypothesis to see if they stand up in reality. The scientist's goal is to demonstrate the falsity of those theories and hypotheses. Scientists attempt to verify and refute the theory in question under the conditions and parameters set by science, with the intent of qualifying, or not, the tentative worthiness of that condition or statement. So why should values and morals not fit into such a structure? Can the researcher not test a moral statement in order to verify or refute the applicability of that statement under parameters set a priori, particularly if the underlying intent is the advancement of individual and social well-being? I think it can. Science and research can help to clarify the conditions of the context in which social policy is to be constructed and applied.

In addition to the realism verses cultural relativism debate, there is often a love/hate relationship on the part of social policy practitioners and politicians for the compilation and analysis of data as a fundamental part of the social policy formation process. It sometimes seems that politicians do not want to have their policy agenda interrupted with the facts. However, there is an implicit understanding by both the politician and practitioner, and by the general public for that matter, that social policy needs to be based on some form of empirical data analysis rather than on pure whim or fancy of those in charge of the system. It also needs to distinguish who the policy will and will not benefit. That said, it is often the case that politicians only want data analysis that confirms their view of the world, and they are ready to dismiss research results when it does not bend to their agenda. There is also a great amount of skepticism about the validity of research results when findings do not confirm the prevailing view or conventional wisdom held by society. Attempts are often made to discredit the analysis or analyst when decision makers are in opposition to what their data suggest. Not only are their data often attacked, but so are the methodology and research design on which it is based. It is critical, therefore, that those engaged in social policy development be extremely competent in conducting and analyzing research. It would be shameful to lose solid policy options because of faulty research design and practices that leave them vulnerable to attack.

Although the social policy research endeavour is filled with many minefields, it is imperative that social policy formation not be constructed in a vacuum, but influenced by the analysis of a sound database. It is critical that the database be constructed on an ongoing basis and not simply a one-off to solve an immediate problem—although that must be done as well, but not to the exclusion of the long-term collection and analysis of data, including building a comprehension collection of baseline data. All too often data are collected and analyzed to solve a particular problem when that problem has a major detrimental impact on some group in society. There may be specific and unique circumstances associated with immediate social problems that need to be researched and decided upon immediately, but it is also critical for social policy makers to be engaged in consistent, coordinated policy making based on data collection and analysis that systematically occurs over the long term as well. What is critical to the research process is that data be comparable over an extended period of time so that long-term changes in the environment can be detected and measured rather than data analysis exclusively dedicated to providing a snapshot of a particular, isolated period in time. Social policy should be a result of a clear understanding of the ever-changing makeup and dynamism of the population and the social, economic, political, and environmental landscape in which it is situated. The social landscape is in constant flux and therefore demands an ongoing research effort to describe its dynamism accurately.

***

Numerous texts deal in detail with social policy research from a methods and analytic point of view, so this volume will examine the subject from the macro perspective and leave the micro presentation to the plentiful volumes available on the subject. This discussion, however, will be different in one other major respect. Most methodology chapters in other volumes view research as a process for determining what exists at the moment or the analysis of a present deficit in society. This volume views research as a method of enquiry for determining what ought to exist in the future, and therefore be value laden, in order to address the present and looming large-scale social and environmental problems that appear to be dominating the current outlook and the future issues on the horizon of the social and environmental landscape. It is recognized that there are present and persistent social problems that require research to address those realities. That said, those in society concerned with social inequality and social injustice have been constantly fighting the immediate short-term consequences of that condition without great effect and without ever moving to the larger discussion that can advance society to the next level of human development. As a consequence, this book and the discussion regarding the practice of research in the social policy process are mostly concerned with the big picture and will mainly focus on societywide change rather than methods dedicated to micro issue remediation. In some cases, research activity can contribute to both the micro and macro picture at the same time; however, not all small advances add up to one big positive, but can, in fact, produce a large-scale negative. For example, food banks were to be a short-term measure for staving off hunger and were probably a positive initiative originally. They have become permanent features on the landscape, however, and may now be a negative development in the larger social picture. Many social commentators now believe they are a barrier to eliminating poverty because they have let governments abdicate their responsibility for grappling comprehensively with this important issue. Simply fighting the day-to-day injustices and failures in the present system does not allow for the necessary contemplation of societywide change that is needed in order to permanently rectify the systemic inadequacies in the system. This book argues that it is the system that needs changing, not the various anomalies in it on which the micro approach tends to focus. Social policy makers can be overwhelmed with current micro problems and not find sufficient time or effort to address the larger structural problems in society that are the underlying cause of many of the problems they fight on a day-to-day basis. This volume is very aware of that potential pitfall and will constantly reflect on, and refer to, the state of social relations in society that produce inequality and social injustice in the world, rather than tinkering at the margins to improve the present condition slightly and, perhaps, only temporarily.

***

This chapter also presents the overarching ontological positions that support the appropriate level of research and social impact assessment of present and potential future social policies. The approach of this book is unique in as much as most social policy research texts present data collection and analysis techniques without placing them in the larger context of expected goals and objectives of the research activity. It deals with how one goes about collecting and manipulating data, but does little, if anything, on determining why one would want to undertake data collection and analysis in the first instance. This volume attempts to answer the following questions: What do we want to accomplish in the research protocol and what effect can be expected from the research activity we employ?

Fundamentally, social policy is about solving social problems through the planning and implementation of activities and programs to ameliorate unacceptable conditions produced by society, but it is also about education. In fact, education may be the foremost activity of social policy making and, consequently, the research function that is in aid of social policy formation. It is important to social policy formation for society to be reflective and determine a vision on which its long-term future would be based. As various members of society examine their situation and educate themselves regarding what is of value to them and instrumental to their success in the future, they are bound to determine for themselves what barriers stand in the way of creating that better life. The processes involved in social policy research are influential in helping people learn about themselves and the social environment in which they live. Fundamentally social policy research, in the first instance, is concerned with asking people what kind of society they wish to live in, and second, how they might eventually reach that state. This activity contributes to individual and collective empowerment—one of the main goals of social policy research and development.

***

Our society seems to be unsure about the role and function of social policy generally and the use of research in the policy development process specifically. In some cases, research is used to support one's philosophical position or is ignored when it does not suit their position. Research outcomes can even be sabotaged or buried so that they do not surface to discredit the political ideology or the agenda of those in power. I have seen notices on my own university's advertisement board by a funding agency that stated they were offering a $10,000 scholarship to any graduate researcher who could produce a case for privatizing healthcare. This seemed a little odd to me given that the function of science is to make discoveries on issues, not make cases for the political position of those in power or an advocacy group. It would be naive to think that this type of inducement does not happen regularly. That said, there are times when the disadvantaged or marginalized in society will undertake research to demonstrate how present practices disenfranchise them in society. But hopefully this does not include making up results. I view this type of advocacy differently than those in power, who engage in research that contributes to that disenfranchisement and furthers false consciousness as discussed previously in this book.

As this book is being written, the government of Canada has recently tabled a budget. In that budget they pronounced two notable and important measures, among others. The first was to declare an increase in the age of eligibility for receiving Old Age Security from sixty-five to sixty-seven. The implementation date is set for some time in the early 2020s, so it will only affect those who are not concerned about retirement yet but will inevitably reach that stage. Allegedly, this measure was instituted to even out the government's expenditure for Old Age Security as the baby boomer generation approaches retirement. The government's rationale for this measure was to stem the increase in recipients when the baby boomers hit retirement age, which, they contend, could not be afforded. The parliamentary budget officer, through his ongoing research effort, notified the government that the increase would amount to less than 1 percent of gross domestic product (GDP) and would not be a burden on the tax system at all. This scenario provides a prime example of the research, producing a conclusion in a direction other than where the decision makers wanted to go for ideological reasons. There may be many reasons why the government wants to enact this policy; however, the stated rationale was found to be inaccurate and inadequate. This example illuminates the value that government places on research in the social policy development process and the modus operandi for decision making. The dismissal of research findings in the foregoing example happens all too frequently in social policy formation, and more attention needs to be placed on the value of sound research in the setting of the social policy agenda. The deferred entry into the pension program comes at a time when the same government reduced taxes on Canada's largest corporations. These two measures taken together clearly demonstrate where social policy sits on their agenda and the value those politicians give to social policy research.

An earlier decision taken by government was to eliminate the compulsory long-form census. The rationale by the government in power at the time was that they could increase the size of the sample by seeking more voluntary contributors. What the government of the day did not understand was the necessity for the sample to be randomly generated, and that the sample size was not as important as making sure all citizens had an equal chance of being selected in the sample. It is clear to social scientists that some groups, such as recent immigrants and the poor, would be less likely to participate in a voluntary census than other segments of society, thus skewing the sample and, therefore, the results of the research. The consequence of this action on the part of government is to cast some doubt on the randomness and legitimacy of the results of the entire long-form census on which much is learned about the need for social policy in society. I might add that this decision to eliminate the mandatory nature of the census was made in the face of great protest by academic researchers, the business community, and civil institutions that rely on the data produced by the long-form census for input into their decision-making process. Rather than consider this action of government to be of malicious intent, I prefer to think of this act as a demonstration of their ignorance for the need for sound research design in the social policy development process. Happily, a new government has just been elected, and one of their first actions was to reinstate the long-form census. This reinstatement of the long-form census will aid social policy researchers immensely as they try to provide accurate analysis in the aid of good policy making over the long-term.

Another measure taken by the previous government in their last budget was to announce strict enforcement of provisions in the tax code for tax exempt NGOs who engage in advocacy or political activities of any kind. The intent here is to stifle opposition that some of these organizations bring to controversial issues that affect their client base and society in general. I am specifically speaking about environmental groups who oppose government plans to undertake projects that these groups deem to be environmentally unfriendly and wish to bring these concerns to the attention of not only parliament but the general public as well. There are additional examples of NGOs that are concerned with social issues, such as poverty, that are subject to this type of government action as well. If they do anything that might be construed as lobbying, including reporting research results, under these new rules, they run the risk of losing their tax-exempt status. This policy has had a sobering effect on the research agenda undertaken by many NGOs. Whether or not undertaking and disseminating the results of focused research on social provision questions will be considered political activity and lobbying is yet to be determined, but if it is, then an even greater pall will be cast over social policy research that has practical value for questions of social importance. At the same time, governments in many countries are muzzling their scientists to keep them from speaking publically about the results of their research, which is often not supportive of government policy. This is decidedly casting a chill inside the civil service, particularly among its research cadre. Again, I am happy to report the new government of Canada has reversed this practice, at least, for the time being.

The measures engaged by many governments and spoken about earlier say something about the social and political environment in which we live. These types of government actions and the reaction against them by civil society will define what kind of society we will create in the future. Divulging and debating research results is part and parcel of social policy making, and good participatory research design can contribute important information to that process. Although it is obvious that the Old Age Security debate previously spoken about is directly related to social policy, the tax-exempt status of environmental organizations may not be quite so clearly connected in people's minds. It needs to be emphasized that social policy is dedicated to defining what kind of society we are creating, and how we treat and define the role of civil institutions in it is an important part of that dialogue. To quote John Shaar (Shaar, 1989, p. 321) on the subject:

> The future is not a result of choices among alternative paths offered by the present, but a place that is created—created first in the mind and will, created next in activity. The future is not some place we are going to, but one we are creating. The paths to it are not found but made, and the activity of making them changes both the maker and the destination.

***

Futurology has been rightly discredited as pseudo-science when it is designed to predict a singular future. Attempting to predict the future is pure folly. However, research that is devoted to creating a range of possible future scenarios based on policy options is critical if policy makers are to make accurate and important decisions about future programs. Given that no one could comprehend the range of variables that might affect a final scenario, predicting an unguided future is designed to fail. This type of futurology views the future as a teleological event rather than something that is created intentionally by the human community.

What is being suggested here is research that focuses on the consequences of our present societal path, and that information offers potential multiple futures and the analysis of their different outcomes. This is vision creation and goal setting, not pure speculation. It also provides society with a framework for debating its values and aspirations. The analysis of a vision for the future is what Shaar is suggesting when he speaks of creating the future in mind and will. A large part of this activity is political, in that policy-making activity is not given over to a group of scientists, professionals, or politicians but

The Role of Research   149

involves carrying out ongoing public discussion concerning societal priorities and asks the question: What kind of future civilization best suits the circumstances of today, and will solve the problems of tomorrow? It rejects the idea of the 'invisible hand of the market' as the sole arbiter for creating the future of society. Research activity provides decision makers with information on which they can render intelligent decisions, and consequently, useful policy.

The research activities that go into developing social policy must focus on both the substance and the process through which it occurs. It should also be placed in a historical as well as a present and future context, unlike most research, which focuses solely on the present. Not only are we concerned with satisfying the needs of today's society and how those requirements can be achieved, as important as that perspective is, but also we need to focus research on our aspirations for the future and the processes that are necessary to achieve those ambitions. And, as Shaar points out earlier, that social policy is about changing the makers of those policies as well as the society in which they live. Advancing the human condition requires self-reflection and education as well as concrete programs and policies to address social inadequacies. Above all we must recognize that all social policy activities—both substantive and educative—are deeply rooted in values. As Wharf and McKenzie (Wharf & McKenzie, 1998, pp. 24–25) make clear when they talk about planning the future, particularly with regard to social policy:

> The approach should be explicitly critical in considering historical, cultural, political, and economic factors; people must be recognized as active agents in shaping as well as reacting to their environment; the life experience of users must be considered and; solutions should promote social justice.

***

With the foregoing providing the research framework for social policy making, we can turn our attention to the activity of needs assessment and impact research. Contrary to the practice of decision making by ideology, politicians also frequently want research to provide them with decisions so they are not held responsible if those decisions do not sit well with their constituents. Often politicians will say that the research dictates what must be done. It is a method for deflecting responsibility. This is quite understandable, given the political polarization social policy formulation often produces among the various constituent groups in society because of its contentiousness and how it is often a reflection of, or in conflict with, one's worldview. It needs to be clarified, however, that research does not make decisions, decision makers do. Research provides decision makers with detailed and valuable information on which decisions can be reached in dialogue with those who will be most affected by the policies that result from those discussions. Decision making is often accomplished through widespread consultation by decision makers with those whom the decision will affect and with those who may have a secondary interest in the subject under review. Research results can inform those discussions considerably.

Given that social policy is made and implemented at multiple levels of society from the local to the national and international forum, the research undertaken and its resulting information will also be located at various levels on the specificity spectrum. Regardless of the level of understanding and analysis required, knowledge comes in three basic fundamental varieties, starting with technical, which is interested in helping us understand the physical world we inhabit. This type of knowledge is usually quantitative in nature and generally answers questions pertaining to issues of 'how much' and 'how many' or 'similarities' and 'differences' between or among variables. When the outcome we desire is to portray or identify the characteristics of the unit under measure, then technical knowledge may be very helpful.

Practical knowledge, on the other hand, is information that helps us understand others and their desires and interests, leading to the manipulation of the system. Manipulation in the sense used here should not be viewed as Machiavellian, but rather, as compassionate in nature, in that it is manipulating the system in favour of the common agreed-upon will. It is argued by many social and political pundits (Krugman, 2007) (Sachs, 2011) that social policy and the political agenda are controlled by the rich and powerful. Sachs has chronicled the relationship between Wall Street, the big banks, and the political system in the United States in a compelling way. The manipulative nature of social policy in this regard is designed to redress that inequality and to change the future for some disadvantaged group, or for an entire community. This is the interpretation of manipulation that is intended here and not the type of malevolence that gives undue preferential treatment to an advantaged group in society at the expense of the larger community and those truly in need. Practical knowledge focuses on the citizen's perception of the inadequacies in the system. It is both quantitative and qualitative in nature. It deals with issues of 'what is'—that is, it identifies the components of the here and now and describes how the system works and the inadequacies it promotes. It often focuses on the entire system and not on the isolated parts within it. It is therefore synthetic in nature rather than reductionist in orientation.

Finally, emancipatory knowledge, which concentrates on freeing ourselves from dominating structures in society, is also often a focus of social policy research. This type of knowledge is usually positional in nature and is not necessarily interested in discovering esoteric truth, but in verifying what is understood by some group (usually an oppressed group of people in society) to be their truth and in their best interest to pursue. It often asks and answers the question of 'what ought to be'. Many forms of feminist research fit this category.

***

Figure 10.1 sets out a simple but classical social policy research process. Of course, completing such an exercise in reality rarely operates in such a linear or straightforward manner with a natural beginning and end. When people are

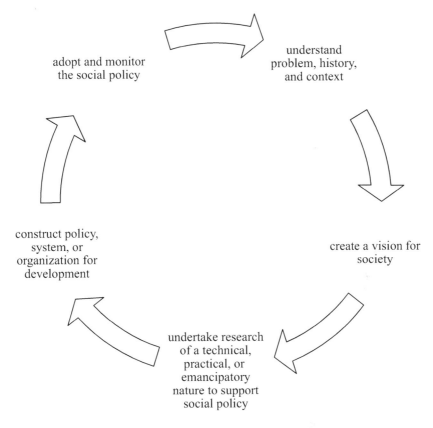

Figure 10.1 Stages in the Research and Planning Process

involved in social policy making, they often wish to skip important steps and jump ahead in the process in order to arrive at solutions without completing the necessary background work, leading toward a result that is acceptable to all concerned parties. Social planning and policy development can be a messy process, but the diagram provides a framework and some guidance in hopes of making it more coherent. It is important to have a framework such as the one outlined here so that everyone in the process has the opportunity to inform and be informed regarding the best thinking on the subjects to be investigated and addressed.

The goal of the first stage in the policy formulation process is to gather as much pertinent information as possible on the issue to be addressed. This objective can become intensive and consume too much of the process if it is allowed to, however, and that can be as debilitating as not collecting and analyzing enough data. The critical thing at this stage is to limit the parameters of what will be obtained and analyzed. Clearly one wants to gather all the pertinent information needed to be well informed on the nuances of the subject under investigation, but not be consumed by the collecting activity itself or overwhelmed by the amount of information collected. This information is used to establish the vision, goals, and objectives for the social policy agenda and should have a citizen participation component to it, preferably driven by those the eventual policy will affect. Research is then undertaken to determine the potential solutions to the problems being addressed and the future policies needed to address them adequately. Once the policy is constructed, then a system, organization strategy, or implementation procedure can be created in order to deliver the policy to the target group. Finally, a research process for monitoring and evaluating the policy over time is established and put into practice. This completes the first round of policy development at which time the policy is reviewed for its effectiveness and revised if need be. The process should be repeated throughout the life of the policy and not simply be a single, one-time event.

This diagram does not address the issue of who should be involved in the process. It is important to stress that the entire process should be highly interactive and engage citizens throughout all of its stages, including understanding and defining the problem to be addressed, its history, and the context in which the policy is to be situated. Perhaps even more important is to engage all interested parties in the vision creation stage of the process. Planners and policy makers, to their peril, have often left citizens out of these critical early stages. When citizens are brought into the process at a later stage, say to discuss an alternative policy drafted and preferred by the professional, it is bound to fail because the potential recipients of the policy may have differing conceptions of the problem itself and likely a different vision on which the policy is to be based. Citizens have a natural interest and stake in determining the vision they will live out as their future. In order to work up to that vision, it is important to engage them in defining and clarifying the context and the problems to be addressed. Citizens and nonprofessionals will bring a different perspective to the discussion than will professionals who have a technical interest but not necessarily an emotional one, and passion is an absolutely necessary ingredient in the social policy development process. The process will come crashing down, as so many of them have in the past, if citizens are only engaged in the solution creation stage of policy making, or worst yet, are asked to support a policy created by some agent without their input and contribution. Many public meetings that I have attended have ended in confrontation between the planning agent and the community because the planner's definition of the problem was either not clearly thought out and properly enunciated or, much worse, not the problem requiring resolution as identified by those who were to be affected by the eventual solution. If the problem is not clear or accurately stated, or it is not the right problem from the perspective of the larger community, then there is no hope of reaching agreement on what to do about it.

There is often great stress in the social policy-making arena. Much of this stress can be attributed to the different ways individuals and groups view the world. Certainly those on the right side of the political spectrum have a distinct way of looking at the world, as do those on the left. That said, I believe that those differences can be surmounted if both sides try and understand each other's point of view and show some willingness to compromise. Additionally, differences can be narrowed through dialogue regarding aspirations and values. At least on the surface much agreement can be found between and among groups on the eventual outcome, that is, a society where all people possess a basic standard of living relative to one another and have their basic needs met. When one group feels they are being exploited by others, then mistrust and conflict are the inevitable result. Without trust in the social policy-making process between and among the parties involved, the social policy-making activity will be in danger of failure.

***

Establishing problem statements often provides a space for great debate and potential confusion. It can also provide the opportunity for all in the debate to come to understand each other's point of view. In addition to variation in values and ways of viewing the world and, hence, differences in defining the social inadequacies to be resolved, there are differences in the priorities for addressing these difficulties in society even when agreement is found on the specific shortcomings to be addressed.

Often problems get expressed in solution form. In my travels as a former consultant, I cannot recall the number of times I heard municipal decision makers define problems in terms of a solution. For example, I have often heard municipal councillors talk about their problems in terms of a need for some type of a facility—for example, our problem is we need a community centre. As you can readily see, the identification of a community centre is not a statement of a problem but an aspiration and a potential solution to an undefined problem. The question 'What problem will the construction of a community centre solve?' needs to be asked and answered in the first instance. If, for example, it turns out that the problem is an increase in juvenile crime, then the construction of a recreation facility such as a community centre may be one potential solution among many to address that issue. There could be less costly alternatives, however, and once the problem is clearly enunciated, then a search for the most appropriate solution can be undertaken.

One of the subsets of problem definition and expression is the perception and distinction between 'need' and 'want'. Confusion is rampant in what constitutes each in the social policy debate. Generally speaking, there are four distinct types of need. The first is normative need. This type of need relies on comparison between and among individuals or groups in society. Communities, particularly in rural settings, compare their position on a number of variables with their neighbours. If a different community has some type of social facility not found in their community, people feel neglected and disenfranchised or somehow diminished. Perceived need relates to perceptions and feelings. Often people will feel that their welfare is being neglected but have difficulty concretely identifying the locus of that dissatisfaction. It becomes a matter of perception. Expressed need, on the other hand, is determined by the use of present services and facilities. If there is overuse of a facility and access to that service is difficult because of that overuse, then it will often be determined that there is need for more of that particular service or commodity. Relative need reflects a comparison of data from one area or community with a provincial, state, or national average. Standards that invoke a ratio of population to a service or facility are a case in point. For example, the need for a hospital or a school is often determined from population size and/or distance to existing services. Each of these ways of viewing and measuring potential requirement for a service are legitimate and need to be recognized as operative in the process when conducting needs assessments. All participants in the process need to understand the point of view of the assessment and what is being measured and what isn't.

Needs of individuals and their wants are often confused. Needs that are considered to be acceptable to an individual and society are the easiest on which to reach agreement. Universal healthcare policy can be considered such an entity. For the most part there is general agreement among the population and decision makers alike that the lack of health insurance, whether a single-payer healthcare system or some other option, is detrimental to not only individual health, but also the healthcare system and society generally. The healthcare sector will have to deal with the uninsured in a crisis situation rather than through prevention, or certainly in a less severe condition, when there is lack of ongoing access to the healthcare system for all members of society. Most advanced societies understand the increased cost to both the individual and the system when people neglect their health over the long term due to the lack of access to the system. Individual and society needs coincide when speaking to the issue of access to healthcare.

We are still on solid ground when the desires of individuals and social needs and social cohesion coincide. Many local governments provide or assist in the provision of recreation services to their population. Local governments understand that recreation programs aid in the health of their citizens and in promoting social solidarity, and therefore see expenditure in this area as legitimate. Individuals, on the other hand, may be participating in some of these activities for reasons other than health or social solidarity but enjoy the service nonetheless. So both individual wants and social needs are satisfied. It becomes more contentious when there is disagreement between some members of society and others and whether the policy domain is clearly within the jurisdiction of the decision-making authority or not. Smoking policy is one of those contentious issues. Although the majority of society understands the importance of a nonsmoking policy in public areas to counteract the effects of secondhand smoke, a considerable number of individuals see a nonsmoking policy as undue interference in the freedom of individual rights, although the eventual effects could be deadly not only to the smoker but to nonsmoking members of the public as well. Also, the gun regulation debate in the United States fits this category. The idea of gun regulation is considered a matter of public health by some and rejected by others.

None of the methods of enquiry for determining need outlined earlier are particularly precise in and of themselves. Their quantitative measurement certainly isn't. The data that assesses need in each of these areas usually come from two sources. The first is the secondary use of existing data. National census counts are a particularly good example of this type of data. Also, social service agencies and researchers periodically launch surveys of targeted populations or the general public to study some potential need or lack thereof for social policy development. Professionally conducted public opinion polls supply information on these types of needs.

Social policy research is often taken up by the focus on content issues such as healthcare provision and poverty reduction. Although these are worthwhile goals, social policy research also needs to examine issues of social change and process. Society has not demonstrated a good track record in the social provision of services, not because it is incapable or unprepared to provide an adequate service in whatever domain it is needed, but because they have been less convincing on the benefits to society than the forces against social policy enhancement are able to mount. Solid research is critical to explaining need in society and the benefits of social policy to the general public.

A number of myths dominate the social policy provision discussion that cause many in society to reject the increase in development of social policy. For example, there is a notion that social payments to the poor produce dependency on the part of recipients and their provision make people dependent on the government. No one has yet convinced me that being dependent on a large multinational corporation such as General Motors or Caterpillar (remember the example from before) is a better option and produces more independence than relying on a government wage, but that is the commonly held view. All of these myths are fodder for social policy researchers, and determining their truth and accuracy would provide an important function in social policy research. Social policy research can focus on exposing false consciousness (see Chapter 3) as well as on providing evidence in establishing need for some particular service.

Those of us who are members of the social policy community have not examined or critiqued many of these myths ourselves, and in numerous instances we accept them without critical examination, therein perpetuating the myth yet again. Much of the social policy dialogue needs to be centred on examining and critiquing the myths in society that work against social policy development. Much of this dialogue and research can be centred in the community development approach, as laid out in Chapter nine. From a research point of view, the discussion of quantitative and qualitative methods and the application of each is also important. It is likely that both methods would prove useful in counteracting false consciousness.

***

In a simplified way, issues that require counting things are best served by quantitative methods. When we need to know how many people feel a certain way about a particular subject, or how many constituents use a service, or where they come from, quantitative data gathering is most appropriate. Also issues of the relationships among variables and what variables fluctuate or correspond to what other conditions in society are main themes for quantitative data gathering and analysis. On the other hand, questions of meaning are more likely than not to be found in data of a qualitative nature. For example, how one feels an organization could improve its visibility in the community is a qualitative question. That said, social policy questions are often multifaceted and complex, so social policy researchers will frequently attempt to use a mixed-method strategy in research that involves both types of data collection.

Many areas of life that social policy speaks to are perceptual and therefore seek qualitative data. On the other hand, some issues are squarely quantitatively based. Take healthcare, for example. Whether or not to increase service in a certain area can be demonstrated by examining expressed need, that is, quantitative data that reflect the number of people who are already engaged in the service and those who would be engaged if the quantity of that service was to be increased. Wait times for healthcare is an example of expressed need and is quantitatively based. On the other hand, the life experience of people who endure long wait times to receive healthcare attention is a qualitative question for the most part. It may also be true that specific sections of the population are not receiving service of a certain nature because of their poverty. This, too, can be demonstrated through carefully collected quantitative data and their analysis. Whether or not a service meets the needs of a specific population can also be determined by using qualitative methods. Qualitatively expressed questions that probe satisfaction levels of a service are frequently engaged and provide useful information for the social policy–producing agency.

It is frequently the case that any given social policy research activity can benefit from both quantitative and qualitative data. Quantitative data explains the numeracy of the situation, and qualitative information provides nuances of the state of affairs that quantitative analysis does not. In most cases, a mixed-methods strategy should be given careful consideration in social policy research.

A major problem arises when those conducting the research are ideologically attached to one technique or another and therefore use the wrong method for explaining what one wishes to clarify. There are a great number among us who steadfastly refuse to engage in quantitative analysis because they feel that this approach in some way diminishes human beings. It is often said that it reduces a person to a number or a series of numbers and the subject loses his or her humanity in the numbers. It, as the argument goes, simply turns people into numbers or statistics, an outcome to be avoided in their view. Equally concerning is the position held by the other side that feels that unless the situation can be explained numerically, the research outcome is not legitimate. A pragmatic approach seems to be more useful. Understanding what one is trying to explain should cause the researcher to select the most appropriate approach or approaches to data collection and analysis. Both forms of data collection and analysis can be very useful in providing a clear, in-depth, and well-rounded picture of the situation that is attempting to be understood and portrayed.

Research in the social policy field is a complex affair. It is not only fraught with technical complexities, but often enveloped in the political process, which obscures it even further. For these reasons, social policy experts need to be well trained in not only the technical aspects of research, but also in terms of what each method can bring to the analysis. To view research in the social policy formation process as a secondary requirement is to diminish its importance to the successful development of much-needed public policy.

References

Harris, S. (2010). *The Moral Landscape: How Science Can Determine Human Values.* New York: Simon and Schuster.

Krugman, P. (2007). *The Conscience of a Liberal.* New York: W.W. Norton & Company.

Sachs, J. (2011). *The Price of Civilization: Economics and Ethics After the Fall.* Toronto: Random House Canada.

Shaar, J. (1989). *Legitimacy in the Modern State* (2nd ed.). New Brunswick, NJ: Transaction Publishers.

Wharf, B., & McKenzie, B. (1998). *Connecting Policy to Practice in the Human Service.* Toronto: Oxford University Press.

Part III

11 Decentring Work

The Role of Meaningful Activity and Leisure in Social Policy Development

When remedies are created to address social problems, leisure is probably considered least, if at all, as a legitimate partner in the battery of therapeutic or life-enhancing strategies. That said, it is always interesting to observe the amount of time most social work agencies devote to creating leisure activities for their clients without officially recognizing its curative and life-enhancing value. It seems that leisure activity often provides the context in which groups of people, including the marginalized and disadvantage, engage during remedial or restorative healing. Society generally considers leisure as an area of life that is casual and without purpose other than to amuse or to help individuals escape the harsh realities of life for short periods of time in order for them to return refreshed to the more serious matters of life. Upon closer observation, however, leisure and meaningful activity appear to play a much greater role in individual and social life construction than most of us might think. It may have value beyond the playful elements attributed to it and provides many of us with purposeful and consequential life-enhancing experiences, perhaps, more so than work in many cases. In the future it may become even more meaningful to life construction as we move from a consumer society to a more nonconsumptive and sustainable existence.

Leisure is often considered a personal and social space for individual escape and refreshment in order for us to return to the more serious undertakings of life with greater enthusiasm and energy. Leisure is seen as a legitimate activity for those who are employed and earning a living. It is often considered a reward for work. Society may not consider it justifiable for the unemployed or for those living on public expenditure, however. Leisure is often viewed as a commodity to be earned through work and an illegitimate activity for those who have not earned it. Notwithstanding that position, those on the margins of society often engage extensively in leisure, not because they necessarily desire to, but because they lack an alternative, mainly work. In some cases the leisure experiences available to the dispossessed and marginalized are not life enhancing but often life destroying. It must be pointed out, however, that this stereotype is just that, a stereotype, and most people on the margins of society engage in socially acceptable and life-enhancing leisure activity when it is made available to them. The problem, of course, is that it is not made available to them in the same quantity as it is for the remainder of society. And, if it is available, it is usually at a price they cannot afford.

Work has been considered by modern society to be the substance of life. It is often said that one's purpose in life is found in one's work. Work as it is conceptualized here means paid work, to be found in the market economy. I stress meaningful work because all work is not meaningful, and therefore some jobs do not engage the worker sufficiently to provide purpose and meaning to life. There are still many jobs that are nothing short of pure drudgery and would not be chosen readily by many of us unless forced to.

The difficulty with the concept that work brings meaning and purpose to life is that it is getting harder and harder to generate meaningful work for all who require it. Additionally, the youth of today are better educated than in previous generations. Many of these educated youth, if fortunate to get employment after graduation, often find themselves in jobs much below the skill level their education would warrant. As a result, many youth are alienated from society and profoundly disturbed about their situation in life. This may be one reason, among many, why terrorist organizations from around the world are able to radicalize and recruit many young people to their diabolical causes. Work as we have conceptualized it in the past may no longer be able to provide human society with the psychological and social rewards it once did. So, a new means for individuals to find purpose in life is sorely needed, and meaningful activity and leisure may provide an alternative for many. In fact, for many people who work full time their real life satisfaction comes from their nonwork time (Mannell & Reid, n.d.).

Leisure activities for the marginalized and unemployed frequently become a substitute for paid work and a replacement for a life that is devoid of positive social interaction typically found in the workplace. It can also allow the marginalized person to escape from the harsh realities of everyday life. Many of us believe this to be an unhealthy distraction from what should be the purpose of life. Leisure does, however, provide a necessary function for those mired in poverty or for those experiencing other social problems, including unrewarding work. Programs offered by social work agencies to the marginalized and those with social and psychiatric problems often contain a large leisure component that provides a context for promoting social interaction, which, as said earlier, is frequently missing in their lives. Leisure activities can provide a therapeutic function in their own right in addition to contributing the more general qualities mentioned earlier. Leisure offers a context and vehicle for therapy and can possess curative attributes that may be useful in solving modern-day psychological, social, and environmental problems. In fact, leisure may be under-recognized for its significant socially integrating contribution to society. In addition to being useful as a tool in the social policy arsenal for counteracting social problems, leisure activities may possess qualities that rival work and the job as an avenue for providing purpose and meaning to life (Mannell & Reid, n.d.). Work has been given sole responsibility for this function in the past, but in a time of increasing unemployment, underemployment, and the fragmentation of work in the traditional workplace, meaningful activities during leisure may take on a heightened role, one that incorporates some of the psychological attributes traditionally found in work. This idea may seem counterintuitive when all of our social and economic problems are couched in economic terms, and society generally sees the way out of most, if not all, social problems through growing the economy. But the spirit of leisure can free society from the life-threatening destruction that is prevalent today through overreliance on economic growth and unsustainable resource use (see Skidelsky & Skidelsky, 2012). We now face a new world that some call 'the new normal', which requires innovative approaches to old and new social and environmental problems alike. The critical solutions to addressing sustainability of the environment in the short and long term will likely break from historical patterns and norms. What is needed now in the face of overwhelming social and environmental problems faced by modern society is a heroic leap of imagination, including the more creative use of leisure in constructing everyday life. New creative approaches to the creation of individual identity and social integration are required. For many, purpose in life will be found in nonwork and leisure activity, not in the workplace, as has been our tradition. Society will be faced sooner or later with developing and constructing a new social order—nothing remains static forever, or it perishes—and meaningful or leisure activity will need to be relied on to play a heightened role in this 'new normal'. If a culture remains static, then it is on its way to extinction. The social and psychological attributes that are found in leisure activity and a pluralistic lifestyle will need to be part of this new approach. The old tried-and-true remedies of the past will no longer effectively deal with the social and environmental problems of the new age, and innovative ideas, including an increased role for leisure in society, can be made part of a mixture of lifestyles that can be eventually incorporated into a new social contract. Because of their intrinsic value, leisure and meaningful activity, which lie outside the market economy, will play a larger role in individual and social life construction in the future than they play today. Less reliance on work and more dependence on individual social and psychological development as a major force in everyday life will have positive benefits for both social construction and environmental sustainability. Of course, a greater reliance on nonwork and leisure activity for providing meaning to life requires an altered arrangement for distributing resources among the population, but that question will be addressed in a later part of this book.

***

Earlier chapters of this book have argued that human society is in the midst of a significant social, environmental, and economic crisis, and in order to overcome these challenges, society needs to transition to a new social order, much as it did when it leaped from an agrarian way of life to the industrial society or from feudalism to mercantilism and then on to capitalism. It is my view that leisure and meaningful activity will play a heightened or perhaps central role in any new social organization strategy that attempts to address the crises that have been outlined previously. It is the purpose of this chapter to outline in brief what that role will look like and how it will benefit the human condition. Other chapters in this book (see Chapters 2 and 3) have made the case for the need for a social transformation, so this chapter will focus on the practical use of leisure in this conversion. Fundamentally, leisure may take on more responsibility for providing life satisfaction or in creating a substitute for work for some and for giving individual purpose and meaning in life for others who may continue to work. Meaningful activity and leisure, as it is conceived here, can reduce humanity's overuse of the natural resources on which the present economy and lifestyle depend. Leisure is not consumption dependent but psychologically driven for the most part. This change contains huge implications and consequences to the economy and our present lifestyle, but it does provide a path to the type of sustainability that we often talk about but don't put into practice in our day-to-day activity.

Many authors and researchers have pointed out time and again how happiness and well-being are not enhanced even marginally by increasing wealth once a minimum threshold is reached. Regardless of that fact, our present social structure continues to increase the production and availability of goods and services that business and industry claim increases our effectiveness and worth as individuals. We seem to be locked into a myth that is based, perhaps, in a previous reality but does not reflect the nature of our present actuality.

Historically, society has always considered work as the only vehicle for individuals to gain self-esteem in addition to providing a method of wealth accumulation and distribution. Industrial society has gone to great lengths to urge people to consume goods and services so that economies will grow and wealth will be created. In the face of that objective, modern society has not left the accomplishment of that goal to chance, but has created the marketing firm to artificially create need for an ever-increasing array of material goods in society. More recently we have transcended the traditional marketing instruments by the creation of the World Wide Web and the Internet. Stealth marketing mechanisms are now employed that impinge on the human psyche without awareness by those targeted. It appears that the overriding goal of commerce is not increasing human happiness, but in driving the consumption of goods higher for its own sake and for the betterment of those in control of the process. As a consequence, we find that humans are serving the economy rather than the economy serving humans. In fact, given our environmental and present and persistent social problems, the idea of the market economy as the sole mechanism for remedying those difficulties may now be more of a false consciousness than it has been historically. As you might guess, commerce through marketing is attempting to take over and control the leisure field as it has done with earlier technologies that freed humans from the time-consuming drudgeries of domestic work. It was these technologies that provided the unobligated time necessary for leisure. The same message on individual worth that was used to sell washing machines in the early part of the twentieth century is now being employed to sell leisure in all of its commercial manifestations. This is an attempt to commoditize leisure rather than leaving it as a personal, private, and social entity.

What is meant in this book when I speak of leisure is all of those activities that address the psychological and social development needs of the individual and society, not simply the extension of commercial consumerism into the leisure realm. Leisure as described and discussed in this book is seen as a self-reflective and social activity that is psychological or physical in nature and gives meaning and purpose to life. Leisure is self-defined. For some, leisure may consist of activities that I would find unpleasant and distasteful and, therefore, would not provide the psychological benefits that would constitute leisure for me. On the other hand, some of the leisure activities I engage in may appear to be purely drudgery to others. So when we define leisure, we need to think about what is taking place within the individual and not focus on the activity itself. Leisure is created for the individual by the individual and not something that is prescribed by an outside agent such as a corporation.

The ever-growing overconsumption on which our economy is built has had negative consequences to the globe's environment on which we so desperately depend for life and has created a global environment that is in jeopardy of being able to continue to support life over the long term. The capitalist economy as it is now configured has led to severe crime, pestilence, and the death of large numbers of people across the globe due to the unequal distribution of the world's resources. Many people remain in poverty in spite of the continual increase in economic growth throughout the world. It has recently been estimated that 46 percent of American citizens are receiving food stamps. McMurtry (1999) has described this situation as the cancer stage of capitalism. If humanity is to continue on this planet over the long term and in a sustainable fashion, then the present social contract, organization system, and basic *raison d'être* for life will need to change drastically, not just be altered or adjusted at the margins. Some of this transition will need to feature the ideas contained in the concept of leisure or, if you prefer, 'meaningful activity', and away from traditional notions of work and the job on which the work–spend–work cycle is constructed. Of course I can hear you asking 'How will we pay for this new order or how will people exist without earning a living?' and that is a subject to which I will turn my attention to in the next chapter.

It is clear that humans thrive psychologically on the recognition given them by their peers, community, and society. One of the human characteristics that has caused *Homo sapiens* to be as prolific and successful in comparison to other primates is their propensity for cooperation, and hence, for social recognition. The need for recognition seems to be universal, although in some societies it may be recognition of the collective rather than the individual. At present, recognition in our society is dependent on our economic success as individuals. This drive has led us to great heights in achieving the affluent society that some of us enjoy today. Economic success has become a double-edged sword, however, as we have become overly efficient at exploiting the world's resources at an ever-increasing environmental cost, including changing the climate of the planet, perhaps unalterably. We have also developed unacceptable inequality between and among the populations of the world. Unlike the other animals on the globe, we have gone beyond satisfying our basic needs and produce goods that may not be essential for increasing well-being, but are now only necessary for the structure and functioning of the economy. This way of living is now on the verge of putting into mortal danger the human race, and perhaps the planet itself. The balance between the system-world and the life-world has become severely skewed in favour of the system-world.[1]

How human society has arrived at this point is a long and complicated story. Voluminous anthropological treatises can recount the history of that journey. I will not repeat that voyage here. What may be germane to this discussion is to summarize the result of that voyage and to offer a new course in order to overcome the environmental and economic decay that has set in. Simply put, human social networks and individual recognition are tied directly to the unending drive for material accumulation and consumption for its own sake and not for utilitarian reasons. However, as John Galbraith (1984, p. 259) so eloquently put it decades ago:

> To furnish a barren room is one thing. To continue to crowd in furniture until the foundation buckles is quite another. To have failed to solve the problem of producing goods would have been to continue man (sic) in his oldest and most grievous misfortune. But to fail to see that we have solved it, and to fail to proceed thence to the next tasks would be fully as tragic.

The more we consume and accumulate, the greater status we are given by the social networks in which we circulate. Of course, a few individuals in every society achieve great recognition for their deeds, not for what they have accumulated, but they are in the minority. Here I think of Gandhi, Martin Luther King Jr., Mandela, and other such notables. But for most of us mere mortals, our path to recognition by our family, friends, and community is tied to what we can accumulate and consume over our lifetime. This is how we as a society symbolize success.

These long-held values and what they mean to social life, I argue, is why our economy is so successful at saturating the world with the vast amounts of consumer goods that appear on the shelves of commercial outlets everywhere. Commerce and consumerism is who we are and how we define ourselves. They define the essence of human life in this day and age. We have created a vast marketing industry to convince each of us how badly we need these goods and services. Shopping now is marketed as a very personal experience, where the individual can discover his or her 'true' inner self and worth as a person. As Marshall McLuhan (1967) in his epic book made clear decades ago, 'the medium is the message'. Accumulating material goods and consuming them is now a psychological experience and not one of survival, at least not physical survival. It may now be more a matter of psychological survival in the consumer society and survival of the economy than enhancing our true welfare. One's ability to accumulate material goods announces to the world who we are and our place in it.

****

Given how apparent the damage to the planet and the unequal balance of resource distribution have become to the human condition induced by the long-held values of society enunciated earlier, the question of what can replace them needs to be considered. There is no doubt that new values will need to be powerful, given how deeply ingrained accumulation and material consumption have become in our modern world. I believe the values of accomplishment and aesthetic consumption may be more utilitarian given the realities of our world today. I am not suggesting here that there needs to be a one-for-one replacement, but that a blending of these new values and the present social markers are required if we are going to alter the present course of destruction to both the planet and the social system. Ideas such as 'shop till you drop' or 'those with the most toys at the end of life wins' cannot be considered satisfying objectives over the long term, or to the maintenance of a healthy planet. The production and consumption of goods and services to satisfy the basic requirements of life will always be needed in some form and to some extent, but their pervasiveness in everyday life and the use of them to measure and give status to individuals must be replaced by new, more sustainable, and equitable social values in the continued evolution of humanity.

The ideas of achievement and aesthetic consumption are values that lend themselves well to restructuring our social organizing system. Coincidently, the objectives of leisure or meaningful activity and not commerce can provide support to this new way of life. The concept of leisure is well positioned to act as a framework for making the transition from a society that organizes itself around material consumption and accumulation to one that expands civilization beyond the need to survive to one that values individual development and accomplishment as its main social goal. Human society is entering an era where it needs to transcend to another intellectual and social plane and one that is built on a new set of values and moral imperative. I have described the coming transition as one from environmental distress and economic crisis to one that is dependent on continued intellectual and aesthetic development of the human species. This transition will conserve the basic resources of the planet and broaden human life on a more sustainable foundation.

The idea of leisure as a legitimate and significant social value around which society can be constructed is not a comfortable notion to many. Their reluctance is a result of being entrenched in the status quo, replete with numerous false consciousnesses, and any significant change in human existence is naturally resisted, particularly when the preferred alternative reduces or minimizes the role of work and commerce in the construction of society's values and myths to which most people have attached their notions of individual purpose, self-worth, and personal dignity. Work and accumulation are so pervasive in present society that they may have taken on the role of an archetype as defined by Jungian psychology. Resistance to new ideas such as those presented earlier may be an evolutionary function, particularly when biology has been the focus for evolutionary progress. But biology may no longer be in charge of our evolution, and culture may now be the paramount evolutionary mechanism for propagating the human species going forward into the future as described in an earlier chapter in this book.

Leisure in the modern world has been considered a frivolous pastime and not to be taken as a serious element in life's struggle. Leisure as conceived here is not such a frolicsome idea. It can combine the psychological and social features of work and 'the job'. Embracing the new values and attitudes of accomplishment and aesthetic consumption as mainstream goals in a new social organization system will be more life sustaining in the long run than by the present values we hold so dear. If, in fact, our human existence is unable to make a transition away from the present form of social organization that has put our environment in great jeopardy and created a huge social distance between the classes of society, then human life as we know it may be in immense peril.

***

It is interesting to note that leisure has been the focus of study by scholars as far back as the Greek civilization. Leisure as conceptualized by classical Greek society was known as Schole and in Latin as Otium. Classical Greek society valued leisure highly—it gave the privileged members of that society space to contemplate and create theories of governance, to explain the natural wonders of the world as they understood them, and to create methods and processes that were the forerunners of our present ideas about science generally and how the universe works specifically. Of course, they were able to indulge themselves in leisure because they possessed a slave class to do much of their labour, and although our society does not condone human slavery, we possess greater artificial labour power through the technology we have created than what was available to the Greeks through human bondage.

One prominent school of scholars (Farina, 1974) views leisure as a mental condition or state of being. This school of thought argues that leisure is the ultimate state of freedom. It is the freedom from the necessity of being occupied and the right to choose activity, or not, without compulsion. Many observers would suggest that it is in leisure where many of the great human accomplishments have been created. It is in leisure, arguably, where all of the great developments in society occur. Leonardo da Vinci, Einstein, and Darwin, for example, were clearly at leisure and not engaged in what we would today define as market-based labour when they were occupied in their great discovery process. Csikszentmihalyi (2014) has coined the term 'flow' to categorize this human condition. Work for many of us provides the environment for creativity at some level; however, many are engaged in jobs of drudgery and find no virtue in their labour beyond the utility of a pay cheque. Those in society who extol the virtues of 'the job' in human satisfaction are usually those engaged in elite and highly satisfying work and overestimate the satisfaction levels of work for those occupied in less creative endeavours. Leisure for many provides the time and space for life-satisfying activity. In an earlier study by Mannel and Reid (n.d.), a large sample of workers reported that escape from the realities and stresses of everyday life and friendship were the two most important states gained through leisure. Many of the participants in this study also thought that leisure could provide many of life's satisfactions, particularly those of a psychological and social nature, usually considered exclusive to the work domain. Personal competence was reported as a variable that could easily be found in leisure, as were nurturing friendships, in addition to escaping the mundane activities of everyday life.

Joseph Pieper (Pieper, 1963) sees leisure as the basis of culture. Pieper contends that leisure is a prerequisite for those incredible moments in history when human knowledge and understanding have advanced perceptively. On a more utilitarian note, Thorstein Veblen (Veblen, 1899) views leisure as a function of social class. His concept argues that each social class can be identified by their leisure pursuits. The upper class in society, he argues, engage in conspicuous consumption, which allows them to display their wealth to their peers and to the society at large. The other end of the social continuum engages mostly in less costly activity and recreation. Their activity allows them to escape the vagaries of life, at least for a short while. Veblen was writing at the end of the Victorian period when visible display of wealth was difficult not to recognize. That said, his ideas about conspicuous display may be more subtle in present-day society but are visible nonetheless.

A later-day notion of leisure is Stebbins' (1982) idea of serious leisure. Stebbins argues that many modern humans engage in leisure in the same psychological and social manner that they bond with work. For some, he argues, leisure may be even more psychologically instrumental to their life satisfaction than their work. He suggests that there are six qualities that distinguish serious from causal or unserious leisure: it occasionally necessitates the need to persevere; it often fills the role of a career; it may sometimes demand significant personal effort based on special knowledge; it may provide some durable benefit to the individual and society; it may possess a unique ethos where participants operate in their own social worlds; and its participants identify strongly with their chosen pursuit.

Stebbins' qualities in many ways are exactly those that one might expect to find when studying the psychological satisfactions and commitments found through work. Certainly these are not the usual qualities that the general public expects to absorb from their leisure. What may be different in leisure than in work is the basis on which the activity is chosen. Leisure is freely chosen and not performed out of necessity, as is often the case with work. Serious leisure may not be enjoyable at all times or without moments of toil and diligence, but can be highly satisfying over the long term and provide purpose and meaning to life. Serious leisure may also have great benefit to society, often in the form of volunteerism or through the creation of a 'work' of art. The health and fitness condition of humans is often dependent on leisure and recreation activity. Certainly social networks are created in leisure spaces. Such technologies as Facebook and Twitter are created for forging social networks, even for those seeking romantic relationships. Leisure as has been demonstrated by the Occupy and Arab Spring movements has been seen to be the forum for creating or changing democracy. Stebbins originally constructed his notion of serious leisure around the acts of volunteering, hobbies, and in being an amateur of some description. Heather Mair (Mair, 2002) has suggested an extension of Stebbins' theory by expanding his basic idea of serious leisure to include civil leisure. The notion of civil leisure is defined as

> leisure based in resistance concerned with creating public discursive space. This definition is exemplified through both the Occupy Wall Street and Arab Spring movements. This notion is important because it emphasizes the extent to which leisure might be re-constituted as a public, collective realm where discussions about society can take place.
>
> (Mair, 2002, p. 213)

Given the different ways leisure has been defined earlier, it can serve as an instrumental vehicle for actualizing the ideas of aesthetic consumption and accomplishment discussed earlier in this book.

***

The obvious question when considering leisure as a major contributor to one's life is the issue of finance. Our society has tied the distribution of resources to work. As a consequence of this relationship, and the passing on of wealth from one generation to the next (Piketty, 2014), we now have an exaggerated and imbalanced distribution of wealth and major inequality both within and among countries. It may now be time to sever, or at least modify, this long-standing relationship between work and wealth creation. In the next chapter I will outline some possible ways to construct an economy that is not so dependent on the relationship between remuneration and work. We need to transition from a work- and production-dominated existence that promotes material accumulation and consumption to a system that is built on serious leisure principles and aesthetic consumption and accomplishment. Leisure can provide the vehicle for that transition, but the question of financing that transition needs to be addressed.

During downturns in the resource-based economy in some regions in Canada, the issue of a replacement for work has been examined. On the east coast of Canada and the United States, for example, the 1980s and '90s' saw the collapse of the cod fishery. This situation presented those who worked and depended financially on the industry with two pressing problems. The first was answering the question, How am I going to feed myself and my family? This, of course, is an economic question and, for the most part, was answered at least temporarily through social policy, including some new government programs to meet this crisis. The second question was, What will I do with myself when I get out of bed tomorrow morning? This is a psychological question with regard to finding purpose in life and in constructing a lifestyle, including a sense of self-worth, that was previously found through the occupation of fishing. Leisure, particularly serious leisure, provides a reasonable response to this dilemma if social policy and social institutions in society can be organized and arrange to facilitate such a lifestyle and societal change.

It is becoming increasingly evident that there may not be enough meaningful work available in the marketplace to accommodate all who wish to work. It may be equally evident that the major goal of industry is to provide wealth to shareholders and to create employment as a secondary objective. The lack of employment was historically viewed exclusively as a developing world problem with little relevance to the affluent world. As a consequence little concern was devoted to rectifying this difficulty, outside of a few NGOs from the developed world that attempted to create small-scale local economic development schemes. Certainly some multinational large firms have moved out of the developed world to underdeveloped economies where they can exploit an unorganized and desperate labour force. The world has been witness to collapsing factories where hundreds of workers have been killed, all in the effort to keep production costs low. This situation is highly unsatisfactory in the long term and cannot be justified.

The migration of manufacturing has had an equal effect on the countries that have lost those jobs. Permanent unemployment is on the doorstep of the developed world and is not exclusively a developing nation problem. It may now receive the kind of attention that it truly deserves. Once it is determined that work and employment no longer include the positive benefit to individuals and society it once did, new alternatives for organizing the system need to be created and proposed. The act of engaging in meaningful activity or leisure—that is, divorced from financial considerations—could provide a very individually satisfying life for many people in society. Retired persons live this lifestyle, and the majority find it very satisfying. Few people on their death bed wish they had spent more time at the office or on the factory floor. Engaging in serious leisure as a life pursuit could take pressure off the economic system to produce, environmentally damaging, and perhaps non-satisfying jobs and alleviate the stress this paradigm places on society and the environment. Additionally, engaging in serious leisure could also produce great benefits to the community through the creation of social capital and community development activity generally. Leisure activities could produce highly beneficial results for humanity on a number of fronts. Even today many volunteers provide valuable service to society and the environment.

Some critics suggest that unless society controls individuals through work and uses the pay cheque as the framework for that control, society's work will not be achieved, and there may be some truth to that argument. There will always be a need for incentive-induced labour, especially over the short-term, and the market system is a mechanism to achieve that goal. I, for one, am not willing to discount the potential of robotics and artificial intelligence to replace human labour in the production process in some not too distant time period, however. But for now, some human labour will be necessary to produce the basic goods and services required by society. Some, maybe a great portion, of this labour will be done willingly by people who find meaning in the task. Leisure takes on different forms and provides dissimilar satisfactions for each of us. Gardening is a horrid task for me, but there are a huge number of people who engage in it every day out of sheer pleasure and without remuneration. Each person will find their vocation in life. As the renowned anthropologist and philosopher Joseph Campbell (Campbell, 2004) would remind us, each of us will need to find our own 'bliss' in life.

No doubt this idea takes us some distance from life's basic imperative of making and spending as much money as possible over a lifetime. A transition in lifestyle as large as the one proposed here would rely on changing our education system from a work preparation exercise to a focus on citizenship. This type of nonmarket-based lifestyle would rely on internal inspiration and organization and not be dependent on the firm or institution for motivation, organization, or control. At present we define freedom as a capitalist notion that emphasizes the freedom to gain unlimited economic resources. The new orientation would define freedom from a different perspective. In this new social organization system, freedom is defined as psychological freedom that is oriented to aesthetic appreciation and to individual and collective accomplishment. The individual is free because of internal criteria that values aesthetic consumption and accomplishment and not on external notions of accumulation and material consumption that is controlled, and controlling, by work and the work institution. In this scenario individuals are freed from the fear of absolute poverty and embark on a life that is designed to engage in meaningful activity and exploration through leisure activity that is of value to the individual and to the community in which they live.

***

The second question posed initially in this chapter, What will I do when I get out of bed the next morning?' when leaving the labour market, whether permanently or partially, has been at least somewhat answered in the discussion earlier. The answer to the first question, 'How am I going to feed myself and my family?'—the economic question—needs to be addressed. In answering this question, only the rudiments will be addressed here. Issues such as world markets will not be talked about, but are expected to operate as usual although with more equality and compassion and with a goal of providing the necessities of life rather than unlimited consumption. Fundamentally, world markets in this scenario will be operated on a basis that recognizes that people are the subject of importance and that economies are intended to support populations, not the other way around.

With regard to distributing resources to individuals, the idea of a guaranteed annual income (GAI) is proposed. This idea is not new—it has been offered by many economists, think tanks, and political parties in the past as a viable addendum to the market system, and it has been the subject of limited experimentation with great success in northern Manitoba in Canada and elsewhere. Some Scandinavian countries are flirting with this notion at the present time. In fact, Finland is implementing such a scheme as this book is being written. It is an idea that allows a plurality of lifestyles from the singular one of the work–spend–work routine we embrace today, to one where an individual is completely devoted to making a contribution to himself or herself and the community or society in which one lives through the meaningful activity or leisure model, and at the same time, not fear poverty.

The guaranteed annual income is a public scheme devoted to providing a basic income or floor through which no citizen would be allowed to fall. Society would determine the level necessary that could be considered adequate support for a person in the society in which they live. The idea of a GAI requires both an ideological/political and operational/logistical discourse. Many questions need to be answered before such a scheme could be thought credible. Although the GAI has been discussed occasionally in a peripheral manner, it has never received the kind of attention that is required in order for it to be taken seriously or be viewed as anything other than a potentially good idea. Perhaps the Finnish experiment will change the nature of that discussion. The GAI is obviously a controversial notion and one that requires great political debate before it can be considered to be at least a partial solution to our economic and environmental problems. A more detailed account of the mechanics of this potential system will be provided in the last chapter, but let's look at some of the potential political and social stumbling blocks such a system might meet.

***

As mentioned earlier in this chapter, the second and perhaps more crucial problem to be surmounted in the dilemma presented by poverty and unemployment is the ideological or political fear the GAI generates among most members of society. During interviewing people experiencing poverty in an earlier research project, we were often told by the interviewees that they were not like the other residents in their social housing project who were also experiencing poverty. They saw in their neighbours stereotypic behaviours that are often used by larger society to define people who are poor. Although they attributed the stereotypic characteristics to their neighbours, they did not see those same characteristics in themselves, but set themselves apart and viewed their neighbours with a certain amount of disdain. This short vignette illustrates the deep-seated psychological and ideological barriers and constraints that face the unemployed and poor in society. Our culture is constructed on the work value principle, and those who are nonconforming are set aside and marginalized in society. This type of stereotypic thinking will be a critical issue to be addressed when attempting to move society onto new paths that may be liberating for society, perhaps even lifesaving, but unconventional and initially frightening for the majority of people who have been indoctrinated in the capitalist system built around the fundamentals of hard work.

Although a GAI may seem logical on the surface for the reasons enunciated earlier, it usually encounters stiff resistance by society when vocalized in the political discourse. Although it may appeal to logic when coached in the proper context, as a standalone idea it often encounters great emotional and negative reaction. It is difficult for Western, perhaps all, cultures to embrace an idea that is counterintuitive to maintaining the status quo. Working and earning one's daily bread may be so ingrained in our collective unconscious that it will take considerable effort on the part of society's leaders to establish a radically different system such as a GAI as a legitimate alternative to our present singular market system. Our brains may be wired from birth to embrace work as a fundamental concept. That notion as explained in this book may no longer be the most useful idea from an environmental or social point of view, however.

Additionally, the GAI is an idea that is friendly to resolving the environmental problems society is creating, as well as freeing up individual creativity that is otherwise stifled through the limiting labour market system. It is an idea whose time has not only come, but is much needed in order for humanity to save itself from environmental catastrophe and social unrest but may not be as yet sufficiently acceptable from a political or ideological point of view to gain complete acceptance. It may take further breakdown in the environmental and social fabric before the concept will get a fair hearing and be seen as an acceptable alternative to an impending disaster. In his book *Collapse*, Jared Diamond (2005) warns us of the impending collapse of our civilization by recounting historical mistakes made by earlier cultures that could not adjust to meet their changing environmental challenges. It appears that the inability to abandon the status quo when it no longer appears useful is a major ingredient in this collapse. We may be at the same point in our history given that we are grappling with recurring problems in the environment and in the social system over and over without resolution. The adoption of new ways of distributing wealth in a more equitable and sustainable manner, such as a GAI, is much needed but is just now entering the political radar. It will take bold leadership and the right historical moment to move to a unique and innovative idea such as the GAI and greater emphasis on meaningful activity and serious leisure as a substitute for work, in the fight to save the human species on this planet.

So what is humanity to do in response to the difficult problems we face and the seemingly unorthodox ideas available to resolve them? So far, the response by politicians and social officials, including academics, has been to focus on addressing the individual problems that perplex us on the ground level. Most of this problem solving dialogue centres on growing the economy and job creation. I see this as a dead end and it will not take humanity to the next level of existence. What is needed, however, is to address not just individual environmental and social problems at the grassroots level, but to examine them at the macro system level as well. I, for one, have come to the conclusion that it is the system that needs changing if we are to make significant progress on the problems that threaten our very existence on this planet, not just stop-gap measures that kick the can down the road for future generations to solve. The final chapter attempts to provide some ideas on the required changes in society that will lead the way to a totally new social contract.

Note

1 The system world is the interpretation of world affairs and structures that reflects the interests of the corporation and government institutions. The life-world is the interpretation of the world that gives primacy to the interests of people as they live everyday life. See Guess, R. (1981). *The Idea of a Critical Theory.* London: Cambridge University Press.

References

Campbell, J. (2004). *Pathways to Bliss: Mythology and Personal Transformation* (D. Kudler, Ed.). Novato, CA: New World Library.

Csikszentmihalyi, M. (2014). *Flow and the Foundations of Positive Psychology.* Dordrecht: Springer Netherlands.

Diamond, J. (2005). *Collapse: How Societies Choose to Fail or Succeed.* New York: Penguin Books.

Farina, J. (1974). Toward a Philosophy of Leisure. In J. F. Murphy (Ed.), *Concepts of Leisure* (pp. 151–154). Upper Saddle River, NJ: Prentice Hall.

Galbraith, J. (1984). *The Affluent Society.* Boston: Houghton Mifflin.

Guess, R. (1981). *The Idea of a Critical Theory.* London: Cambridge University Press.

McLuhan, M. (1967). *The Medium Is the Message.* Toronto: University of Toronto Press.

McMurtry, J. (1999). *The Cancer Stage of Capitalism.* London: Pluto.

Mair, H. (2002). Civil Leisure: Exploring the Relationship between Leisure, Activism and Social Change. *Leisure/Loisir: Journal of the Canadian Association for Leisure Studies, 27* (3–4), 213–237.

Mannell, R. C., & Reid, D. G. (n.d.). *Changing Patterns of Work and Leisure: Perceptions of Workers in Selected Work Organizations in Six Ontario Economic Sectors.* Guelph, Ontario, Canada: School of Environmental Design and Rural Development, University of Guelph.

Pieper, J. (1963). *The Basis of Culture.* New York: Random House.

Piketty, T. (2014). *Capital in the Twenty-First Century.* Cambridge, MA: The Belknap Press of Harvard University Press.

Skidelsky, R. & Skidelsky, E. (2012). *How Much is Enough?: Money and the Good Life.* New York, NY: Penguin Books.

Stebbins, R. A. (1982). Serious Leisure: A Conceptual Statement. *Pacific Sociological Review, 25* (2), 251–272.

Veblen, T. (1899). *The Theory of the Leisure Class.* New York: Palgrave Macmillan.

12 The Way Forward
The Great Transformation

This book has been devoted thus far to critically analyzing the present social and environmental conditions that characterize today's society. It has critiqued the primacy of the market and laid bare its shortcomings in attending to the well-being of the public and recommended a foundation for building a new social contract based on an altered set of fundamental values. It stressed the importance of the social policy community as an appropriate vehicle for implementing the social change necessary to assist humanity through this next great social transformation. To complete this discussion, it is important to examine some of the possibilities for moving this project forward.

Although this book argues for a change in the macro approach to the next generation of social policies, particularly in regard to poverty, well-being, and the environment, it is recognized that human progress on the social policy front has made solid strides during the capitalist epoch. The recent Nobel Prize winner Angus Beaton (Beaton, 2013) would want us to recognize that the wellness of humans across the globe has increased greatly since the beginning of the twentieth century and even more remarkably since the end of World War Two. Life expectancy at birth is now greater than any previous generation in the developed world, if not quite yet in the developing parts of the globe. Today, surviving birth is almost assured for most women, which was not the case at the beginning of the twentieth century, although it has recently been reported in the United States that maternal mortality is greater now than it was in 1990. However, there are still too many poor and marginalized people throughout the world in spite of unprecedented economic growth and affluence. As explained earlier, we are experiencing a rapid increase in the separation between the rich and poor, and there is some evidence that the middle class is being hollowed out, particularly in America, if not in all Western nations. Collective human progress and life standards may now be reaching their potential in the modern capitalist system, so it may be time to revitalize and rejuvenate humanity's social system by rethinking the purpose of the economy and human development.

People are living longer than ever before thanks to better nutrition and medical technology. Certainly the discovery of germs and the antibiotics to cure the diseases caused by them has increased life expectancy astronomically. That is not to deny the differences in life span depending on which part of the globe one lives. The unequal distribution of resources throughout the world is accountable for much of that difference. There appears to be great inequality between the developed and developing world, even today. Perhaps more importantly, human society may be reaching the upper limit to increasing human health and well-being, relying solely on individual wealth creation and the market mechanism for those increases.

The ability to pay for better nutrition and increased access to medical care may have reached its limits of effectiveness. After all, how many doctors can you see before their advice becomes redundant? How many calories can you consume before they become detrimental to one's health and are no longer producing increased benefit? The abundance of food and affluence has produced an epidemic of obesity unseen in humanity before. If there are advances to living standards and greater longevity yet to be made, and I think there are, they will come from a different system, one that utilizes genetic knowledge and gene replacement or reconstruction rather than the present medicinal approach to life enhancement and well-being. The present approach depends on pharmaceutical companies to produce new medicines, and they do so with an eye on what is profitable and not necessarily on what is in the public interest. The new approach laid out in this book is likely to require a collective advance rather than an individual one that sees healthcare as a commodity rather than a social good. The next generation of responses to health and wellness is liable to be a collective, societal-driven event and one that is fraught with all types of ethical questions we will need to answer with an eye to what is truly in the public's, not the corporation's, interests.

Many of the recent advances in living conditions have also been detrimental to the environment. It is argued in this book, hopefully successfully, that we have reached the limits of what we can unthinkingly dump into the environment without considering the consequences. We are now at a crossroads where those 'things' we once saw as increasing our well-being are now detrimental to our very existence. We can no longer live in a throwaway society. The air, land, and water we share communally will have to account for the externalities to which they are subjected by our growth-dependent economy.

This concluding chapter is devoted to providing suggestions not only about what could be done to produce a more equitable and sustainable future, but also how society might go about doing it. Describing how society can implement the enormous, but important, changes to the social system that have been described throughout this book is no doubt daunting, but critical if humanity is to survive over the long term. It is not sufficient to provide an analysis and then leave the reader asking how and on what basis does society move toward this new vision. Providing a quasi-blueprint is no mean task, however.

I want to make it clear, it is not sufficient to simply attack the issues of poverty and climate change directly; we must also change the social system that has produced such conditions. One can argue that capitalism as practiced by our society has inevitably led to the problems we now face. As a consequence,

Klein (Klein, 2014, p. 155) reminds us when she quotes A People's Declaration from Kima Forum, in December 2009, that what is required is, 'System Change—Not Climate Change'. I would also extend this sentiment to include rectifying the poverty and inequality issue as well as addressing climate change. Klein goes on to explain this idea by quoting Miya Yoshitani, "It is the fight for a new economy, a new energy system, a new democracy, a new relationship to the planet and to each other, and food sovereignty, for indigenous rights, for human rights and dignity for all people" (p. 155). As Klein suggests when referring to the present system,

> [The] economic model is failing the vast majority of people on the planet on multiple fronts . . . Put another way, if there has ever been a moment to advance a plan to heal the planet that also heals our broken economies and our shattered communities, this is it.
>
> (p. 155)

Undoubtedly, the future will be constructed through a complex and wide-ranging process involving many citizens and groups in society, and to think we might know how it will turn out exactly is naive. In fact, no matter how much effort one would want to put toward creating the future, no single person or some imaginary invisible natural process will decide it. It will likely be a messy and highly uneven process involving many debates and skirmishes. We see that happening now with the Occupy and Arab Spring movements. The difficulty of the task should not prevent us from thinking about the values we would want embraced in any new social form that is created and from attempting to provide some thoughts on social design. There is no doubt that the future will be created by some group of people in society and hopefully with wide-ranging participation and consultation that engages the public broadly and does not just give lip service to their input. The participatory process to accomplish the task of reconstruction must have the widest representation possible from all segments of society. Given that the future society is not a predetermined path that we are marching toward, society at large, not just the elite, should be involved in its construction. The major question of who will design the future is of primary concern. Will it be created through democratic drift or by intelligent design that involves all citizens in the process? If we simply let our politicians and business leaders create the future for us, then we will certainly get more of the status quo. They seem to be locked into a certain pattern of thinking that suits them, but will not produce the type of future required to maintain life on this planet in a more equitable and sustainable way. The elites have had their chance; now it is time for collective action and change from the bottom up.

Much of the present political thinking about the future and the economy is a result of intense lobbying by business, so we know where they will want to take us. If we want a different future, one that rests on social equality and on a sustainable environment, we will need to institute a public process that does not leave decision making solely in the hands of those who hold power at the

The Way Forward   179

moment. Historic trends would suggest that the leaders of today want more of the same destructive economics we now experience and are not interested in new approaches to progressive change. Why would they, when they have taken great pains in the past to order a life that benefits them handsomely but leaves others behind? It is estimated that the average corporate CEO will make the same amount of money by noon on the first day of the year that will take the average worker the whole year to earn. This exploitation is not sustainable. A sustainable and equitable future will only result if it is based on a wide-ranging, rational, broad discussion that takes into account all aspects of life and is not simply based on economic concerns. We can no longer afford to exploit the environment and the general public as if they don't matter.

In spite of the daunting challenges presented by the size of the problems needing to be resolved, ideas to kick-start the discussion are urgently required. The future is not teleological, but constructed. The question of who might lead us in constructing that future is left open ended, and whether one is involved in helping to create the end result or is part of someone else's strategy can be determined by each of us. Whatever future is eventually reached, it will need to be based on a great leap in the collective social imagination and not simply by tinkering around the margins of the present system. Our gaze needs to be comprehensive and far reaching. It must include thinking about what type of society we want to build for the long-term. It needs to avoid the trap of simply negotiating a minimum standard of living for the most unfortunate members of society in order to stave off the threat of immediate social unrest. Social policy should graduate from establishing remedial stop-gap measures to creating innovative social development projects and be comprehensive in the grand sense. We must create a society that is socially just and mindful of the needs of all members of society and the health of the planet and not be simply dedicated to protecting the privileged among us, as seems to have been our tendency over recent history.

Individualism cannot be given sole prerogative in guiding future life. Humans are, by nature, social animals, and our continued existence depends on our collective behaviour. There is no justification for the extremes in wealth and power that exist today, no matter what false consciousness is created by those in power. So, in addition to creating an inclusive process, we need to determine the basic values on which the next iteration of society will be built. Perhaps this is the most critical first step in the process. All models of the future social system can be built around a set of fundamental values society holds dear. Articulating those values may be the first step in the process. I have offered some suggestions on that question in earlier chapters of this book, but this part of the process should not be short-circuited in order to get to potential, unwarranted solutions prematurely.

***

A number of issues need to be addressed as we move to a new social contract. These issues can be summarized as the need to break away from the consumer society and adopt a conserver society; the need to equal out the distribution of resources so that there is limited inequality enabling everyone in society to receive sufficient resources to live a comfortable life; to remove the leftover false consciousness that exists from earlier days that now inhibit rational thought about future needs; orient education toward accomplishment and away from job skill training and consumption; direct education at all levels toward collective social engagement and community participation rather than pure competition; focus on developing rational rather than emotional (ideological) thinking when addressing the big issues of society; raise the level of consideration for the environment as a primary ethic; and create new social markers for society that move away from material accumulation and consumption and toward aesthetic consumption and accomplishment.

Underpinning all of these fundamental changes is the requirement that our civilization transition from a consumer society to something more sustainable in the form of a new social contract that moves away from material consumption and accumulation and toward aesthetic consumption and accomplishment as its main social goals. Aesthetic consumption moves us away from material consumption that devours great amounts of energy in the production and distribution of goods, and takes us toward a type of consumption that is based on low energy inputs and that requires short distance distribution systems. Aesthetic consumption is directed at satisfying the individual's intellectual and aesthetic senses rather than the ego-enhancing display of wealth on which much of our present material consumption is based. Fashion for the sake of fashion is not a component of aesthetic consumption. Likewise, accomplishment is the companion motivation to aesthetic consumption. Accomplishment satisfies the need to create, regardless of the field of endeavour. Accomplishment is intellectually and socially satisfying and speaks to the inner need for purpose in life and self-actualization. And it is doubtful that capitalism, as it is now constituted and practiced, can accommodate these new social values.

Collective action, perhaps headed by an entrepreneurial government (Mazzucato, 2014), needs to facilitate establishing these new values in society, but not to exert absolute control over their construction. The makeup of this new order has to be constructed collectively after thorough, in-depth, wide-ranging public discussion—not the type of token consultation with which we are all too familiar. We need a greatly modified new form of capitalism that sees strength in cooperation and is not solely devoted to rugged individualism. Collective rationalism, not individual power, should be adopted as the framework for future development. This new type of approach will require a good slice of oversight by public bodies in order to avoid singular groups taking advantage of institutions such as the economy, and therefore re-creating the type of distorted capitalism to which we are now subjected. We have recently demonstrated that our society is willing to give up some of our freedoms for security when we are confronted by so-called threats of terrorism, and we may need to adopt some of this attitude as we confront real threats to our basic social system and the health of the planet.

In the following diagram, I have attempted to depict in the large sense a future that moves us away from a society based on consumption and accumulation to a modified and directed capitalism that is oriented to aesthetic consumption and accomplishment in order to achieve the goals of social equality and the ecological rehabilitation of the planet. It is further argued that only by moving away from an economic structure that is so dependent on consumption will we be able to address the pressing issues of poverty eradication and climate change, among other environmental and social issues that need our greatest attention.

Figure 12.1 summarizes the major components in the transition from the present capitalist structure that is solely based on an economic system of relations to a 'new social contract' that features limited inequality and environmental sustainability. I have not given a name to the new social contract simply because it is not clear at present just what values or social organizing system will describe its features best, although I have offered some possibilities throughout this book. Those characteristics will become clearer as society embarks on a consultation with itself and identifies its construction more clearly. As mentioned previously, the new system will reduce the influence of the system-world and increase the power of the life-world. The system-world will also increase the presence of the state, not necessarily as provider, but as facilitator of the nation's business and international affairs. Featured in this transition are the public instruments that are removed from economic policy and supervised through social policy. For example, the idea of social assistance or welfare has been constructed on the economic model in that it is a

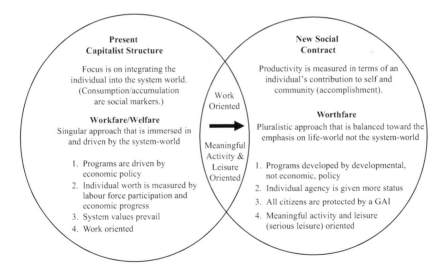

Figure 12.1 Transition from the Status Quo to a New Social Contract

Note: See Stebbins (1982) for an explanation of serious leisure.

meagre stop-gap measure meant to encourage those in the system to re-enter the labour market even when the prospects of that are dim, either because of the lack of available jobs or individual inadequacies. Worthfare[1] in the new social contract replaces the concept of welfare and is a developmental notion and meant to be a permanent part of the social fabric, along with the GAI, that lifts people permanently out of poverty and allows them to be equal participating members of society. The worth of individuals in the Worthfare policy society is no longer driven by their participation in the labour force. Individual productivity is measured by each individual's ability to be of use to themselves and the community/society in which they live. Work or one's job does not determine value in society. Each person is accepted and seen to be worthwhile because of their personal accomplishments and individual uniqueness, whether they are in or out of the labour market. Some, maybe many, will gain their sense of purpose and self-actualization through meaningful activity or in leisure. Research (Reid, 1995) suggests that many already find great meaning in life during their leisure pursuits, and work for them is simply instrumental to providing an income.

Figure 12.1 provides a quick snapshot of two very different social constructions and the basis on which each rests. The circle on the left essentially portrays the distorted capitalist system we live in at present, and the one on the right contains elements on which a different and more sustainable capitalism could be developed. Essentially the diagram suggests that society needs to move away from material consumption and accumulation, which seems to be the goal of present capitalist society, and replace these old values in the new social contract with the markers of accomplishment and aesthetic consumption. This will greatly assist humanity to address the pervasive issues of climate change and poverty because the basis on which society rests is quite different and does not rely on exploiting either people or the environment, which leads to a more egalitarian society. The goal of the new social contract is to diminish the accumulation of individual wealth and the overexploitation that pursuit produces.

One of the formidable goals of present society is to integrate the individual into what Habermas and the Frankfurt School (Guess, 1981) have described as the system-world, and the new social contract would change that focus to the life-world by giving more agency to the individual and groups in society. Also, the system-world would be rebalanced, giving more weight to governmental institutions and reducing the power of corporations in the new structure. This transition places emphasis on the welfare of each individual in society and reduces the imperative for accumulating wealth for no apparent reason other than for gaining power in the social system. An outcome of this conversion will require institutions to serve citizens rather than members of society serving social institutions, as they do at present.

The consumption and accumulation pursued in the present system by each of us are directly tied to work at the individual level, as opposed to the new social contract, which views work as only one avenue for self-expression and for gaining purpose in life. The new social contract also emphasizes meaningful nonwork and leisure activities as legitimate avenues for individual accomplishment and for constructing a sense of self-worth and dignity so vital to human existence. This change would provide more options for gaining purpose in life, which is greatly lacking for a growing number of members of our society, particularly for youth. In this scheme, individual sustenance and welfare can be gained through work or through a guaranteed annual income (GAI), or a combination of both, but the absolute dominance of work simply to accumulate as much wealth as possible is a diminishing imperative in the new social contract.

***

Whether it was hunting and gathering, as during the early years of human existence, or fragmented work in the industrial epoch, work, in some form or another, has formed the *raison d'être* of human existence down through the ages. At present, it is the vehicle on which wealth and consumption are constructed. Some would argue it is what gives essence to life. In Jungian terms, it has become an archetype, and perhaps as strong as the God or Hero archetype as defined by Jung (Jung, 1990). Work has been a strong force in all societies throughout human existence. However, the capitalist industrial system has taken it to unprecedented heights. The psychological and social meaning of work in the capitalist system cannot be overstated for its importance in giving purpose to the individual in present society. Even today those who work are revered by society and those who do not are chastised and viewed as deviant. In an individual-oriented society, one's industriousness and success in the market economy denote one's station in life. More specifically, what one is able to accumulate as a result of his or her work effort sets him or her apart from fellow members of society. This alone may spell the doom of the human species in the long term, however, as natural resources on which consumption depends become ever so scarce and will be eventually depleted unless conserved (Harari, 2014). The process of converting those resources into finished products is polluting the environment as well. It is said that the oceans are accumulating discarded plastics at an alarming rate. Plastic deteriorates at a rate based on temperature, and when those products enter the oceans, the temperature in that environment is not sufficient to continue the breakdown process.

To continue to accumulate wealth at the expense of others in the community and to drain the life from the natural environment in such a cavalier manner as we have been doing over the last century or longer will doom humanity over the long term. At present individual success is based on consuming natural resources at an unsustainable and destructive rate and without regard for the environmental damage that type of spendthrift behaviour generates. The major stratagem in the diagram promotes a transition from a work-oriented, wealth accumulation- and material consumptive–dominated society to one that focuses on meaningful activity and leisure which is oriented toward personal accomplishment and aesthetic consumption as society's predominant social values. Work in the new social contract, although necessary in order to produce the goods and services humans depend on for their everyday care, will no longer be regarded as the centrepiece of culture. Individual purpose, self-expression, and dignity will be found in many different ways than solely through the work environment.

In the pursuit of individual wealth humans have fished out the oceans, poisoned the land, and denuded vast areas of forests. This condition is a direct result of the exponential development and indiscriminant use of technology in the production process. We now fully recognize we are changing the climate of the globe. It is now difficult for slow-moving cultural change to keep up with the social and environmental transformations we are producing through the extensive overuse of technology in the production of goods and services that we may not really need. This practice will inevitably result in the imminent collapse and destruction of the world's natural resources unless we reconstruct our social value system. Humans are causing untold damage to the very environment on which we depend for life. As a result of this situation, the diagram makes the fundamental recommendation that the social values in all societies need to move from material consumption and accumulation to accomplishment and aesthetic consumption. Our ability to accumulate and consume should no longer provide the basis on which we construct our social relations, individual life purpose, and self-esteem. As this consumptive philosophy of life plays itself out, it will become increasingly seen as antisocial. The proposed transformation in the *raison d'être* of society will be accompanied by a more equal sharing of the remaining resources on this planet. In this scenario, work that is so damaging to the environment must give way to more mindful and human-enhancing forms of activity, which can be found in the concepts of meaningful activity and serious leisure as defined by Stebbins (Stebbins, 1982) and as indicated in the diagram. Work in the new social contract is devoted to satisfying the needs of humanity, but in a reduced and more responsible form. Present institutions such as 'marketing' that creates imperatives out of unnecessary wants will need to be moderated or extinguished altogether. The fundamental alteration in social values as suggested in this book would go a great distance in dealing with the social and environmental ills that plague present and future society. This change carries with it the introduction of a guaranteed income to combat poverty and introduces a method for distributing resources on a more equal basis. It would also make the physical and psychological need to work in the marketplace less imperative, and therefore, less destructive to the environment.

***

It has been argued earlier in this book that distributing resources to people solely through the market economy is no longer efficient or effective and is blocking the advancement of society in moving to the optimal next stage of appropriate human development. What we see clearly in the social organizing system of today is that the market itself has become sacrosanct, not the welfare of the general public to which it should be subservient. Society has lost its understanding of what the economic system was intended to accomplish, and its original purpose has become drastically distorted. Andrew Ross Sorkin (2010) in his book, *Too Big to Fail*, relates a story that chronicles the machinations inside the firms of Wall Street during the 2008 financial meltdown when he tells us that Secretary of the Treasury Hank Paulson knew that Wall Street's leverage problem could not end well. He also knew that firms would never rein themselves in; they were blindly chasing one another. He always reminded himself of a remarkably telling question that Charles Prince, the CEO of Citigroup, had asked him the year before: "Isn't there something you can do to order us not to take all of these risks?" (Sorkin, 2010, pp. 12–13). It is clear from this anecdote that those in charge of the huge financial firms on Wall Street and elsewhere throughout the world cannot help themselves; they are addicted to increasing profits for their shareholders and their firms, regardless of the consequences. They are playing a game of trying to outdo each other and don't understand, or don't care, that they have the fate of all society and the planet itself in their hands. If there ever were any notions of responsibility on the part of the captains of industry and finance for social responsibility and planetary welfare, it has been lost. This state of affairs indicates that there is need for alternative ways to distribute society's basic resources in addition to, or perhaps in place of, the market that takes us out of this gambling mentality of Wall Street and the other financial centres throughout the world. Perhaps one of the ways to take pressure off the 'growth at all costs' mentality is the introduction of a GAI in addition to government regulations that outlaw many of these antisocial practices. The problem is that under present circumstances big business and banks have too much power in the corridors of government for this toxic situation to change. Regulations will need to be put in place to regulate the relations between government and business.

***

The GAI has been discussed in a number of advanced countries over many decades. Finland is now implementing such as system as this book is being written. Economists, social commentators, and pundits agree that, conceptually, it is an idea whose time has come. However, these same economists, pundits, and social commentators do not agree on the best mechanism by which such a scheme could be implemented. Further, there is some skepticism that such a system could be paid for without raising taxes. Others feel quite strongly that the present social welfare budget and other government programs, including some business subsidies, could provide for a generous GAI if it were collapsed into a single reservoir of funds. These issues give the reader some feeling for the technical problems to be overcome before such a scheme could be adopted, but there is no doubt that some version of the idea is feasible if there was sufficient political will to first create and then engage such a system. Certainly, the general attitude in society that holds that individuals who do not earn their living in the marketplace are, at best, somewhat less than productive members of society, even free riders, needs to be addressed. Perhaps first and foremost, society will need to redefine what it means to be a productive citizen. A definition that goes beyond simply defining productivity as solely the result of earning a living through the market mechanism is required. Productivity would need to be redefined on a much broader basis than it is at present and embrace concepts that include all activities that add to one's sense of purpose and self-worth and contributes to society's well-being. The concept of Worthfare discussed earlier provides a suggestion for how the new social contract could define productivity.

The idea of a GAI is to set a minimum floor through which no citizen is allowed to fall. Those who earn the amount set as the floor or do better through the market economy would not receive any payment by way of public expenditure. Those who earn a little would receive the difference between what they earn and the designated amount set as the GAI. Those who earn no income through the market mechanism would be fully compensated to the set level guaranteed in the GAI. As long as the floor is set at an appropriate level, this system not only addresses the income part of the poverty issue, but could go some distance in dealing with the environmental concerns described throughout this book. This scheme would allow people to opt out of the market economy and accomplish satisfactions through other forms of meaningful activity that are satisfying to themselves, of importance to the human community, and nondestructive to the environment. In spite of the positives of this scheme in dealing with the poverty issue, the GAI system does not address the problem of unacceptable inequality and the distorted compensation that some at the top end of the remuneration spectrum receive and where a few individuals take exorbitant amounts of wealth and resources out of the system at the expense of the majority of the population. Certainly setting income tax rates higher at the upper end of the income scale would be one method for dealing with this problem. But the problem may be more complicated than an increase in taxation will address, so this matter will be revisited throughout the rest of this chapter.

Let's address the logistical and operational issues that need to be dealt with in order to establish the factors inherent in such a scheme as the GAI in the new social contract. The first question that comes to mind when this idea is proposed is, Can our society afford such a scheme? In societies that have not been adequately providing for their poor, historically, the answer is likely no, at least on first glimpse. Those countries will need to undertake a more fundamental debate and determine the amount of inequality they are willing to endure and at what level they are willing to support their poor. This discussion should also include the consequences to society for not establishing an adequate level of support if that should be the outcome of the debate.

For those countries that do support their poor in some fashion already and provide subsidies through tax policy to the less fortunate, the answer to the question is likely yes. It becomes a matter of arranging the resources that are already dedicated to social programs and other sector subsidies in a manner that focuses solely on poverty eradication and on supporting a lifestyle that embraces the ideas of aesthetic consumption and accomplishment. In most developed countries, governments provide social assistance, food assistance (in the United States known as food stamps), disability payments, pensions, and, in Canada, equalization payments to the poorer regions of the country. In addition to direct payments to those in need, governments in most countries of the West provide subsidies to agricultural producers, including family farms and large industrial agriculture companies, and to a variety of other producers such as oil companies, one of the main contributors to climate change. It is estimated that governments across the globe are providing $450 billion in subsidies to oil companies for the exploration and production of oil and gas. This comes at a time when most governments are trying to wean their economies off carbon-based energy. A GAI would also require less bureaucracy, which would save huge amounts of money that could be made part of the GAI budget. When all of these programs, including oil subsidies, are collapsed into a single pool, there is an adequate amount of capital to provide a generous GAI to those who would want to avail themselves of such a system. Qualification for receiving the GAI and what constitutes generous is also a matter to be determined in the political arena.

What might form the rudiments for administering such a system? I prefer the negative income tax model. That is, governments guarantee a certain amount of annual income to all citizens regardless of how that income is constructed. Let's, for the sake of discussion, set the income level at $25K. This is the level at which no one in society is allowed to drop below. Those earning more than that amount in the market economy would receive nothing from the program but would, of course, contribute to it by paying income and other forms of tax. Those who earn nothing would receive the full $25K. Those who make some money but not $25K would be provided the difference between what they earn and the set floor of $25K.

Not a realistic proposition you say? In addition to Finland cited earlier, this has been tried as an experiment successfully in one Canadian small community in Manitoba called Dauphin with a population of 8,251 people. The headline in the Huffington Post on 12/23/2014 "A Canadian City Once Eliminated Poverty and Nearly Everyone Forgot About It" says it all. This article reviews an experiment to implement a GAI of $10,000 (a reasonable amount of money at that time) over a five-year period from 1974 to 1979 to see what would happen. All reports at the time, including the Huffington Post article cited, were very positive, as the headline would suggest. What happened to it, and why has everyone forgotten about it? The only reasonable explanation to that question would be that it is not politically acceptable in a capitalist economy because it defies the inherent tenets of the capitalist system as currently conceived. So it has been conveniently forgotten about, except for a few people who are committed to encouraging a society without poverty who continue to talk about it and hold it up as a positive example of what can be done.

I can hear the critics already; it would go something like this. Those who earned less than the proposed $25K mark would not bother to work at all and receive the whole $25K from government coffers rather than from their own effort. There can be incentives to encourage engagement in positive types of services and activities needed by society in order to qualify for this benefit for those who are overly concerned with the emotional issue of free riding. As for me, I am not concerned at all with this seeming problem, given that advanced society is not likely to reduce the present unemployment rate much over the short or long term as it now stands, so it might be a moot point. We seem to be in a situation where our governments are artificially trying to create jobs in order to distribute money rather than letting jobs create themselves because society needs that particular task done. It seems that what was once the goal of producing goods and services required by society has now become the means to achieving some other end such as personal income, and not a very efficient vehicle for realizing that aim at that. Perhaps a better alternative is to support people with a basic social wage and allow them to creatively contribute to society using their own ingenuity and in their own fashion. This moves control of the individual from an outside agent, such as the corporation (or in earlier times the landlord or church), to the individual. This transition will provide a new meaning to the concept of freedom.

Encouraging people to be of use to themselves and the community in which they live can be a requirement for gaining access to the GAI, and those activities can be determined by the participant in the program and reviewed if necessary by some quasi-judicial body. I dare say that some very creative and helpful activities would result from such a requirement. The second concern would be affordability, but I have answered that critique a certain amount already when I spoke about collapsing present government programs into a pool of capital and devoting those funds to a GAI. For some, the issue remains how we can engage in a program such as the GAI and continue to reduce taxes. My answer to that concern is that we have already reduced taxes too much in order to run an ineffective public enterprise and an inequitable economic system. Most pundits and social critics are concerned with the present public debt and want to cut social policy and programs in order to eliminate government deficits and eventually abolish the debt. This continual focus on tax reduction and laissez-faire capitalism will only produce more inequality and environmental catastrophe if we continue along this path. So, from my point of view, this attitude of cutting taxes at any social cost is no longer morally supportable.

There is also the notion that raising taxes will reduce the number of jobs in the economy. The view of classical economic theory that there is a corresponding decline in market activity for every dollar raised in tax has never been proven. In fact, some administrations have increased both taxes and economic activity at the same time in the United States and elsewhere, which suggests the opposite of the conventional wisdom is true. This provides more evidence of the false consciousness syndrome described in an earlier chapter. Regardless of that argument, with the institution of a GAI, the pressure is off government to create jobs. Jobs are no longer the sole mechanism for income distribution, which would go a long way to solving the environmental crisis we now face.

There are those who argue that governments appear to be insolvent. This may be a result of too much tax slashing even as the nation's private wealth is increasing at the same time. I have chronicled in other parts of this book where those at the top end of the income ladder have benefited handsomely from these tax cuts and other public policies initiated by governments, and the burden for producing tax revenues for present social policy has been placed on those at the middle and lower end of the income ladder. In a society that engages in such equality-producing initiatives as a GAI, the objective of that society is to lift up all people in society and not just the rich among us. 'Lift up' is defined here as providing sufficient resources to those at the lower end of the income scale so they can live an adequate life and not simply engage in idle talk and rhetoric about all people being lifted by a rising economy through the trickledown effect of the market. We have lived through that scenario before and we should not to be fooled again.

***

In addition to the mere survival of the marginalized among us, society must be concerned with the notion of equality and justice for all (which includes the idea of limited inequality) and develop a social system that arranges more fairly the distribution of resources among the population and provides a purpose in life and one worth living for all members of society. We need a social transition as profound as when society leaped from hunting and gathering to an agriculture-based civilization. Politicians, and society in general, rhetorically talk about justice and equality for all, but little progress has been made in spite of all the talk. It is now time to get serious about making monumental changes to the system if we are to truly construct a civilization that will be sustainable into the future rather than just giving lip service to it.

The notion of poverty is an antiquated term and negative in connotation and needs to be replaced with a positive expression that indicates our condition as a species. There will be no need for such a word as poverty when the condition no longer exists. That said, the word and connotation poverty congers is needed to give politicians and general society a concept that describes the dire consequences for those experiencing it, but when the condition is eliminated the notion of well-being will better describe the mission of social policy. We must not let politicians and society off the hook at present, however, by using more benign words such as well-being until the condition of poverty has been eradicated completely. Then and only then can we think of social policy in terms of focusing solely on well-being and social development rather than on the remedial action social policy must be geared to at present. The concept of well-being also embraces highly developed states of health, democracy, and education, in addition to truly eliminating financial poverty, and that, too, needs to be a focus for society in the new social contract.

***

This book urges society to reduce the strength of the motivations for accumulation and material consumption as the major social values that defines one's success in society at present and replace them with aesthetic consumption and accomplishment as the new mechanism for social relations. Not only will this speak to environmental issues by reducing unneeded consumption, but also the basis on which meaningful activity will be pursued by individuals and society collectively in the future. Future human society will be better served by rewarding accomplishment rather than simply engaging in a system that 'beggars thy neighbour' in an attempt to accumulate as much wealth as one can.

As indicated in Chapter 6, this book advocates the adaption of social well-being indicators to replace measures such as the GDP as the touchstone for judging the condition of the social life we live. And, although descriptions of the GDP and concepts of well-being were introduced in that chapter, there is need for greater explanation of their nuances, given their importance to the new social contract.

Many schemes in the literature today present the idea of well-being as an alternative to the GDP measure. I argued earlier in Chapter 6 that the GDP is a false consciousness as a complete measure of how each member of society is faring, so a new or additional measure is required to determine more accurately how all people in society are doing; that is, whether or not they are becoming better off in terms of their quality of life and well-being as the years progress. Such a measure can be found in the Canadian Index of Wellbeing (CIW). This measurement includes education, democratic engagement, community vitality, healthy populations, environment, time use, leisure and culture, and living standards (for a further explanation of the variables that constitute each of these areas, see the CIW web page) as important indicators of well-being. In this and similar schemes, notions of well-being are based on a fundamental principle:

> It begins with the belief that the cornerstone value as Canadians is the principle of shared destiny—that our society is often best shaped through collective action; that there is a limit to how much can be achieved by individuals acting alone; that the sum of a good society and what it can achieve is greater than the remarkably diverse parts which constitute it.
> (Canadian Index of Wellbeing, 2009, p. 5)

The 2011 CIW report (Canadian Index of Wellbeing, 2011, p. 1) begins by making the comment that

> When we ask our friends, how are you doing? we certainly do not expect the answer, my economic outputs are up. We want to know if our friends

are doing well, if they are healthy, how their families are doing, if they have jobs that cover the bills, if they have seen a good movie recently, or have been out with friends.

This is a convincing argument to the advantage of using a composite measure rather than a singular focus such as the GDP. It is quite certain that the GDP has value as a gross measure to make comparisons of one country's economic activity with another. It is constructed, however, as a single focus that can be misleading when used as a solitary gauge for measuring the quality of individual and social functioning. The multiple indices used to construct the CIW composite measure provide a much more comprehensive look at what contributes to a satisfying life than does the single, albeit important, measure of economic activity. Each of the domains, as the CIW refers to them, includes a number of indicators that comprise each area, and none of these sectors depend solely on a single indicator. For example, the living standards domain in the CIW includes after-tax median income, income distribution (ratio of top to bottom quintile), incidence of low income (LICO), CSLS Economic Security Index, long-term unemployment, employment rate, CIBC Employment Quality Index, housing affordability, wealth distribution, persistence of low income, and food security. Bringing these measures together into a composite score provides a broader picture of the economic health of individuals and the society in which they live than does the GDP. Each of the domains in the CIW includes several variables that collectively provide a deep and wide definition of that domain. And when all of the domains are included in a composite score, a more robust and sound picture of individual and social health is presented beyond a single variable score such as the GDP. We must broaden our notion of what constitutes a healthy society beyond the GDP measure to a gauge such as the CIW or some other comprehensive estimate that includes the varied indices that reflect the values and aspirations of that society.

***

The discussion here has laid out the barest of policy changes that are needed by society if we are to transition from a society that favours indiscriminant exploitation of the globe's natural resources and the potential environmental disaster that activity will inevitably produce, and the astronomical inequality that exists in the present system, which unavoidably leads to crushing poverty. The question of how society moves forward on this agenda needs to be addressed. In addition to the concrete policies suggested earlier, a process will need to be put in place that can provide a plan for moving forward toward the goal of building a new social contract. This process must provide a forum for carrying out wide-ranging discussion and an opportunity for educating the public, including our officials, about the impending disaster humanity faces and the need for the considerable social reform, including complete system reform. The idea put forth by the social learning model of development can provide the framework for moving forward.

Social learning is defined and described by (Friedmann, 1987, p. 81) as

> knowledge derived from experience and validated in practice, and therefore it is integrally part of action. Knowledge, in this view, emerges from an ongoing dialectical process in which the main emphasis is on new practical undertakings: existing understanding (theory) is enriched with lessons drawn from experience, and the 'new' understandings then applied in the continuing process of action and change.

Taplin and Clarke's paper (Taplin & Clarke, 2012) on the theory of change amplifies Friedmann's basic notion of social learning.

In the 'Theory of change', Taplin and Clarke (Taplin & Clarke, 2012, p. 1) state that "Theory of change is a rigorous yet participatory process whereby groups and stakeholders in a planning process articulate their long-term goals and identify the conditions they believe have to unfold for those goals to be met". They lay out a highly participatory and straightforward planning model for implementing and stimulating social change. The change model is intended for a small group or community-level intervention. Needless to say, applying such a well-accepted method for engendering change at a national or international level would be a larger and more complex task, but with great care and diligence, their ideas regarding change theory could prove very useful in providing a framework for implementing Friedmann's notions of social learning. One might consider the cascade model of development that requires discussion to begin at the smallest levels of society and continue up the size scale by repeating the process over and over again at all levels and stages. This model of implementation would require feedback up the system and down again continuously throughout the process.

The first and most basic outcome of social learning must be to diminish false consciousness that has formed our values and motivations historically and then build a realistic understanding of the present needs of society and the requirements of the individuals that live in it. Future human needs would also need to be constructed within the physical limitations and confines of the planet and its systems. The goal of this exercise is to create a new social order, one that is more sensitive to individual and social needs and planetary requirements. This can be accomplished through direct intervention in the social system with the intent of providing a more realistic reflection on the social and economic needs of all citizens, rather than the aggrandizement of the few. In Habermasian terms, social learning attempts to decrease or rebalance the system-world, which has dominated social values, in favour of the life-world,[2] which focuses on the basic needs of maintaining human, and perhaps, all life on the planet.

***

The transition to a new order that reflects the thoughts contained in this volume may require some form of world government as described by Redner

(Redner, 2013) in his book titled *Beyond Civilization*. The ultimate creation of a new social, and perhaps international, political order remains a political decision, and part of the process leading up to that decision needs to be the engagement and implementation of a society-wide discussion with the purpose of creating the framework on which the new international social order could be fashioned. Some present nations such as the United States are likely to balk at the notion of giving over any sovereignty to an international body, let alone embrace the idea of some form of global government. The problem at the moment is that we are partially there and running into trouble—not because too much responsibility has been passed to international bodies, but because we have not given them enough mandate or responsibility. The major private companies across the globe are multinational corporations who for all intents and purposes provide a form of world corporate government. Perhaps they can provide some encouragement with regard to the success of reaching beyond established political borders in this new age.

At the time of this writing, Greece is undergoing a financial breakdown in its banks and fiscal system as a result of their unsustainable debt. Under the nation-state organizing system, the way out of this dilemma for Greece is to devalue their currency. Given that they share the Euro with other European nation-states, they have lost control of their own monetary policy, so they cannot use this mechanism for debt reduction. What levers they have left to them to address this problem remains through austerity measures and, as we have seen, this approach has not been successful, but has actually put them further behind. Each nation in the European Union (EU) maintains sovereignty over its fiscal policy, but some smaller countries in the EU have accumulated such debt that fiscal policy is now ineffective to deal with the issue. If the European Union had both monetary and fiscal policy available to them, they might have the necessary instruments to address this crisis and other fiscal concerns more effectively. We have in effect globalized the economic system, but have not done the same with the governance structure to any extent. This deficiency presents a huge barrier in moving forward to create an integrated system that is appropriate for dealing with many social problems, including our antiquated economic structure, and the environment.

Any effort to rectify the present condition will need to address false consciousness that emphasizes the uniqueness and, perhaps, the feelings of superiority of one country over another. For example, the idea that the United States is the best country in the world is contested, yet that notion is still part of the world's false consciousness. Although it does lead in some areas such as military strength and financial accumulation, it does not compare well to other countries when it comes to the eradication of social problems or in developing social cohesion and solidarity. In fact, it is woefully down the scale on most social measures and indices that are produced by reputable independent research bodies. The historically positive role for nationalism is diminishing in the face of the present and future problems facing the globe. In the final analysis, resolving the issues of poverty and climate change will depend on cooperative, coordinated action at the world level and not on individual country power in isolation to others. No individual country can on its own protect itself against climate change. Only through cooperative effort and the dedication of all countries in the world can CO_2 emissions be reduced and the world's climate brought into homeostasis. So a new social order must look to revamping the present international organizations that exist and give them a renewed mandate to address some of the problems outlined earlier that will determine the fate of humanity on this planet and that remain irresolvable by individual nation-states acting alone.

If such international organizations, such as the United Nations, World Bank, and International Monetary Fund,[3] were mandated to take on this heightened role, this arrangement would be contingent on all countries engaging in cooperation and in developing agreed-upon solutions that would meet a set of fundamental requirements. Each country may undertake a unique approach to meeting these requirements, but meeting them is necessary for gaining or continuing membership in the international community. Issues such as setting parameters for limited inequality and establishing a global mechanism, perhaps a restructured version of the market system for resource distribution, could replace the dysfunctional international markets that exist today. The international organization created or designated to provide such a coordinating function would need to be given taxing or fining powers in order to orchestrate a more egalitarian world order. For example, take the myriad number of professional sports leagues that exist throughout the world that attempt some form of parity among the teams. Many of them have instituted a salary cap and luxury tax. Under this scheme, once a team exceeds the salary limit set by the league, it is fined by the governing body based on how much they have exceeded that limit. It is possible to establish an inequality limit to which all countries agree and then those that exceed that limit would be subject to a tax which would then be redistributed to those countries at the bottom of the scale, much like the GAI at the individual level. This principle would also need to be incorporated by member countries in order to address the inequality issue, which creates an enormous gap between the rich and the poor that is increasing at an accelerating rate. This approach to addressing inequality could have great positive effect in reducing the extreme income separation that exists throughout the globe and in redressing the poverty issue that appears so entrenched within countries. It would also change the perspective of the economy, making it less rewarding for someone to exploit the natural resource base in an unrestrained manner as it is being done at present. This system or a facsimile of it has the potential to bring the economic system and environment back into equilibrium. Although these initiatives may seem drastic, humanity is at a point in history where a transition of this magnitude is required to bring human made devastation back from the brink.

Other authors such as Piketty (Piketty, 2014) have provided different schemes to achieve similar results. Piketty favours progressive taxes. This would not only include a progressive income tax but also a progressive tax on capital and inheritance. Piketty's proposed progressive tax would amount to almost 100 percent on what he considers to be exorbitant sums of money, those earned by the top 1 percent and less as one works down the wealth scale. His suggestion is sound in terms of redressing inequality and subsequently poverty, but even Piketty realizes that there would be great opposition to his proposal. In fact, there would be great opposition to any proposal, including the one I presented earlier, by those in power who have the most to lose. Regardless of this natural opposition, if the world leaders are serious about combating climate change and poverty, measures this drastic would need to be adopted and put in place.

It is clear Piketty's proposal of a progressive tax on income as well as on capital and inheritance would go a long way in solving the problem both he and I are concerned about. I believe my proposal for dealing with inequality by enacting a scheme like the various professional sports leagues have adopted in terms of a salary cap and subsequent luxury tax has a greater chance of success, however. I say this for one single reason: it requires implementation and oversight at the national level rather than giving it over to an international body in the first instance—an uploading that many would find unpalatable at the very least. Certainly the international community would have an oversight role to play by monitoring each country to make sure all nations were following the same rules, but the mechanism for enacting the scheme is best left as local as possible. Nation-states would be charged with introducing and collecting the appropriate tax in the first instance, which would make the scheme more palatable to most societies. Also, Piketty's progressive tax does nothing for reducing inequality between and among nations but solely focuses on redistributing financial resources within a nation state.

It is recognized that the international institutions that exist at present are inadequate to meet this challenge. Those mentioned earlier such as the World Bank and IMF have potential for reconstruction to suit this increased responsibility, but the renovations required are beyond the scope of this book and will need to be addressed elsewhere. Let me just say that if this scheme were to be adopted, then organizational renovation of these institutions would need to be considerable or new institutions created that could adapt more quickly to the job.

The legitimacy of the institutions named earlier would need to be enhanced dramatically for this scheme to work. All the countries of the world, including the most powerful ones, would need to move closer to the acceptance of a world cooperative structure through these institutions than they appear willing to do at present. In fact, there could be a two-tier governance structure where monetary and fiscal policy are given over to the first tier and all other policies that affect individual cultures left at the country tier. Such entities as the form of democracy and justice for individual countries would be left at the country tier. There would need to be meaningful penalties or sanctions put in place for nonparticipation or noncompliance to collectively made decisions. This would mark an extreme departure for some countries such as the United

States. At present, many powerful politicians and lobbyists in America possess great disdain for these types of international institutions, or for any form of government intervention beyond the barest minimum, for that matter. There must be no mistake about it: many of those in power across the globe see such institutions restraining their activities and position of power in society and will resist such ideas with great vigor. But this resistance is what has us perpetuating, and unable to solve, the problems outlined earlier in this book. Until we do something dramatic, these problems will not get resolved and we will be taken closer to the brink of disaster as time goes on.

We are witness today to a titanic struggle between opposing ideological forces. The right side of the spectrum is symbolized by the Tea Party in America. Their view of the world is one where governments are given a diminished role in society, and they would certainly not want to consider any type of internationally shared governance system. They believe in individual freedom and responsibility and disdain any notion of collective action by governments. It is this ideological view that is taking us down the destructive path that we are on, however. This view not only permeates the economic realm, but predominates in many other aspects of life as well. For example, it is this view that believes the right to bear arms takes priority over public health and safety. They also believe individuals need to arm themselves in order to reduce gun violence, a conclusion that escapes me and is inscrutable to much of the population around the world. They see increasing gun ownership as the only possible measure for decreasing the mass shootings so prevalent today. At the very least this demonstrates a lack of creativity in dealing with a huge problem in society. This view will try desperately to create a false consciousness around the ideas laid out here, but which will be better understood by the more progressive side of the political spectrum. Regardless of the looming battle over these ideas, a social learning process must proceed to put these and other ideas on the table for discussion. We must not allow those who yell the loudest to intimidate the rest. Rationality must prevail in the end if we are to enhance environmental and social functioning.

There are plenty of attempts at present to start this type of social learning process. Witness the so-called Occupy movement. This movement could be considered the beginning of such a dialogue as envisaged in this book. Many felt the Occupy movement to be weak because of its reluctance to outline a tangible set of demands, or as many pundits observed, outline 'what they wanted'. What many observers and critics failed to understand was that the goal of this movement was not to achieve tangible policy change immediately, but to start a dialogue on the kind of society members of the collective want to eventually achieve. What it wanted was for society as a whole to address the inequality issue and the pending environmental disasters faced by humanity and not propose solutions prematurely and designed by the few. That approach would have been to repeat the mistakes they were protesting against. They felt, and rightly so, that it was too early in the process to be offering solutions to unclearly defined problems. What the Occupy movement wanted was to begin a dialogue about the future, based on what has been described as an unsatisfying and unworkable present condition, and to engage as many people as wanted to be involved in that discussion. Western society, and perhaps all human societies, have become accustomed to demands that are concrete in form and lead to direct policy changes, but that was not the modus operandi of the Occupy movement. The Occupy movement is dedicated to encouraging or providing a forum for dialogue so that all members of society, if they so desire, can actively participate in creating their collective future, one that is suited to achieving their needs and not just in rewarding those with means and power with more means and power.

This brings us to the conclusion of this text. So far the main body of the book has analyzed and critiqued the state of the present environmental and social situation at the global level. This critique has come to the conclusion that the environment and people of the globe have been exploited in order for certain segments of the population to live at a very high level as the majority squeaks by. The system that promotes indiscriminant wealth creation has also caused severe environmental problems. Because of the inequity this system has produced, the very process of it can no longer be tolerated or absorbed by the environment and a new foundation for ordering society must be constructed. This construction must be built around the values of aesthetic consumption and accomplishment rather than, as it has been historically, through material consumption and accumulation.

Chapter 3 explained how society through false consciousness has been perpetuated in the social fabric from which it now needs to be extricated. This chapter has offered a path that society could pursue to rescue itself from the impending social and environmental disaster if it so wishes. There could be many other future scenarios in addition to the one presented in this book that society may chose after long and careful deliberation. This book has presented what needs to change and what that change might look like in the large sense. What is left unsaid until now is how the transition of society might be brought about. This is no easy task and it is filled with potential stumbling blocks and divergent end points but an important contemplation nonetheless.

***

First it must be admitted that a transition of this magnitude will be a long and tortuous process. It will take the commitment and education of most citizens around the globe who come to understand what is at stake for humans and all other species. In fact, this collective awakening is likely to be the first task. This mission is liable to take a generation or more to complete, and there is no guarantee that amount of time is left before the environmental and social system collapses. It has already been stated that the planet is hotter now than at any time in its history, and the only question remaining is what action can be taken to stop that upward trend.

There is no doubt that the transition spoken about throughout this book will need involvement from both the top and bottom of the social structure. The top can provide a champion or group of champions that see the potential calamity the world faces and have a willingness and the courage to do something about it. Their role will be one of funding and lending their credibility to the project. Dedicated funding is needed for the concentrated and passionate groundwork required in order to educate the public about the present and future reality and to overcome the false consciousness that has been built up by the system-world and its agents for at least the last half century or more. For this project to be successful it will need to create a force as powerful as what has become known as Madison Avenue, the advertising agents for the capitalist system and the primary creator and purveyor of the false consciousness that pervades society today. Such forces continue to be perpetuated but, unfortunately, to spew an unworkable mythology and false consciousness. Entities such as the 'Americans for Prosperity' and other libertarian institutions want more unregulated use of the natural resource base and a heightened individualistic society, requiring less government, and will continue to work for that end (see, Mayer, 2016). In opposition, the scientific community continues to provide evidence of the destruction that outlook is creating. Many individual large donors continue to fund these institutions and what is being suggested here is the creation of champions on this scale, to combat these forces and created a new dialogue on social and environmental change.

This campaign needs to engage informal education processes at the grassroots level to build a committed population to reverse present thinking, and to create an apparatus that will shepherd in a new future that is created collectively and in society's best interests. This future will feature the life-world and bring the system-world back into proper balance with it. These types of informal education campaigns have been created and used to emancipate populations in the past. Here I think of The Cody Institute of eastern Canada in the 1960s and '70s that helped company town employees emancipate themselves from the complete domination of the company. This type of experience can provide a model on which a campaign can be created although the scale is so much different. These small-scale community interventions and social organizing institutions can be used to create a larger force to undertake the social transformation discussed throughout the pages of this book. As mentioned previously, a recent example is the Occupy movement, which may have sputtered but was on the correct path. This grassroots movement sprung up spontaneously and without any foundational support, and once support is provided this type of action has the potential to produce solid results.

This is a huge undertaking and will require great effort and considerable time to achieve, let there be no doubt about it. Given the pending environmental disaster before us and the present state of social conditions in most societies across the globe, such actions as the Occupy movement have a great role to play as the future unfolds. That said, no movement on its own and without wide-ranging popular support will gain enough strength to take us into the new sustainable and egalitarian society that we all desire. In the end all citizens will need to participate in creating the conditions they believe will lead to a sustainable planet and healthy social system.

Notes

1 A Worthfare (developmental policy) approach would take us forward to a holistic conceptualization of the individual with unique and distinct needs and abilities that are directly related to the capacity of that individual to be of value to themselves and the community in which they live. This would become the new definition of productivity. The Worthfare model includes a guaranteed annual income (Reid, 1995) as the method of tackling the poverty issue. As conceived here, the Worthfare model recognizes that all individuals will not find a place in the market economy, but that through nonwork and leisure activity each can make a contribution to themselves and their community that will, in the long run, be of great value to them personally and benefit society generally. What may be needed most to make this approach work is some encouragement and social engagement skills in the form of poverty reduction and lifelong learning. The goal of this model for development rests on the vision of establishing a personal sense of self-worth and dignity through poverty reduction and engagement in community activity and service, and not solely dependent on entry into the market economy as ultimately desirable as some may want that to be. Reid and Golden (2005).
2 See Guess, R. (1981). *The Idea of a Critical Theory: Habermas and the Frankfurt School.* London: Cambridge University Press, for a treatise on Habermas's notion of life-world and system-world.
3 It is understood that the present international organizations would need considerable reconstruction if they were to take on such a task as described here.

References

Beaton, A. (2013). *The Great Escape: Health, Wealth, and the Origins of Inequality.* Princeton, NJ: Princeton University Press.

Canadian Index of Wellbeing. (2009). *How Are Canadians Really Doing: The Report of the Index of Wellbeing.* Waterloo, Ontario, Canada: Canadian Index of Wellbeing.

Canadian Index of Wellbeing. (2011). *How Are Canadians Really Doing? Highlights: Canadian Index of Wellbeing 1.0.* Waterloo, Ontario, Canada: Canadian Index of Wellbeing and the University of Waterloo.

Friedmann, J. (1987). *Planning in the Public Domain: From Knowledge to Action.* Princeton, NJ: Princeton University Press.

Guess, R. (1981). *The Idea of a Critical Theory: Habermass and the Frankfurt School.* London: Cambridge University Press.

Harari, Y. (2014). *Sapiens: A Brief History of Humankind.* Toronto: McClelland & Stewart.

Jung, C. G. (1990). *The Basic Writings of C. G. Jung* (V. de Laszlo, Ed.). Princeton, NJ: Princeton University Press, Bollingen Series.

Klein, N. (2014). *This Changes Everything: Capitalism vs. The Climate.* Toronto: Penguin Random House Knopf Canada.

Mazzucato, M. (2014). *The Entrepreneurial State: Debunking Public vs. Private Sector Myths.* London, UK: Anthem Press.

Mayer, J. (2016). *Dark Money: The History of the Billionaires behind the Rise of the Radical Right.* New York: Doubleday.

Piketty, T. (2014). *Capital in the Twenty-First Century.* Cambridge, MA: The Belknap Press of Harvard University Press.

Redner, H. (2013). *Beyond Civilization: Society, Culture, and the Individual in the Age of Globalization.* New Brunswick, NJ: Transaction Publishers.

Reid, D. G. (1995). *Work and Leisure in the 21st Century: From Production to Citizenship.* Toronto: Wall & Emerson.

Reid, D. G., & Golden, B. L. (2005). Non-Work and Leisure Activity and Socially Marginalized Women. *Canadian Review of Social Policy*, (55), 39–65.

Sorkin, A. R. (2010). *Too Big to Fail.* London: Penguin Books.

Stebbins, R. A. (1982). Serious Leisure: A Conceptual Statement. *Pacific Sociological Review, 25* (2), 251–272.

Taplin, D. H., & Clarke, H. (2012). *Theory of Change Basics: A Primer on Theory of Change.* New York: ActKnowedge.

Index

aboriginal populations: residential schools, establishment 112–13; welfare 118
absolute poverty 122–3; example 123; health/education issues, absence 124
accomplishment 8, 23, 59, 161, 167–168, 170, 170, 172, 180–4, 190, 197
accountability 138
accumulation: imperative 58–9; motivations, strength (reduction) 190; pursuit 182–3; values, replacement 59
achievement, ideas 167
active social policy (poverty) 99
adaptive behaviour/characteristics, reproduction 35
adjustment: concept 29; security, contrast 29
advocacy: activities, NGO engagement 147–8; objectives, fulfilling (success) 137
aesthetic consumption, ideas 8, 23, 167, 180–4, 190, 197
Affordable Care Act (ACA) 14
Africa: Gini coefficient 120; poverty, assessment 87–8; quasi-recolonization, status 119–20
agenda 138
Agricultural Adjustment Act of 1933 83
alternative development, community development (incorporation) 128–9
American Dream, The 45–6
American Fascists (Hedges) 40
Americans for Prosperity 198
analysis, amalgam 68–9
anticipatory play 36
Arab Spring 9, 69, 178; Facebook/Twitter usage 170
artificial intelligence, potential 172

bankers, bonuses 25–6; limitation 28
banking system 46
banks, too big to fail categorization 26–7
Basic Needs approach 95–6
Beaton, Angus 176
belief systems: civilization nonacceptance 44–5; creation 44–5; values, connection 57
Beverage Report 85, 86; tabling 86
Beverage, William 81, 84–5
Beyond Civilization (Redner) 48
biological determinism 51–2; consistency 58; ideas, usage 55–6; problems 52
biological evolution 32, 35; idea, prominence 52
biological impulse, idea 52–2
biological systems, shaping 35
biology, culture (influence) 35
Blackmore, Susan 52–4
boundaries, term (usage) 66
Brazil, GDP (increase) 6, 75, 120–1
Britain: bankers, bonuses (limitation) 28; movement conservatives, impact 9; social reform, support 85; welfare state, consideration 79–80
bureaucracy, reduction 187
Bush, George W. 30

Campbell, Joseph 172
Canada: budget, tabling 146; Employment Insurance Program 29; First Nations, marginalization 6; government, rationale 147; hard times, acceptance 94; mixed economy, construction 83; movement conservatives, impact 9; poor, homogeneous population (perspective) 95; population, poverty 75; public/

Index

private debate 105–6; relative poverty 89; resource-based economy, downturns 170–1; retirement age, increase 82; single-payer system 105–6; social policies 82
Canada Housing and Mortgage Corporate Act (1985) 107
Canada Pension Plan 88
Canada, welfare state *81*; consideration 79–80; origin 80–81
Canadian Index of Wellbeing (CIW) 97–8, 190; report 190–1
Canadian Senate Standing Committee on Agriculture and Forestry, poverty study 88
Canadians, life (quality) 97–8
Cancer Stage of Capitalism 28
capacity building (CB) 127–8, 131–2
capitalism 163; collapse 35
Capitalism, Cancer Stage 28
capitalist society, goal 182
capitalist structure: components *181*; transition 181–2
capitalist system, dominance 58
capital system, near collapse 27
carbon-based energy 187
carbon dioxide emissions 194
celebrity culture 58
change: resistance, evolutionary standpoint 54; theory 192
checks/balances, system 139
chief executive officers (CEOs): bonuses, excess/problems 19–20; salary, worker wages (comparison) 179
children, home-schooling 112
China: economic rise 119–20; gross domestic product (GDP), increase 6, 75, 120–1
Christian-based NGOs 119
Christian right, intolerance 114
chronic disease, WHO focus 102
CIBC Employment Quality Index 191
cities, poverty 88
citizen engagement: occurrence 7, 126; success 135
citizen groups 129
citizen participation (CP) 14–15; approach 135–6; Arnstein's notion 136; concept, usage 136; framework 134–5
citizenship, defining 115
citizenship participation, Arnstein's model 135
civilization, transition (requirement) 180

civil leisure 170
Civil Works Administration 84
class-based society, celebrity culture 58
classical economics 23–4
class warfare, result 134
climate change: impact 23; issue, attack 177–8
Cody Institute, The 198
collaboration 138
Collapse (Diamond) 174
collective human progress 176
collectiveness, spirit 81
collective rationalism 180
colony, role 118
communicable diseases, concern 103
communities of interest 129
community: community-level intervention 192; education (enhancement), CD (impact) 132–3; fragmentation 132–3; mobilization 138; participation 138; reach 138; services 110; usage 188; utility 138; wealth accumulation, problem 183–4
community-based development (CBD): implementation 131; term, interchangeability 130–1
community building 126; components *127*; idea, impact 7; initiatives 131; social capital, impact 131
community development (CD) 127–8, 141; definitions 128; definitions, possibilities 129–30; focus 128; incorporation 128–9; method 129–30; movement 130; negatives 133; process 130; program 129–30; term, interchangeability 130–1; top-down approach 133; values 128
community-level intervention 192
comparative advantage 36
composite measure, usage 191
compulsory long-form census, elimination 147
conflict resolution 138
Conscience of a Liberal, The (Krugman) 21
consciousness: falseness, dispelling 40; impact 40–1; present form 41
consumer society: psychological survival 166–7; transition, requirement 180
consumption: imperative 58–9; increase 8; pursuit 182–3; values, replacement 59
contact with external agencies 138
context-specific skills, identification 132

cooperation/collaboration 138
Co-operative Commonwealth Federation (CCF) 81
creativity, absence 196
crises, series 8
critical mass 138
CSLS Economic Security Index 191
cultural dialogue 40
cultural environment, impact 59–60
cultural evolution: backward-gazing process 36; occurrence 38–9
cultural institution, superimposition 48–9
cultural model 71
cultural relativism 40, 142–3; realism, contrast 143
cultural truths, impact 42–3
cultural values, acquisition 9
culture: adaptive mechanisms 37; adaptively 38; defining 33–4; evolutionary device 32–3; failure 48; force 40; framework 32–3; ideas 32, 55; influence 35; knowledge 34; organizing force 3–4; portrayal 37; rules/standards, sharing 34; survival, product 37; system 34

Darwin, Charles 33, 38–9, 168; theory, interpretation (Spencer) 80
data collection/analysis 156–7
Dauphin, poverty (elimination) 187–8
da Vinci, Leonardo 168
Dawkins, Richard 52
decentralization, centralization (contrast) 30
decision making 138; approaches 63; power (local level) 30
deinstitutionalization 104–5
delegated power 138
deliberation, opportunities 67
democracy 138; form, change 115; importance 126; oppression 47; overarching issue 115–16; volunteer sector, impact 137
democratic drift, recycling 12
demonstrated competence 138–9
developed world, housing (responsibility) 107
developing countries: poverty 123; problems 101; social services, mandate 124
developing economies, dependence 121
developing world: social policy 118, 125; development, origin 6; vaccination, absence 103

development: cascade model 192; top-down model, reliance 66
developmental mandate 139
Diamond, Jared 174
disability payments 187
domestic work, drudgeries 164–5
Douglas, Tommy 81
Dust Bowl 82–3

early childhood, cultural environment (impact) 59–60
Ebola, infection 100–1
economically poor, numbers (trend) 121
economic model 71
economic question 172–3
economic success, problems 165–6
economic system: cultural past, combination 54; intention, societal misunderstanding 185
economy: composite measure, usage 191; exaggeration/dysfunctionality 20–1; growth, capitalism (impact) 20; jobs (reduction), tax increase (impact) 188–9; market economy, impact 164–5; new economy 22–3; overreliance 27–8; resource-based economy, downturns 170–1; skewing 19–20; survival 167; world economy, transition 113–14
education: absence, impact 91; community education (enhancement), CD (impact) 132–3; individual education (enhancement), CD (impact) 132–3; low levels 91; provision 112; state-supplied universal education 112–13; universal education 113; universality 112
Einstein, Albert 168
emancipatory knowledge 150–1
Employment Insurance Program (Canada) 29
entitlements 19–20
entrepreneurial model 71
environment: catastrophe, dangers 23; deterioration 56; exploitation 46; overconsumption, negative consequences 165; protection 23
environmental determinism 55–6
equality, importance 189
equalization payments 187
Europe: bankers, bonuses (limitation) 28; inequality, identification 9
European Union (EU): fiscal policy sovereignty 193; population, poverty 75

evolution: biological evolution 35; biology/genes/DNA, role 33; culture/false consciousness 32; Darwinian theory 80; products 41
execution of power 139
expressed need 154
external agencies, contact 138

Facebook, social network usage 170
faith, correctness 45
false consciousness 32–3, 40, 43–4; advertising agent usage 198; creation 45–6; derivative 49; impact 197; issue, addressing 193–4
family poverty, violence (experience) 92
Farm prices, decline 82
Federal Emergency Relief Administration 83
feedback, term (usage) 66
feudalism 163
Few Good Men, A 45
financial pie 78
financing, issue 104
First Nations: community building 132; individuals, absolute poverty 122–3; marginalization 6; reservations, housing (Canadian responsibility) 107–8
First Nations People: House of Commons apology 113; status, inequality 116
First New Deal 83
fiscal policy, EU sovereignty 193
fittest, survival 80
flow, term (usage) 168–9
food banks, impact 17
food stamps, usage 187
Frankfurt School 182
free market mechanism 48
free riding, emotional issue (concern) 188
Friedmann, John 65, 68
future needs, planning 38
futurology 148

Galbraith, John 60, 166
Gandhi, Mahatma 166
gender equity 139
genes, operation 52
geographic community, homogeneity 129
George, Lloyd 84
Ghana, community building 132
Gilded Age 21
Gini coefficient 120; elevation 121–2
Glass-Steagall Banking Act 84

global mechanism, establishment 194
global problems 19
government-funded medical system, introduction 81
governments: challenges 101; collective action 196; financial restraint/cutback, policy makers (impact) 17; social assistance 187
Great Depression 79–80, 82; progressive political policies 21
great recession 21
Greece, financial breakdown 193
greed, impact 9
gross domestic product (GDP) 146–7; computation 44; economic measure 43–4; increase 6; measure 43–4, 96–7, 190; progress 75
growth at all costs mentality, pressure (reduction) 185
growth scenario 25
guaranteed annual income (GAI) 173, 182–3, 194; access 188; bureaucracy, reduction 187; consideration 8; funds, usage 188; impact 186; institution 189; introduction 185; logic 174; requirement 187; usage 185–6

happiness, morality (linkage) 142
Harris, Sam 42, 45, 142
healthcare: challenge 100–1; cost, increase 102; private provision, public provision (contrast) 105; rationing 106
health concerns 91
Hedges, Chris 40
history deniers 33
HIV/AIDS: epidemic 101; problem 103–4
homelessness: crisis *111*; risk 108; shelter, absence 108
Homo economicus 19, 43
Homo sapiens 19, 165–6; prolificness 165–6; social world interpretation/creation 3–4
House of Commons, blanket apology 113
housing: affordability 191; policy, local specificity 108; prices, increase 26; responsibility 107; social policy, relationship 107–8
Housing Services Act 109
Housing Stability System 111–12
human behaviour: learning 53; memes, instructions 52–3

humanity: collective problems, solution 39; crisis 11; evolution, cultural values (acquisition) 9; needs, satisfaction 184; problems response 174–5
humankind, future 39
Human Resources Development Canada 96
humans: backward-looking nature 41; condition, challenge 55–6; condition (advancement), self-reflection/education (requirement) 149; consciousness, understanding/developing 41; culture 334; evolution, culture/false consciousness 32; existence, reason 183; genetic/environmental determination 53; governing 51–2; hunting/gathering 54; intervention 62; large-scale human cooperation, myths (basis) 37; social construction, ideas 47; society, challenge 56–7; system, intervention (support) 63–4
hunting/gathering 183

ideological forces, struggle 196
implementing experience 139
incentive-induced labour 172
inclusiveness 139
income: distribution 191; poverty, relationship 122; progressive taxes, usage 195; tax rates, increase 186
India, GDP (increase) 6, 75, 120–1
individual education (enhancement), CD (impact) 132–13
individualism, impact 179
individuals: psychological/social development needs 165; society, control 171–2
industrial era, change 11
Industrial Revolution 79–80; requirements 36
inner self, discovery 166–7
institutions, legitimacy (enhancement) 195–6
insurance system, basis 85
interaction opportunities 67
interest rates, escalation 26
International Monetary Fund (IMF) 120, 124–5; mandate 194
international NGOs, social development/welfare policy provision 120
interneuronal connections, shaping 59–60
invisible hand 46–7

Jews, extermination 51
jobs (reduction), tax increase (impact) 188–9
justice: importance 189; principles 23

Keynesian state (KS) 62; central idea 62–3; objectives 62–3; poverty/marginalization 75; theory, implementation 79; theory, suggestion 63
Keynes, John Maynard: ideas 85; philosophy 80
Kima Forum 178
King, Jr., Martin Luther 166
King, Mackenzie 81
knowledge: conception 67; types 150–1
Krugman, Paul 9, 21
Kusnetz, Simon 97

large-scale human cooperation, myths (basis) 37
large-scale social/environmental problems 144–5
large-scale social/human problems, social policy (impact) 7–8
leadership structure 139
leaders, historic trends 179
learning process, decision feedback 67
legitimate authority 139
Lehman Brothers, failure 9
leisure: activities 162–3; civil leisure 170; contribution 170; creative use 163; frivolity 168; mental condition 168–9; personal/social space 161–2; role 161; self-defining 165; serious leisure 169–70; social value 167–8; state of being 168–9
life: bliss 172; domains, understanding 12–13; guiding, individualism (impact) 179; leisure, contribution 170; life-satisfying activity 169; maintenance 178; meaning, discovery 182; minimum requirements, meeting 76; quality, themes (importance) 18; span, differences 177; standards, progress 176; work, impact 162
lifestyle: egalitarianism/balance 21; pluralistic lifestyle 163
life-world, system-world (balance) 166
linkages, formation 139
living conditions, advances 177
local level, decision-making power 30
longevity 139

long-form census, randomness/ legitimacy (doubt) 147
long-term intervention 95
Low-Income Cut-Off (LICO) 191; provision 95–6
Low Income Cut Off measure (Statistics Canada) 76
low income, incidence 191
Low-Income Measure (LIM) 96

McLuhan, Marshal 166–7
Madison Avenue 45–6
Mair, Heather 170
Mandela, Nelson 166
manufacturing: migration 171; shift/decline 28
marginalization: First Nations 6; Keynesian state 75
marginalized, leisure (impact) 162–3
Market Basket Measure of Poverty 96
market economy, impact 164–5
market system: manipulators, bonuses 25–6; restructuring 194
Marsh Report 81–2
Massey lectures 60
material accumulation, psychological social perspective 58–9
material consumption 167; motivations, strength (reduction) 190; psychological social perspective 58–9
material consumptive-dominated society, transition 183–4
maternal health, focus 102
maternal mortality, increase 176
McNamara, Thomas 41, 47, 54, 59
meaningful activity: engaging, act 171; preference 165; role 161
meaningful work, availability (decrease) 171
means-tests public assistance 85
medical care, access (increase) 177
medical technology, improvement 176–7
medicine, advances 104
memes 39; instructions 52–3
mental health problems 91
mentally ill individuals, institutionalization 104–5
mercantile system, class-based arrangement 36
mercantilism 163
middle-class society, disappearance 21
Middle East states, creation 119
Millennium Goals 123–4
mind, purpose 47–8

minimalist model 71
mixed-method strategy, usage 156
morality, linkage 142
Moral Landscape, The (Harris) 42, 142
movement conservatives 9
multinational corporation, dependence 155

National Housing Act of 1944 107
National Industrial Recovery Act 83
National Labor Board, development 84
national poverty level 87
National Reclamation Act 84
nation-states, tax collection 195
nation, welfare 97
natural/social environment, human hunting/gathering 54
nature/nurture debate 53
need: types 153–4; want, perception/distinction 153–4
neoconservative movement 9
neuroscience, impact 59
New Britain 85
New Deal 79–80; First New Deal 83
New Democratic Party 81
new economy: construction 91; impact 22–3; social transition 22; transition 24
new normal 163
New Orleans, neighborhoods (reconstruction) 92
new social contract: economic system basis 181–2; status quo transition *181*
new society, frameworks/blueprints 24
Nicholson, Jack 45
nongovernmental organization (NGO) 171; attention, dilemma 124–5; Christian-based NGOs 119; intervention 95; operation 87; private school establishment 112; sector, involvement 13; social policy 142; tax-exempt NGOs, tax code provisions 147–8; Western-based NGOs 16
nongovernmental organization (NGO) social policy: development/delivery 142; provision 118
nonmarket-based lifestyle 172
non-market decisions 13
nonparticipation/noncompliance, penalties/sanctions 195–6
normative need 153
North Africa, Arab Spring 9
North America: bankers, bonuses (limitation) 29; Occupy movement 9
nutrition, improvement 176–7; payment ability 177

Obama, Barack (healthcare reform) 14
Occupy movement 9, 69, 178; Facebook/Twitter usage 170; impact 196–7
Old Age Security 82; debate 148; eligibility 146; system 88
older adults, poverty risk 88
on-the-ground concepts 61
on-the-ground resources 126
On the Origin of Species (Darwin) 33
Organisation for Economic Co-operation and Development (OECD), poverty calculation 96
organizational structure 139
organizational system, dominance 57
Otium 168
overconsumption, negative consequences 165

Parents without Partners 92
participation levels 130
participatory process 178
partnerships, development trend 137
pensions 187
People's Declaration (Kima Forum) 178
perceived need 153–4
personal dignity 168
Pieper, Joseph 169
Piketty, Thomas 194–5
planet: maintenance 167; preservation, human value/moral question 142–3
planning: approaches, continuum 65; macro approaches 69; theories 67
planning/implementing experience 139
Planning in the Public Domain (Friedmann) 65–6
pluralistic lifestyle 163
policy: analysis 66; development, theoretical approaches 65; formulation process, goals 151–2; policy-making activity 148–9
policy making: context 51; solution creation stage 152
political activities, NGO engagement 147–8
politicians, public (tensions) 15
poor, psychological/ideological barriers/constraints 173–4
populations: challenges 101; mass migration 5–6
poverty: absolute poverty 122–3; active social policy 99; alleviation, experiments 80; assessment 87–8; Canadian Senate Standing Committee on Agriculture and Forestry study 88; capitalist countries, approach 78; causes 55; city poverty 88; condition, eradication 189–90; consequences/outcomes 91–2; definition, complication 96; definition, derivation 89; depiction *90*; description, perspective 122; devastation 79–80; difficulty 95–6; education, absence (impact) 91; elimination (Dauphin) 187–8; elimination, barrier 145; emotional responses 77; experience 173–4; family poverty, violence (experience) 92; horizontal/vertical dimension 93–4; impact 92; income, relationship 122; issues 87; issues, attack 177–8; issues, government focus 77–8; Keynesian state 75; manifestations 122; national poverty level 87; negative connotation 189–90; OECD calculation 96; older adults, poverty risk 88; progress 4–5; reduction 93; relative measurement 76; relative poverty 97; risk 88–9; roots/outcomes *90*; self-referential definition 76; Senate hearings 76; social circumstances, deterioration 86; treatment 90; UN definition 122; understanding 78–9, 94; young adults, poverty risk 88–9
power: delegation 138; execution 139; holding 66
practical knowledge, definition 150
preferred policy option 107
Prince, Charles 185
prisons: operation 29–30; privatization 30
private schools, NGO establishment 112
problems: definitions, subsets 153–4; humanity response 174–5
problems, rank-ordering 56
problem statements, establishment 153
productivity: idea, redefining 46–7; increase 77
progressives, number 124
progressive taxes, usage 194–5
propaganda 45–6
proven track record 139
psychological survival 166–7
public housing stock 109

quasi-recolonization, state 119–20

radical planning: approach 65–6; identification 68–9
Rajneesh, Bhagwan Shree 41–3, 45
realism: cultural relativism, contrast 143; importance 143

recognition, path 166
relational variables 131
relative need 154
relative poverty 97
religion, impact 30
reproductive success 37
research/planning process, stages *151*
residential schools, establishment 112–13
Residential Tenancy Act 109
resource distribution 173; balance, inequality 167; market system, restructuring 194
resources: mobilization 139; resource-based economy, downturns 170–1; sharing 184
"Rethinking Poverty" 123
reverse migration 94–5
robotics, potential 172
Roosevelt, Franklin Delano 83; plan 62
rural citizens, migration 94–5

"Scale of Insurance Benefits and the Problem of Poverty" (Beverage) 85
Schlesinger, Jr., Arthur 82
Schole 168
school-leaving age, minimum 112
second Gilded Age 21
Securities Act of 1934 83–4
Security Plan 85
self-esteem: gaining 164–5; impact 92; poverty-induced issues 92–3; problem 92
self-expression 182–3, 184
self-help, notion 130
self-reflection 55–6; requirement 149
self-worth 168
senior-level governments, participants 110
serious leisure 169–70
severe acute respiratory syndrome (SARS), impact 103
Shaar, John 148
sharing, history 139
single-issue-oriented associations (citizen groups) 129
single-parent social assistance recipients/participants, research 92
single-payer system (Canada) 105–6
smoking policy 154–5
social analysis, focus 25
social assistance, government provision 187
social capital (SC) 127–8, 131; concept, difficulty 132–3

social circumstances, deterioration 86
social cohesion 139
social constructions 182
social contract, necessity 22–3
social design 178
social development: democracy, importance 126; international NGO provision 120
social goals 24–5
social institutions: construction 34–5, 91; evolutionary products 41
social insurance: department unification 85; scheme 85–6
social issue, resolution 65
socialized medical system 105–6
social justice, overarching issue 115–16
social learning: bottom-up approaches 68; definition 192; model, characteristics 67
social marginalization, poverty (impact) 92
social mobilization, bottom-up approach 68
social morals, realism (importance) 143
social needs/cohesion, relationship 154
social networks, creation 170
social order, development/construction 163
social policy: activity social policy (poverty) 99; basis 15–16; construction 17; developing world 118; development, origin 6; domain, substance 4–5; establishment 61–2; experiment, interruption 80; focus 25; formation 143–4; formation, difficulty 69–70; formulation, basis 13; housing, relationship 107–8; implementation 150; macro approach 176; manipulative nature 150; measure 76–7; multitiered set 134; nongovernmental organizations, impact 142; non-market decisions 13; policy-making arena 152–3; policy-making process 15; policy-producing agency 156; poverty, relationship 5; provision, power division 30; role/function, uncertainty 146; system, manipulation 150; theory, domains *64*; two-tiered set 134; understanding, problem 12; universal application 134
social policy development: absence, root cause 120–1; inhibition, problem 119; meaningful activity/leisure, role

Index

161; planning theory 61; research activities 149
social policy formation: research/planning process, stages *151*; research, role 141
social policy provision 118–19; myths 155
social policy research 155; ideological attachment 156–7; mixed-method strategy 156; principle 141–2; problems 143–4; support, ontological positions 145; usage 155
social problems, common-sense solution 16
social reform: planning model 66–7; top-down activity 66
social services, mandate 124
social solidarity 154–5; term, usage 133–4
social spending, increase 78
social structure, involvement 198
social systems, decisions 58
social transformation, need 164
social values, levels (separation) 57
social vision 68–9
social welfare, origins 80–1
societal-wide myths, impact 45
society: accumulation-dominated society 183–4; aspirations 13; challenge 56–7; change, contemplation 145; culture, force 40; day-to-day operation 62; differentiation, increase 9–10; equality 23; exploitation 46; fiscal functioning 127; goals 182; institutions, ideologies (impact) 48; limited inequality 23; path, consequences (research focus) 148–9; person's theory 4; policy changes 191; problem 13–14, 110–1; psychological/social development needs 165; resources, minimum level 115; social/environmental problems 163; social issues, social policy (impact) 5; transition 183–5; transition, difficulty 197–8; values, implementation (social/environmental policy role) 4
Sorkin, Andrew Ross 185
South Africa: Gini coefficient 121–2; gross domestic product (GDP), increase 6, 120–1
special-interest lobby group, identification 137
species: evolution, biology/genes/DNA (role) 33; self-conception 41

state, presence (increase) 181–2
state-supplied universal education 112–13
status quo, transition *181*
steady-state, term (usage) 66
strategic thinking 68–9
Structural Adjustment Programs (SAPs) 124–5
structural coherence 139
sub-Saharan Africa, poverty populations 121
suffering, morality (linkage) 142
supernatural forces 39
survival of the fittest 80
symbolic meaning systems 34
system-world: balance 198; life-world, balance 166

taboo: generation 42; impact 42–3
target setting 139
task-oriented action group, focus 67
tax-exempt NGOs, tax code provisions 147–8
Tea Party 196
technical expertise 139
technological culture, experience 37
technological development 44
Tennessee Valley Authority 83
terrorism, threats 114, 180
theory: structure 70; term, usage 61
therapeutic model 71
Too Big to Fail (Sorkin) 185
totalitarian movements, genius 114
track record, proof 139
traditional authority 139
traditional belief system 139–40
transformation 176
tribe, collective wisdom 47
tuberculosis (TB) 101; resurgence 103
Twitter, social network usage 170
two-tier governance structure 195–6
two-tier system, operation 106–7

unacceptable inequality, problem 186
unemployed: governmental motivation 77; leisure, impact 162–3; psychological/ideological barriers/constraints 173–4
unemployment rate 86–7
United Kingdom, Industrial Revolution 79
United Nations mandate 194
United States: equality, identification 9; Gini coefficient 121–2; maternal mortality, increase 176; welfare state, consideration 79–80

universal education 113
uncontaminated land 59
urban centres, rural citizen migration 94–5

vaccination, absence 103
values: clarification 143; determination, realism (importance) 143; distribution 67; formation 192; ideas 167
Veblen, Thorstein 169
veto power 67
violence, family experience 92
voluntary associations, success 137
volunteerism 46–7
volunteer sector: impact 137; role 136

want: confusion 154; need, perception/distinction 153–4
wealth: accumulation, impact 183–4; ego-enhancing display 180
wealth creation 20, 197; increase 121–2
welfare model 71
welfare policy, international NGO provision 120
wellbeing: GDP surrogate status 97; measure 97–8

well-being, increase 166
wellness, defining 43–4
Western-based NGOs, impact 16
work: availability, decrease 171; decentring 161; domestic work, drudgeries 164–5; increase 8; life substance 162; preparation exercise 172; psychological attributes 163; role 162–3; society consideration 164–5; work-oriented society, transition 183–4
workplace, productivity (increase) 77
World Bank 120–1, 124–5; mandate 194
world economy, transition 113–14
World Health Organization (WHO), UN creation 102
world population, increase 123
World Vision 119
World War II: poverty, progress 4–5; progressive political policies 21; wealth creation 20
World Wide Web, creation 164
worth, discovery 166–7

Yoshitani, Miya 178
young adults, poverty risk 88–9

Printed in the United States
By Bookmasters